MARKED

FAYTENE KRYSKOW
FOREWORD BY LOU ENGLE

a generation of dread champions rising to shift nations

MARKED

DESTINY IMAGE® PUBLISHERS, INC.

P.O. Box 310, Shippensburg, PA 17257-0310

"Speaking to the Purposes of God for This Generation and for the Generations to Come."

This book and all other Destiny Image, Revival Press, Mercy Place, Fresh Bread, Destiny Image Fiction, and Treasure House books are available at Christian bookstores and distributors worldwide.

For a U.S. bookstore nearest you, call **1-800-722-6774**.

For more information on foreign distributors, call **717-532-3040**.

Or reach us on the Internet: **www.destinyimage.com**.

ISBN 10: 0-7684-2819-X

ISBN 13: 978-0-7684-2819-3

For Worldwide Distribution, Printed in the U.S.A.

1 2 3 4 5 6 7 8 9 10 11 / 13 12 11 10 09

Dedication

This book is dedicated to the King of the nations, Jesus Christ, and to the reformers of old who blazed a trail, set a pace, and who are now watching in that great cloud of witnesses cheering us on.

I pray that we make them proud and that we bring many nations to the feet of our King so that both His and their labor is not in vain. The fullness of their promise is found in us (see Heb. 11:40).

Acknowledgments

Special thanks to my amazing team at the time of writing this book (summer 2008 through spring 2009): Tamara Crampton, Sarah Sonne, Jonathan Chan, Amy Good, Robin Noel, Sven Johnson, Sarah Bencic, and Beck Poulson. With TheCRY Canada 2008 and the deadline of the book's manuscript only eight days apart, I could not have done them both without your help and grace. Thanks for quietly walking past when the bright orange earplugs were in my ears, for chipping in around the house, for the shoulder massages to keep my hands typing, for listening to me read and read and read—and then for doing the same yourself; your eagle editing eyes were amazing. You are the real deal, and you are some of my modern-day heroes.

Thank you to Leigh-Anne and Jason for the last-minute photo shoot to get a picture of me with the current hair color. You guys are the best, and I am sure a few people, who otherwise would have been looking for a blonde, will be thankful. We will see how long this look lasts.

Thank you also to my faithful intercessors who prayed these pages into reality over the last year! When you get your copy, I hope you hold it like proud mothers and fathers too!

Thanks to James Goll, Stacey Campbell, Patricia King, Pastor Sunday Adelaja, John Arnott, Tom and Kate Hess, David Mainse, Bill and Gwen Prankard (my pastors), Missy Lindsay, and Giulio Gabeli who, in the midst of your busy schedules, found time to peruse these pages and write a few words of endorsement.

Thanks to my board and advisory team who, time after time, blow me away with your support, faithfulness, and wisdom. Your insights were needed and appreciated at many key moments. You amaze me. Thank you especially to Patricia King. I am convinced that you have saved my life on numerous occasions, and I will forever honor you for it and the amazing example of Christ that you are.

Thanks to Destiny Image Publishers! Ronda, you are the best. Thanks for seeking me out and encouraging me to get this manuscript pounded out—thanks also for the editing grace! You have an amazing team of professionals and tenacious lovers of God (Dean, David, Angela, Jonathan, and the many others I did not meet in person). Thanks for marrying the two and for even breaking grammatical rules at times to illustrate it! Thank you for serving the Body of Christ so phenomenally.

Thanks to my awesome family and to Mom and Dad for simply being that—my awesome family. Here's another book for the collection, Mom! Dad, you will be glad to know that your Youth Juice kept me going. You are the best, for real.

Most importantly, thank You, Holy Spirit. I am crazy in love with You and could not have pulled this off without Your presence in my midst. You make life…well…beyond words.

Endorsements

For years we have had prophetic forerunners who have been declaring a new day is coming. But now a new generation is arising who believe the report and are doing something about it. They say it is time to "Cross on Over!" In fact, some of these new justice riders are already doing something to reverse the moral decay of society. Faytene Kryskow is one of the next generation champions who is leading the charge. I marvel at the courage of this young Joan of Arc for our day. It is an honor to commend to you both her life and ministry, as well as this excellent, penetrating treatise. Read, weep, and *act!*

James W. Goll
President, Encounters Network
Director, Prayer Storm
Author, *The Seer, The Coming Prophetic
Revolution, Prayer Storm,* and many others

For a well-read person like me, unfortunately, it has become almost impossible these days to get a book in hand that I actually learn something from! However, this book by Faytene Kryskow has been absolutely wonderful in that I have not just read yet another book, but I have been truly blessed and enriched by taking in the contents of its pages. Thank you for this inspiring work that will benefit generations to come!

Remain blessed in HIM,
Pastor Sunday Adelaja
Senior Pastor and Founder
The Embassy of the Blessed Kingdom of God
for all Nations, Kiev, Ukraine

When I dream of a righteous, radical, principled, focused, and Spirit-empowered generation who will carry the torch of the Lord in this hour, I immediately think of Faytene Kryskow. I have known Faytene for years. Her faith, her commitment to the Body of Christ, and her tenacious pursuit of righteousness and truth have always impressed me. She does not merely pen her thoughts, but rather her deep conviction that flows from diligent study as well as proven and tested experiences in the Lord. Faytene Kryskow is always worth receiving from. Read. Be blessed, and become a revolutionary, just like her, in Christ.

Patricia King
Founder, Extreme Prophetic and XP Media

Faytene Kryskow, firmly believing that "Righteousness exalts a nation, but sin is a reproach to any people" is calling and championing her generation of youth to press into God and governments to change nations, for revival and the well-being of peoples everywhere. She leads the way for a new generation of world changers and history makers who are following her lead and making a massive difference.

John Arnott
Toronto Airport Christian Fellowship

Marked—A Generation of Dread Champions Rising to Shift Nations! The title alone should begin to stir you. But this book is much more than just a great title; it is a clarion call to all who desire to see Jesus receive what He asked for, the nations of the earth. Faytene Kryskow has brilliantly proclaimed not only a prophetic message of hope that nations can turn to God but also an incredible story of how it is currently happening. I am convinced there is a new breed of revivalists emerging in the earth today who are being raised up to answer the cry of God's heart for the nations, and Faytene is at the forefront of this new breed. In the last few years, there has been a major shift in how the Body of Christ thinks. No longer are we only trying to build good local churches, but we realize that our call is to take cities and disciple nations. But with that realization must come new revelation. This book is part of that new revelation. The message of hope and encouragement is such a vital message in this hour. So many Christians are ready to go and they have a heart to shape world history; they simply need hope and courage to do what God has called them to do. This book will both inspire and challenge you as you pursue seeing the nations of the earth given to Jesus as His inheritance.

Banning Liebscher
Lead Pastor, Awakening Youth Movement
Bethel Church, Redding, California

Faytene Kryskow is a 21st-century, Kingdom of God woman. She lives, inhales, dreams, and communicates the Kingdom with urgency and passion. For such a time as this, she has been born and raised up. She does not take her mandate lightly; rather she leads with diligence. She talks with authority, but more importantly, she walks in authority, not her own, but with the rights she's relinquished to the King of Kings. She fearlessly approaches the Throne of Grace, has touched the King's scepter, and is not found wanting. In my wife's poem "Palace Style," she writes:

> Sons of thunder, bold as lions
>
> are Your righteous ones
>
> confronting whitewashed sepulchers, brooding vipers
>
> The King's daughter, all glorious within
>
> if I die, I die; lays down her life for Kingdom causes.

Faytene is one of these. She is treading where few have gone before because, indeed, she is a trailblazer, following hard after Jesus. "And from the days of John the Baptist until now the kingdom of heaven suffers violence, and the violent take it by force" (Matt. 11:12). Now is the hour for a generation of dread champions to arise and take the Kingdom of God by the force of the Holy Spirit to earth. This generation's absolute surrender and submission to God's Word and love for the lost and dying will reverse demonic decrees, save another generation of babies, shift the heavenlies, and ultimately shift the nations, giving the Son of God His rightful inheritance. Will you be *Marked* by Jesus? We fervently exhort you to "eat this scroll." Jesus is coming soon!

Pastor Tom and Kate Hess
Jerusalem House of Prayer for All Nations
Israel

On August 23, 2008, Faytene Kryskow led "TheCry," a movement impacting Canada and its government. Thousands of Canadians standing on the lawn facing the "Peace Tower" heard Faytene describe the pros and cons of four pieces of upcoming legislation. Never have I heard before such gracious, yet powerful, wisdom-filled words. Faytene is without doubt the most outstanding spokesperson for the emerging generation of leaders.

David Mainse
Founder, Crossroads Christian Television, Canada
Author, *God Keep Our Land* and
Impact Canada 100

As with Joan of Arc, God has used Faytene as a mighty prophetic voice for this generation to influence key national leaders and to ignite and perpetuate political, godly reform in the Canadian Parliament. Faytene has legislated in the heavenlies with prophetic and strategic intercession on the Canadian Capitol Hill and has met with over 300 members of Parliament, to include the Prime Minister himself, for the purpose of challenging the controversial moral issues of her nation. This provocative and inspirational volume chronicles the emergence of an army of anointed reformers who will diplomatically confront kings and leaders of nations with the truth of the Bible, providing biblical foundations and key principles to shift and shape moral legislation throughout nations. A must-read for apostolic and prophetic giftings!

Missy Lindsay
Christ For the Nations,
Granddaughter of Gordon and Feda Lindsay

This book is a must-read for every apostolic and prophetic leader, ministry, church company, and network. The biblical expositional truths and revelatory insights shared by Faytene Kryskow will cause every reader, whether they be scholars or not, to be enriched in their understanding of the clear mandate in Scripture to establish the Kingdom of God in the transformation of nations. Faytene's 21ˢᵗ-century language and writing style is relevant and refreshing. She brings a Josiah anointing from a life dedicated to national transformation that continues to be a torch blazing brightly for many across Canada. This book is destined to become a classic for generations to come.

Giulio Gabeli
Senior Apostolic leader
Westwood, Vancouver

In every generation, a few voices rise above the noise of political opinion and religious rhetoric to declare, "Thus says the Lord." Preachers, evangelists, and revivalists all have an essential function in the Body of Christ, but it is often the reformer God uses to shake believers out of complacency and to impact society. Faytene is one of those unique voices.

In her first book, *Stand On Guard*, Faytene Kryskow skillfully documented Canada's righteous foundations and spoke prophetically of God's heart for the nation. In this book, *Marked*, she shows believers that, while we honor the past and fix our eyes on the future, God is calling believers to action now. As her pastors, we have witnessed many of the amazing events she shares in the following pages. God is honoring her courageous obedience to declare the Word of the Lord in both spiritual and political arenas and to model a life of holiness. He has raised her to national prominence to influence political policy and to inspire a generation of righteous reformers. *Marked* will inspire you to rise to the challenge, to respond to the voice of the Spirit, and to usher in His prophetic purpose in your nation.

Rev. Bill and Gwen Prankard
Evangelist, Pastor, Dominion Outreach Center
Ottawa, Canada

Every man gives his life for what he believes and every woman gives her life for what she believes. Sometimes people believe in little or nothing, and they give their lives to that little or nothing. One life is all we have; we live it and it is gone, but to live without faith is more terrible than dying. Even more terrible than dying young.

—*Joan of Arc*

Contents

Foreword

Why do the nations rage,
And the people plot a vain thing?

The kings of the earth set themselves,
And the rulers take counsel together,
Against the Lord and against His Anointed, saying, "Let
us break Their bonds in pieces
And cast away Their cords from us."

He who sits in the heavens shall laugh;
The Lord shall hold them in derision.

Then He shall speak to them in His wrath,
And distress them in His deep displeasure:
"Yet I have set My King
On My holy hill of Zion."

"I will declare the decree:
The Lord has said to Me,
'You are My Son,
Today I have begotten You.

Ask of Me, and I will give You
The nations for Your inheritance,

And the ends of the earth for Your possession.

You shall break them with a rod of iron;
You shall dash them to pieces like a potter's vessel.'"

Now therefore, be wise, O kings;
Be instructed, you judges of the earth.

Serve the Lord with fear,
And rejoice with trembling.

Kiss the Son, lest He be angry,
And you perish in the way,
When His wrath is kindled but a little.

Blessed are all those who put their trust in Him (Psalm 2).

All governments derive their authority from the higher government of God. When kings become renegades and conspire together, throwing off the fetters of God's laws, the Lord has a word to say to them. He is not politically correct, and He is not happy. He speaks to them in His deep displeasure. Why? Because God's laws were given by loving design for the well-being of His creation, families, and children. To change God's fixed moral standards by legal decree is to bring hurt and destruction to people.

But God has another hill that is above every other capitol hill. Upon that governmental hill, He has installed His Son, Jesus, as Prime Minister. The installed Son and great Intercessor is now enjoined by the Father to ask Him for the nations as His inheritance. The government of God rules the nations through the new and glorious administration of prayer. From that prayer meeting on Zion's hill, kings and judges are warned to realign their laws with the laws of God and to do homage to the Son, God's rightful Regent over the earth.

The Church, that heavenly governing body in celestial counsel with the Sovereign Ruler of the universe, binds and looses in prevailing prayer the rebel powers of renegade kings and judges. Kings are haunted and converted with dreams like Nebuchadnezzar, or they are judged and removed like Herod. God is the one who raises up kings and brings them down as the Church prays for all those in authority.

I see a new breed of believers arising from the ashes or from religions that fail to transform the earth into the resurrection power of

Christ born out of fasting and prayer. An Esther generation is beginning to step onto the stage of history with this imperial prayer vision burning in their hearts: "the kingdoms of this world have become the kingdoms of our Lord and of His Christ..." (Rev. 11:15). They are not living for self-preservation; the cry of "if I die, I die" is the new sound. With their three-day Esther fasts, they appeal to the Supreme Court of Heaven who overrules the supreme courts of earth. Pro-abortion laws and political perpetrators like Hamon begin to tremble, totter, and fall.

This is not just hype or rhetorical fantasy. Even now in Canada, a great prayer movement has arisen to challenge the governmental gates of death and their decrees of destruction. Righteous men have been promoted to the highest places of governmental influence. Faytene Kryskow, who is like a daughter to me, has, like Esther, risked everything to step onto the stage of Canadian history. As she is calling the youth of Canada to prayer and fasting, they are now seeing visible change take place. She has stepped into the very governmental halls of Canada with her young maidens and mighty men speaking to and praying for Parliamentary leaders. Amazingly, the scepter of favor has been stretched out to her and the benevolent Kingdom of Heaven is transforming the halls of justice. Laws and ideologies are changing. Abortion has become a wedge, and it is being driven into the conscience of Canada.

So read again the biblical account of Esther and watch the fasting prayer meeting moving the unseen hand of providence, reversing decrees, and raising up the righteous. Then as you read this book, you will see once again an Esther-Mordecai movement stirring. Kings and queens are shaking as a nation begins to return to loving submission to the Son, installed on His holy hill. The Son is pleading mightily, "Father, give Me the nations as My inheritance."

Lou Engle
Director, TheCall

19

I have often noted that those who are the most able to help others are those who have walked the long road from the bottom to the top, from failure to victory. By taking the long road, they have had to face—and overcome—every obstacle that presents itself before victory is achieved.

Faytene's capacity for nation-changing is huge, not because she started at the top with a silver spoon in her mouth, but because she has conquered most of the things that the rest of us use as excuses. In my mind, there is no next-generation leader I know who is more capable of writing a book on transforming nations than Faytene Kryskow—Faytene started with self-transformation, then worked to see transformation among the poor of the earth until she realized that justice for all comes when kings and leaders rule in righteousness. She has taken the long way home and understands clearly why and for whom she is laboring to see nations transformed.

What I love about Faytene is that she seeks to really *do* what the Bible says. When she reads "Go into all the world," she does it. When she discovers "disciple nations," she says "OK." Undaunted by the magnitude of the call, she simply begins with what she has and watches God take her "loaves and fishes" and shifts an entire government. I live in the nation where Faytene is impacting government policies. I regularly write e-mails to politicians in response to Faytene's communications to the Church to get involved. I have watched with my own eyes Faytene and her small band of committed disciples begin to change the very mindset of a nation from liberal to biblical values—law by law, media presentation by media presentation, Facebook group by Facebook group. What Faytene writes about is not theory—it has happened and it is happening. The kings of my nation are being discipled in righteousness, in part through Faytene's ministry.

I cannot conclude without commenting on Faytene's character. Rarely have I met a person with as much integrity as Faytene. She works tirelessly, selflessly, continually. She is filled with honor for all those in authority. She never complains, always prays, and is a supreme example to those of her generation. I simply love who she is in every way. As one who has traveled to the nations of the world and worked with those who are changing nations, I can say that Faytene is a bright light among shining stars. She is a leader of leaders, and I am honored to introduce this book to you. This is a manifesto on nation changing, and you can take the principles and begin to change your city or nation. If you read between the lines, you will catch the spirit of its author—abandoned commitment to "love justice and do mercy" and unabashed love for Jesus. This is the spirit of a nation-changer. This is Faytene Kryskow.

Stacey Campbell
Be a Hero
Revival Now!
Founder, the Canadian Prophetic Council
www.beahero.org

Preface

Before you embark upon the pages of this book I first of all want to thank you in advance for the time you will be spending with me. We could be spending our time in many different worthy ways, and yet for some reason, in God's divine plan, we find ourselves here together—me typing, you reading, and Holy Spirit brooding upon us, desiring to impart something that will *mark* us for His purposes in this hour of human history. I don't know about you, but I want to be marked and set apart as a carrier of His heart, revelation, and intent for the nations of the earth. And so, it is truly my prayer, as we set out together on a journey through these few hundred pages, that a pure DNA strand from Heaven will be woven into our souls (nothing plastic), and that we will go forth from this contact point manifesting that DNA in the earth.

As I set my heart before God in these moments, I am struck with a specific thought: *God's heart burns for nations.* Jesus came for them. He died for them. He rose again and left us with the authority to ransom them. I do not claim to be an expert in all these things, but one thing I do know is that God truly is raising up a generation of dread champions[1] who will give their lives contending for the fullness of their, and His, inheritance. We can't get away from it. Part of this inheritance is nations, real nations. According to Psalm 2, Jesus is asking; He is asking for your nation, and He is asking for mine. Just as He burns for nations, it is my prayer that both you and I will burn to give Him the desire of His heart.

What you are about to read is many things. *First of all,* it is a challenge from Scripture regarding the clear biblical mandate to influence our nations for Christ. If you have never thought of this as part of your life's mandate, my prayer is that, after you have read the first few chapters, you will be thinking, "How did I ever miss this?" It is all over the Guidebook that Holy Spirit has given us, the Bible.

Second, in many ways, this book is my heart on pages. It reveals a lot of my personal journey, theological processing with the Lord, and the testimony of how God has raised up a band of mighty young men and women over the past three years to influence the Church at large and the main political leaders of my nation. I love the stories because they are so authentic, so unexpected, so real, and such solid proof that God is truly in the habit of using the foolish things of the world to confound the wise (see 1 Cor. 1:27).

When I was totally apolitical in nature, God plucked me from serving in the social gutters and inner-city streets of my nation, and then from the back woods of West Africa, and transplanted me smack in the epicenter of my nation's political affairs—prophesying to leaders and influencing policy. Why? Maybe simply because He is God and He does what He wants to do or because He truly is passionate for the affairs of nations and is looking for anyone who will carry His heart into the midst of them.

Throughout this journey, God has poured out revelation of unavoidable principles that have guided our ministry team as we have sought to radically obey the call He was laying before us. He has also poured out *ridiculous* favor and grace upon us to carry out the mandates that He has put in our spirits and that burn as unquenchable torches. This means we have some really great stories to share [smiles].

As we have walked a step at a time, following the voice of our God, we have walked right into places that most in my nation only dream of— even the most rigorously trained, educated, and financed individuals in our nation. It is quite hilarious actually. As a group of underfunded and undereducated young adults, we have been given audience with more Parliamentarians than any organization in the nation and mind-blowing favor on so many fronts, only to find out after the fact that what we were experiencing was not "normal." Time and time again, whether after receiving an unexpected invitation to a Parliamentary reception, after receiving a call from national media wanting to write another story or publish another intern's article, or after leading a prayer gathering of thousands of committed Christians from across Canada, my team and I have looked at each other and said, "I cannot believe this is our life. How did we get here?"

In the last three to four years, we have stood in the midst of one of the most incredible national reformation periods our nation has seen in recent history. These pages are birthed out of these experiences and stories. As you read the testimonies and hear of the fruit, my prayer is that the truth that *God can do anything with nothing* will deeply impact you. Give Him your two loaves and five fishes and watch Him feed a nation!

Third, woven throughout this book, you will find a thread of prophetic revelation and insights for the hour we are living in—both my own prophetic insights and a few words from others by whom I have been deeply impacted. The cat is out of the bag: yes, I believe God talks today. My best friend is invisible, but don't worry, I am not depressed, bi-polar, co-dependant, extremist, or delusional, and I don't need Prozac to dumb it all down. I'm simply convinced. Once you have "met" Someone, it does not matter how many people tell you that that person does not exist or does not communicate. You know better because you have met that Someone. Because, by God's grace, this is my reality, it is the place from where I write.

John 10:27 says that His sheep hear His voice and that they will not follow the voice of another. If you struggle with the worldview that God is truly a good and relational Father who speaks to His kids on a regular basis, then you may have a hard time with most of this book. Almost all that we have walked in, as far as effective national reformation and influence is concerned, has somewhere along the way been inspired by His voice. I am really sorry if that seems freaky. Joel 2 says that the Lord utters His voice before His army, and the thought of Him leading us by it actually brings me great comfort. Because this book is written to the global Christian community, not the secular, I have taken the liberty to speak freely from my experiences in God.

My belief is that, as long as what we believe Holy Spirit is speaking (through dreams, visions, inner-audible voice, etc.) is in alignment with the Word of God, we are well within the boundaries. Because of this, to the best of my ability, I have been careful to make sure that every revelation and insight is clearly framed by just that—the Word of God. If you do not believe in the premise of John 10:27 (that those who belong to Him hear His voice), then I joyfully invite you into these pages anyway to partake of the insights, wisdom, and principles. I believe you will find that their merit stands regardless. Truth is truth and wisdom is wisdom. Period.

If you have never heard His voice, but want to, I pray you will experience this for the first time as you journey with me. My prayer is that the prophetic revelation shared in these pages will impart inspiration into your heart, just as it did mine when I first received it. I also pray that you will receive revelation of the hour we are living in and the awesome call that we have to live our lives to bring Him glory.

I would also like to make another small but essential disclaimer—especially for those of you who may skim the book at parts and thereby not catch the fullness of my heart at points. I burn for righteousness and holiness; I love it. My love for it comes out of a love for God though, not crusty religious effort. It is worship. I want to love what He loves because I love Him. I fully acknowledge that the only way we can walk in righteousness and holiness is by His empowering grace; we can't muster it up through efforts of our flesh.

We are not strong enough without Him. There is no getting around that. As a New Testament believer in Christ, I am so thankful that His empowering grace is part of our inheritance. We are under grace and not law. I feel the grace of God alive and pulsating through me continuously. Furthermore, the truth is that I would not be motivated to do anything for my nation or world if it wasn't. Without the grace and empowering presence of God, I would be a couch potato. His fire burns in me and propels me to fight for what He loves.

Most of our nations, however, are not completely submitted to Christ and, therefore, Old Testament laws are still very much in action, just like they would be for an unbeliever. The law of grace is applied after a person receives Christ's atoning sacrifice. Because I am not primarily speaking about God's dealings with an individual in this book, but God's dealings with *nations*, I do pull on principles as they are revealed in Old and New Testament Scriptures alike.

Please know my heart, that at any time in which I am bringing forth a point of conviction, it is with the total awareness that it is only the grace of God that can bring us as individuals into His fullness—and it is only the grace and mercy of God that will redeem our nations. This is precisely why we need to cry out for it. Like Lot and his family in the midst of a community whose hearts were turned away from God, our call is to go forth and minister God's grace in His name by cultivating the good and resist-

Marked

ing the bad, being salt and light in nations where many have not yet bowed their knees to the revelation of His love and goodness.

Finally, I want to say thank you again in advance for your time in perusing these pages. Your time is your life, and your life is invaluable. I pray you will be *marked* with many things as you read. *Marked* with insight and wisdom. *Marked* with passion and vision. *Marked* with consecration and hunger for God. *Marked* with strategy and tenacity. *Marked* with strength and ability. *Marked* with a spirit of honor and grace. *Marked* with great courage, great faith, and great boldness. *Marked* for Christ, no matter what the cost. If this is your prayer too, then simply say it with me now, "Bring it on, Lord! *Mark me.*"

Let's head in.

Endnote

1. If you are not familiar with the term *dread champions*, please see James Goll's word of insight in the Appendix.

PART I

Righteousness and the Nations

Why do the nations rage, and the people plot a vain thing?
(Psalm 2:1)

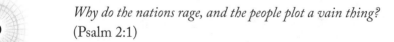

CHAPTER 1
Rule, Subdue, and Make Disciples of Nations

"...All authority has been given to Me in heaven and on earth. Go therefore and make disciples of all the nations..." (Matthew 28:18-19).

Since the beginning, God has been interested in partnering with humankind in keeping life and order in the earth. After several days of creation, He turned His face toward all that He had done:

> *Then God said, "Let Us make man in Our image, according to Our likeness; let them have dominion over the fish of the sea, over the birds of the air, and over the cattle, over all the earth and over every creeping thing that creeps on the earth." So God created man in His own image; in the image of God He created him; male and female He created them. Then God blessed them, and God said to them, "Be fruitful and multiply; fill the earth and subdue it; have dominion over the fish of the sea, over the birds of the air, and over every living thing that moves on the earth"* (Genesis 1:26-28).

What an awesome day that was. Not only had God created something in the physical realm that was a reflection of His heavenly image, but He had extended the hand of fellowship to humankind by commissioning them with authority to watch over and keep care of all that He had created. I find this text so intriguing.

First of all, He said to them, "Be fruitful! Increase!" There is something inherent in the nature of God that loves growth and wants to take over! Recently a preacher friend of mine, Banning Liebscher, said something that I wholeheartedly believe in. He said, "The new breed of revivalists that God is raising up has a 'take-over' mentality. They are convinced that God has called them to take over the world!"[1] If we really believe that we are created in His image, this should not be a surprising statement. Actually, it resonates deeply in my spirit.

> "THE NEW BREED OF REVIVALISTS GOD IS RAISING UP HAS A 'TAKE-OVER' MENTALITY. THEY ARE CONVINCED GOD HAS CALLED THEM TO TAKE OVER THE WORLD."

Because God is so good, the fact that He has a "take-over" mentality is amazing news. I had a defining moment a few years ago as a new Christian when I was in a late-night conversation with a deep-minded friend of mine. He had wrestled with theology for years, and I was really hungry for God, so I was picking his brain for everything I could learn. As we mused regarding the awesomeness and magnificence of God, he suddenly stopped and, with a look of wonder in his eyes, said, "Aren't you glad God is good? He is God. That is a fact. We have to submit to what He decides. Aren't you glad that He is actually *good*? He could be bad, but He is not. He is good."

He is good, and He wants to take over the world! That is great news. There is one clincher, however. The clincher is that He has chosen to execute the expansion of His Kingdom through His people. Whether or not His take-over plan advances in fullness depends on our obedient response to the command: multiply!

> WHETHER OR NOT HIS TAKE-OVER PLAN ADVANCES IN FULLNESS DEPENDS ON OUR OBEDIENT RESPONSE TO THE COMMAND: MULTIPLY!

I believe this command to be fruitful and multiply was not only about making babies, though it was that. It was not simply about bringing people to the saving knowledge of Christ, though it was that as well. Making disciples is clearly paramount to the heart of God. However, in addition to all this, I believe, when the Lord commanded His creation made in His image (us) to be fruitful and multiply, He was also saying,

> I want you to get this goodness inside of you out! Any good seed that I have put in you is meant to be sown into the earth and multiplied. If I have given you compassion, then sow it into

32

the earth and multiply it. If I have given you love, then sow it into the earth and multiply it. If I have given you wisdom, then sow it into the earth and multiply it! *Multiply* for God's sake (literally)!

In God's divine design, we are created to multiply and expand our boundaries for the glory of His name. This is really important to the Lord, which is why it was the first thing He told us to do. Boil it down to the bottom line: you were created to take over the world with the love and the ways of God. In Genesis 1:28, I believe He took this to another level saying,

> I am not only calling you to advance and fill the earth, but I am also commissioning you to subdue it as you go. That means rule over all of creation. Rule over the fish, the creatures, the land. Rule over everything!

SUBDUE (KABASH): TO FORCE, TO KEEP UNDER, TO BRING UNDER CONTROL, DOMINATE OR TREAD DOWN. DOMINION (RADAH): TO RULE, DOMINATE, TREAD DOWN, PREVAIL OVER, REIGN OVER OR SUBJUGATE.[1]

The word *subdue* in Genesis 1:26-28 is the Hebrew word *kabash*, which literally translated means to force, keep under, bring under control, dominate, or tread down. The word *dominion* is the Hebrew word *radah*, which means to rule, dominate, tread down, prevail over, reign over, or subjugate.[2] As a "free-thinking" younger person in our post-modern world, I honestly squirm a bit when I hear words like control, dominate, or subjugate.

Furthermore, with the echo of the Crusaders in our global history, I can imagine that most non-Christians would freak out to hear Christians speaking zealously about controlling, reigning over, or subjugating the earth! (It is chapters like this one that get people like me maligned in national secular media as whacko-freaky, right-winged, narrow-minded, Nazi, and woman-hating [I never quite understood that particular accusation against me since I am a woman].) However, if feelings of anxiousness are aroused when expounding these Scriptures and God's intent to rule in the earthly realm, I think it is because we do not really understand the heart of God and the ways of God.

> ...IF FEELINGS OF ANXIOUSNESS ARE AROUSED WHEN EXPOUNDING THESE SCRIPTURES, I THINK IT IS BE-CAUSE WE DO NOT REALLY UNDERSTAND THE HEART OF GOD...

During this day, age, and Western culture mindset, most people, especially in my age group, recoil at the talk of authority. Yet sane reasoning shows that we need godly authority to keep peace and order in any society. Just ask any person who lived through the slaughters in Rwanda or the current crisis in Darfur. There is control, domination, and subjugation that is bad, and there is control, domination, and subjugation that is good. The good kind of control restrains the teenager who wants to gun down his classmates, restrains the pedophile or rapist from being on the loose, restrains the thief from looting, and restrains the employer from exploiting. It is the type of control that keeps streets safe, markets stable, and governments accountable. It is the type of control that simply keeps things in order. This is exactly what the Lord was commissioning Adam and Eve to do. He was commissioning them to keep the world in order. Like the good gardener who keeps the weeds and pests under control and cultivates good healthy soil for productive plants to flourish, so Adam and Eve were to go forward into the earth to weed out the bad stuff and cultivate the good in every sense. This was the first commission ever given. Guess what? Nothing has changed in this regard.

> LIFE SEEMS HARDER NOW FOR THE DESCENDANTS OF ADAM AND EVE, BUT OUR CHALLENGE IS STILL THE SAME: RESIST THE BAD STUFF AND CULTIVATE THE GOOD.

MASTER (MASHAL): TO RULE, HAVE DOMINION, OR EXERCISE DOMINION OVER.

When sin entered the world, Adam and Eve's mandate was complicated in an instant. Sin, death, and all its destructive consequences were now loosed in the earth. Only three chapters later, in Genesis 4:7, the Lord exhorted Adam and Eve's son, Cain, saying, "If you do what is right, will you not be accepted? But if you do not do what is right, sin is crouching at your door; it desires to have you, but you must master it" (NIV). The word *master* in this text is the Hebrew word *mashal,* and it means to rule, have dominion, or exercise dominion over. Wow. Sounds similar.

In spite of the complication that came with the entrance of sin and death into the world, the challenge remains the same: take control over the bad stuff, don't let it rule. It is true that the job is a lot harder now because, through their sin, Adam and Eve empowered satan to have authority in the earthly realm. The garden disobedience was a battle won for satan and a battle lost for humankind—for sure. Life has become harder for mankind, but our challenge is really still the same: resist the bad stuff and cultivate the good. The call is to begin with our own hearts and inner-lives, but we don't stop there.

Several thousand years later, satan cunningly waved his Garden of Eden win in the face of the Son of God Himself, Jesus Christ.

Luke 4:5-6 relays this encounter:

> *Then the devil, taking* [Jesus] *up on a high mountain, showed Him all the kingdoms of the world in a moment of time. And the devil said to Him, "All this authority I will give You, and their glory; for this has been delivered to me, and I give it to whomever I wish."*

KINGDOMS (BASILEIA): THE TERRITORY OF A RULER, RIGHT TO RULE, OR AREA SUBJECT TO THE RULE OF A KING.

AUTHORITY (EXOUSIA): THE LIBERTY OF DOING AS ONE PLEASES, PHYSICAL POWER, MENTAL POWER, STRENGTH, INFLUENCE, RULE, OR GOVERNMENT.

The word *authority* in this text is the Greek word *exousia*, which means the liberty of doing as one pleases, physical power, mental power, strength, influence, rule, or government. The word for *kingdoms* is the Greek word *basileia,* which means the territory of a ruler, right to rule, or area subject to the rule of a king.

Satan was flaunting the fact that, because of Adam and Eve's sin in the Garden of Eden, he now had power, influence, and rule over territory in the earth. In our modern expression we might say, "he gained authority in the nations." What used to be the domain of God, after being given over to the free will of His creation, had now become a battle-ground where satan did indeed have legal access and authority.

[SATAN] WILL ONLY TEMPT US WITH THINGS THAT ARE OF VALUE TO US, OR THE VERY THING THAT GOD HAS ACTUALLY DESTINED FOR US TO POSSESS...SATAN TRIED TO TEMPT [JESUS] WITH THE VERY THING HE HAD COME FOR.

Satan is not stupid, misguided perhaps, but not stupid. He will only tempt us with things that are of value to us, or the very thing that God has actually destined for us to possess. Knowing that Jesus was the prophesied Messiah, the rightful Heir of the nations of the earth, and that He had a holy love for humankind—a love that wanted humankind restored to the Father in Heaven—satan tried to tempt Jesus with the very thing He had come for: authority over the nations.

JESUS, OF COURSE, DID NOT TAKE THE BAIT. HE KNEW THAT HIS FATHER IN HEAVEN HAD A NARROW PATH FOR HIM TO WALK TO CONQUER THE DOMINION OF DARKNESS.

Satan tried to lure Jesus into disobedience to the Father by offering Him the sphere of influence he had tricked Adam and Eve out of, in the Garden of Eden, millennia earlier. In classic satan style, he sought to lure the Christ through the carnal nature. This, of course, would have been a much less painful route than the Cross. This is one of satan's classic maneuvers. He will deceitfully, sleekly try to deceive us into taking through unrighteous avenues the very thing the Lord will give us if we simply do it God's way. Satan knows that, if we take his bait, though we may acquire a level of what we are after, he will be able to abort the fullness of our destiny and ultimately rule over us. Whatever you submit to will rule you (see Rom. 6:16). So satan tried to lure Jesus by saying [paraphrased of course], "Just bow down to me, Jesus. Bow down to me, and I will give You the very thing You are after; I will give You the kingdoms of the earth."

Satan knew that for Jesus to bow to him would have been a transgression of the first commandment, "You shall have no other gods before me…" (Exod. 20:3). If Jesus had bowed, it ultimately would have led to the abortion of His mission. If He had bowed to satan, joined his fold, and had taken the "shortcut" to dominion over the Kingdoms of the earth, He would no longer have qualified as a sinless, unblemished sacrifice for our sins a few years later on the Cross at Calvary.

Jesus, of course, did not take the bait. He knew that His Father in Heaven had a narrow path for Him to walk to conquer the dominion of darkness. Seeing with the eyes of eternity and wisdom, in Sonly obedience, He did not resist the cup that His Father had for Him to drink. There was no shortcut mentality in His mind—only total abandonment to the will of the Father.

My main point in this opening chapter is to emphasize this: satan tempted Jesus with the very thing Jesus was after, the kingdoms of the earth. Jesus came not only to redeem the souls of men but to take nations. He came to win it *all* back.

Authority Won Back at the Cross

We see this powerful truth demonstrated again in what is commonly termed the *Great Commission*. This commission is found in Matthew 28. Jesus had just defeated satan's dominion through the Cross—overthrowing death, hell, and the grave—once and for all. It was the ultimate victory and ransoming of authority. He then imparted this authority back to man, who was created in the image of God, by declaring to His disciples,

...All authority has been given to Me in heaven and on earth. Go therefore and make disciples of all the nations, baptizing them in the name of the Father and of the Son and of the Holy Spirit, teaching them to observe all things that I have commanded you; and lo, I am with you always, even to the end of the age (Matthew 28:18-20).

JESUS, THE SECOND ADAM, WON BACK WHAT WAS ORIGINALLY GIVEN TO THE FIRST ADAM. HE WON BACK DOMINION IN THE EARTH.

There are two points in this text that are paramount revelations we need to walk in as believers. The first is this: Jesus got the authority back. The word *given* in verse 18 is the Greek word *didomi*, which can be translated to give back to someone something which originally belonged to them or to return something to its original owner. That was the transaction of the Cross. Jesus, the Second Adam, won back what was originally given to the first Adam. He won back dominion in the earth.

ADAM AND EVE WERE GIVEN THE GARDEN OF EDEN. IN THE POST-CROSS WORLD, WE ARE GIVEN NATIONS.

Second, out of this position of authority redeemed, He then turned to His disciples—us—and commissioned them—us—to take that dominion authority and to go forth to make disciples of nations. He commissioned them to teach the nations to obey all the ways of the Lord. The word *nations* is *ethnos*, which can be translated tribes, people groups, the human species at large, pagan nations, Gentile nations, or—ready for this?—literally, *nations*.

Greek scholars who did the work of translating the Word of God worked diligently, sentence by sentence, to translate the Bible in the way that they believed most accurately extracted the meaning of the original text. With this in mind, I find it amazing that, in Matthew 28, when translating the word *ethnos*, they did not choose the words: *pagan nation, tribes,* or *cultures*. They chose the word *nations*. Why? I believe it is obvious: it is the word that most accurately portrays the intended meaning of the text. I also have faith, of course, that their hand was guided by the Divine who was jealous to get a message across. The message was simple and strong—Jesus came for nations.

NATIONS (ETHNOS): TRIBES, PEOPLE GROUPS, THE HUMAN SPECIES AT LARGE, PAGAN NATIONS, GENTILE NATIONS OR…LITERALLY *NATIONS*.

We are to make disciples of the heathen, yes. We are to make disciples of every people group and culture, yes. We are to make disciples throughout the human race at large, yes. But furthermore, the text is clear, we are to take the authority that Jesus won back at the Cross and make disciples of nations (literal nations) and teach nations to obey all that the Lord has commanded. We are to teach them His ways. Adam and Eve were given the Garden of Eden. In the post-Cross world, we are given nations.

Recently in the middle of preaching this message at a conference, I received an on-the-spot insight regarding the "commissions" Jesus gave His disciples. This revelation profoundly impacted me and relates to everything we are talking about. In Matthew 10, Jesus is commissioning His disciples to go and do the works of the Kingdom. In this chapter, He gives them several instructions. Specifically, in verses 7 and 8, He says to them,

> *"And as you go, preach, saying, 'The kingdom of heaven is at hand.' Heal the sick, cleanse the lepers, raise the dead, cast out demons. Freely you have received, freely give."*

This is a pre-Cross commission. Jesus had not yet secured His victory in the realm of time, though He was advancing His Father's Kingdom at every move and sending His disciples to do the same. Even though they were doing major damage to the kingdom of darkness, the total redemption of the authority that was lost in the Garden of Eden had not yet taken place. I find it riveting to think that the pre-Cross commission Jesus gave His disciples in Matthew 10 was to preach the Gospel, heal the sick, cleanse the lepers, raise the dead, and cast out demons. The post-Cross commission was to go, with full authority redeemed, and make disciples of nations.

39

I have heard it said that the preaching of the Gospel with signs and wonders following is "basic Christianity." I agree. When His disciples were still "in training" with Him, Jesus sent them forward to function at that level—to preach the Gospel with a demonstration of resurrection power. I believe in Matthew 28 He took it up a notch and was basically saying,

> Take all that I have shown you. Take the signs, take the wonders, take the healing power, take the resurrection power—and now use your faith to also make disciples of nations. Turn them to Me. Change the way they think and behave. With My power backing you up, disciple them.

With all this in mind, this is the summary of what I believe Jesus is saying in Matthew 28.

> Listen, guys, when Adam and Eve allowed sin into the earth through their disobedience, satan gained ground; he got authority. This is why he could try and tempt Me with the kingdoms of the earth when I was fasting in the desert; many of them were in his grip. But I have some really good news. I legally defeated satan by offering Myself as an unblemished atoning sacrifice for your sins. I have taken that authority back. He lost his ground. It is Mine again. Now guess what? I am giving it to *you*. I am giving it to you just like it was given to the first Adam in the Garden. I am the Second Adam, I have won the authority back, and now I am giving it to you, My disciples. You are now being commissioned with this authority to *go* and make disciples of nations. Go, be fruitful, multiply, subdue, take dominion, and teach them to obey what I have commanded. Work to establish My Kingdom on the earth as it is in Heaven. I am the Second Adam, and you are inside Me and My victory if you are My disciples. So *go*; just know that you don't have to do it with your own strength. I won't leave you. I am giving you My Spirit to help you. Run like you mean it. You are now My ambassadors in the earth; you are the salt

of the earth. Let your light shine before all men. You have a message—speak it to nations.

Of course, Jesus was commissioning His disciples to preach the good news that He is the Messiah and that if any person believes in Him they will be saved from eternal judgment. They were commissioned to preach the good news of Jesus' sacrifice, proclaiming that all now have the opportunity to come into relational restoration with the Father, His eternal Kingdom, and all that His Kingdom contains. However, the Gospel they were to preach was about more than just a free ticket to Heaven. It was about making disciples. A true disciple does not only know her teacher relationally; a true disciple does what her teacher does. To disciple a nation means to teach that nation to do what Jesus would do.

TO DISCIPLE A NATION MEANS TO TEACH THAT NATION TO DO WHAT JESUS WOULD DO.

To teach a person to walk in the ways of their Savior, Jesus Christ, means to teach them to be light in the earth, pushing back the darkness around them just like Jesus did during His earthly ministry. The true disciple of Christ is not just one who is forgiven, but is one who is also walking in Kingdom truth and sharing it wherever he goes.

41

This was the mandate. Go into all the earth. Preach the good news of the Kingdom of God. Make disciples of nations. This is our divine inheritance in Christ because it is His divine inheritance. Let us have hearts that truly respond to this great commission and say, "Jesus, I long to give You the full reward of Your sacrifice. I long to bring nations to Your feet. Raise me up and use me to disciple nations and teach them to obey all that You have commanded."

Let's do it, Church.

Endnotes

1. Banning Liebscher is the director of Jesus Culture, the young adults ministry at Bethel Church in Redding, California. Find out more about Jesus Culture at www.jesusculture.org.

2. Definitions throughout the book have been taken from the Greek lexicon based on Thayer's and Smith's Bible Dictionary plus others; this is keyed to the large Kittel and the "Theological Dictionary of the New Testament." These files are public domain. The Hebrew lexicon is Brown, Driver, Briggs, Gesenius Lexicon; this is keyed to the "Theological Word Book of the Old Testament." These files are considered public domain.

CHAPTER 2

Righteousness and Justice Are the Foundation of God's Throne

Righteousness and justice are the foundation of Your throne.
Mercy and truth go before Your face (Psalm 89:14).

In my initial years of full-time Christian ministry, I had the privilege of serving with World Vision Canada in Vancouver as the city director of a ministry called NeighbourLink. Day after day, I worked to coordinate various churches in the city to be the hands and feet of Jesus to the poor and afflicted. It was such an awesome season and a privilege to serve the Lord in this way. We connected volunteers with elderly people who needed help with shopping, housecleaning, and other random tasks; we assisted shut-ins who needed food delivery, single moms needing rides to doctors' appointments, and more.

Week by week, we saw many turn their hearts toward God and get healed as they came into contact with Christian volunteers who were filled with the love, mercy, and power of God. In all honesty, however, though I loved the results of the work we were doing as a ministry in the city, the actual position I was in drove me a bit nutty.

I spent most days frustrated with the feeling of being chained behind a desk. My daily function was primarily administrative. This is great if your passion is administration; however, mine definitely is not. I love to get out on the streets, get my hands dirty pulling people out of dumpsters, sharing words of life with the lost, and seeing people healed in the name of Jesus. My heart burns for the hands-on, face-to-face encounters with the broken and suffering.

**I DID NOT REALIZE THAT THE LORD WAS KEENLY INTER-
ESTED IN WORKING REVELATION INTO ME AS I SERVED.**

Even though sitting at a desk day after day answering calls, leaving messages, opening mail, and going to meetings with senior pastors (who were mostly 30 years older than me!) was borderline torture for me, I knew that the Lord was asking me to be faithful in this position. So I was. I did not realize that the Lord was keenly interested in working a foundational revelation into me as I served Him, day after day, facilitating hundreds of volunteers to do His acts of mercy. God was laying a foundation in my spirit that would be essential for the seasons ahead.

Every morning I went into the office an hour or two before we opened in order to spend time in prayer and worship. Jesus needed to be the first priority of each day, both for me and for the ministry. I would pick up my guitar, sit on top of my desk, with pens on one side and a computer monitor on the other, and I would bellow my heart out in song before Him! These times with Him were so sweet, until the torment began. Not a torment from hell, but a torment from Heaven.

**...EVERY TIME I WOULD...WAIT UPON HIM IN SILENCE, I
WOULD SEE OR HEAR THE WORD *JUSTICE*.**

Have you ever had God speak something to you over and over and over and over, but you felt like you just didn't quite "get it"? A friend of mine calls this dynamic "the numbskull anointing." Whatever you call it, I had it. Almost every time I would close my eyes and wait upon Him in silence, I would see or hear the word *justice*. I would think, *Justice? Justice? Justice!? Um, God, I don't get it.* The word *justice* was a vague word to me—you know, one of those words that you hear used a lot, but if you had to explain what it actually meant, you would be at a loss for words. I had never really heard a teaching on what biblical justice was, why it mattered, or how it fit into our daily lives with God. In all honesty, when I heard the word *justice,* I would think of a courthouse and some older man with a black robe and a gavel who would send bad guys to jail. I saw no connection between older men in black robes with gavels and finding volunteers to help seniors with grocery shopping. It was a mystery. So I did what seemed to make sense—I asked God to explain Himself.

I HEARD A VOICE IN MY SPIRIT SAY, *PSALM 89:14.*

As I began to seek Him more earnestly about justice, one day while I was in prayer, He responded vividly. I heard a voice in my spirit say, *Psalm 89:14*. Immediately I rushed to look it up in my Bible and read the words of this Scripture, *"Righteousness and justice are the foundation of Your throne."* Jackpot! I was so encouraged by this word of knowledge. However, I still did not understand what He was trying to tell me. Call me thick-headed. So I began digging into the Word of God. Like a wild gold miner, I grabbed my Bible reference books and began to search it out. Let me share with you some of what I found out.

JUSTICE (MISHPAT): JUDGMENT, THE ACT OF DECIDING A CASE, THE EXECUTION OF THAT SENTENCE, THE JUST AND RIGHT ATTRIBUTES OF GOD OR MAN, OR THAT WHICH IS PROPER AND RIGHT.

JUSTICE IS SIMPLY THE ACT OF MAKING SOMETHING THAT IS WRONG RIGHT AGAIN.

45

The word *justice* in this Scripture is the Hebrew word *mishpat*, which means judgment, the act of deciding a case, the execution of that sentence, the just and right attributes of God or man, or that which is proper and right. Bingo! The portion of the definition which said, "That which is proper and right," hit me like a two-by-four in the gut. I then remembered that I had heard somewhere that justice is simply the act of making something that is wrong right again. The example: when a broken bone was fully mended. Justice is the act of mending a broken bone and making it "right" again.

The profound thing about that analogy is that when a bone is mended, it is actually stronger than it was prior to the break because of the extra calcium that forms around the break point. In the same way, the act of enforcing justice where injustice has prevailed serves to not only reestablish that which is right, but actually strengthen it. Wow! An amazing historical example of this would be the Holocaust of the Jews by Nazi Germany. When the Allied forces defeated the Germans, not only was justice reestablished, but it was strengthened. Ever since that moment in global history, there has been a resolve in many nations of the earth to ensure that nothing like the Holocaust ever happens to the Jewish people again. That is an overt global illustration of what it means to strengthen justice.

RIGHTEOUSNESS (TSEDEQ): THAT WHICH IS RIGHT, WHAT IS NORMAL OR THE WAY THINGS SHOULD BE, RIGHTNESS IN SPEECH AND ACTION, RIGHTNESS IN DE-LIVERING THE OPPRESSED, VINDICATION OR VICTORY OVER THAT WHICH IS WRONG.

FOUNDATION (MAKOW): FIXED OR ESTABLISHED PLACE.

THRONE (KICCE): THE SEAT OF HONOR, THE SEAT WHERE A ROYAL DIGNITARY SITS, THE PLACE OF AU-THORITY, OR THE PLACE OF POWER.

The word *righteousness* in Psalm 89:14 is the Hebrew word *tsedeq*, which means that which is right, what is normal or the way things should be, rightness in speech and action, rightness in delivering the oppressed, vindication, or victory over that which is wrong. The word *foundation* is *makow*, which means fixed or established place; and the word *throne* is *kicce*, which translates to the seat of honor, the seat where a royal dignitary sits, the place of authority, or the place of power.

...I AM HUNGRY THAT GOD WOULD NOT ONLY VISIT OUR CITIES AND OUR NATIONS, BUT THAT HE WOULD STAY.

So, boiled down, what Psalm 89:14 is saying is: *doing the right thing and delivering the oppressed is the foundation of the place where God will sit!* OK, now God was getting my attention. I don't know about you but I am a revival freak to the core. Even more than that, I am hungry that God would not only visit our cities and our nations, but that He would stay. We want Him to find His resting place with us (see Ps. 132). We want Him to sit and remain. According to Psalm 89:14, the place where He will sit is the place where righteousness and justice are firmly established.

He then unfolded it all to my heart, "Faytene, you are working to establish righteousness and justice in your city as you serve here day after day. Every time you pick up the phone, lick a stamp, or run an errand to advance the cause of righteousness and justice, you are working to build a throne for My presence in this city. This is a high calling." That put my day-to-day responsibilities in a totally different light! This was revival strategy! From that revelation onward, I had a skip in my step, even in the midst of the administrative tasks that I detested. My whole perspective changed! When people asked me, "What do you do for a living?" I would tell them, "I'm a throne builder; I am working to build a throne for Jesus in my city." I love it!

On an individual level, I would see this on a regular basis as those we were serving surrendered their hearts to Jesus Christ and, by doing so, gave Him a place of rulership in their lives. But what God was speaking to me about was not just regarding individuals, it was about my city. Furthermore, what about a nation?

I am now almost a decade down the road from my season of service at NeighbourLink and my primary focus is national reformation and revival. However, the revelation of Psalm 89:14 lingers as a strong reference point in my spirit: *righteousness and justice are the foundation of His throne.* But let's now take it from the gutters of society to the other end of society's structure, which is the topic of discussion for most of this book. I was simply a city-wide ministry director, but what about those who are influencing decision making at the highest levels of authority in our nations? Does God care about this level? Should we? If so, what does caring look like? What does caring act like? Good questions, I think.

LOOKING INTO THE EYES OF JUSTICE

I HAD NO IDEA I WOULD BE HEADING INTO ONE OF THE MOST UNSTABLE NATIONS IN ALL OF AFRICA AT THAT TIME.

These types of questions took on an entire new meaning for me a couple years later when, in 2000, I bought an open-ended ticket to Liberia, West Africa, to do mercy missions work. Why Liberia? Well it's simple: because God was speaking to me about serving African children and, as I prayed about it, this was the nation I believed He was calling me to go to. I had no idea I would be heading into one of the most unstable nations in all of Africa at that time. Moreover, once there, I found out that Liberia was one of the last places most missionaries wanted to go. This was because of how dangerous and devastated it was. It was a nation that had been ripped to shreds by tyrant leadership and by civil wars.

I had often prayed, "Lord, send me where no one else wants to go!" I suppose He took that prayer seriously. He sent me to the bushes of war-torn Africa perhaps because He was lacking volunteers willing to go to that particular region of the earth; only He knows for sure. Now He sends me to Parliament. Hmmm…

…IT IS ESTIMATED THAT 200,000 PEOPLE WERE BRU-TALLY MURDERED, MOSTLY IN FACE-TO-FACE COMBAT.

Within the decade prior to my going to Liberia, it is estimated that 200,000 people were brutally murdered in that country, mostly in face-to-face combat. That's a lot of death considering bombs weren't dropping. When I stepped off the plane, the Liberia I greeted was full of corrupt and selfish leadership at the highest level. It was also full of men and women, young and old, whose lives had been deeply traumatized by the brutality and cruelty of war, and full of orphans who were starving and dying of disease—all of these ones struggling inside the borders of a nation gone wrong.

I want to say, however, that although I am sure my mother did not get much sleep during that season, I am thankful for the chance I had to be there. It was a privilege to be serving in Liberia at that particular time of their history. People sometimes ask me, "Was it hard?" My response, "It was very hard, but very good. There is no better place to be than in the center of the Lord's will, no matter what the cost or discomfort level." In His will I was, and the satisfaction of knowing it was deeply rewarding.

I lived with a group of beautiful elderly Catholic nuns near a leper colony. Every week I would go into the villages surrounding the town that

I was living in and I would look for Jesus. I would look for what He was doing so that I could partner with Him. This pursuit led me directly to some of the most vulnerable in the nation: the abandoned and starving children. I remember the first little one I met. Actually I don't think I will ever be able to forget him. His name was Saye, which means firstborn son. He found his way into the back row of a little mud-hut church. I had come to visit that Sunday morning because one of my Liberian friends was speaking. I wanted to support my friend and also visit the village, as I had never been there before.

I will never forget the first time I laid eyes on Saye. He was tiny. He wore a man's red t-shirt that was much too big for him. It had holes from the wear and was faded from the sun. The shirt drooped down over his one shoulder a bit and extended to just above his dusty knees. It was all he was wearing—like a dress. He captivated my attention immediately as he looked down at the ground and then rolled his big brown eyes upward at the "white lady" to see if she—me—was looking back. I am not sure if he was in awe because he had never seen white skin like mine before, if he was just curious, or if he was actually hoping I might notice him back. Likely it was all of the above.

His eyes were big and brown like a teddy bear's and he had this sweet little button nose that made me want to squeeze him. His cheeks still had baby fat and were cute and rounded. Looking at his face, I couldn't really tell what kind of a state his body was actually in. I sat beside him and smiled as we continued to listen to my friend share his message with the church congregation. After the service was over, our plan was to make some house visits in the area. There was a boy just up the road who had recently given his heart to Jesus, and my friend wanted to see how he was doing.

> HIS EYES WERE BIG AND BROWN LIKE A TEDDY BEAR'S
> AND HE HAD THIS SWEET LITTLE BUTTON NOSE...
> LOOKING AT HIS FACE, I COULDN'T REALLY TELL WHAT
> KIND OF A STATE HIS BODY WAS ACTUALLY IN.

Saye stuck to me like glue. He did not say anything, but he was my new best friend; I could tell! As we walked, he took my hand. It was a bit of a long walk so, once I felt I had enough of his trust, I motioned to pick him up. He lifted his arms to indicate that it was OK. This is when the dagger hit my heart.

As I lifted him into my arms, I realized how physically fragile he was. He was so boney, skinny, and frail that I thought I was going to break him if I held him too tightly. Underneath that large red shirt and behind those big brown eyes and pudgy cheeks was a starving child. I was forever changed by what I was feeling as I held him in my arms—I will never be the same again. It is one thing to see a starving child on a late-night infomercial back in North America; it is totally another thing to hold one in your arms and look into his eyes when he is only a few inches from yours. It was not an option; I needed to find out this boy's story and be part of the answer for him.

...BEHIND THOSE BIG BROWN EYES AND PUDGY CHEEKS WAS A STARVING CHILD.

I found out that Saye was a product of the war. His father was nowhere to be found. There was a man some thought might be his father, but this man refused to take responsibility. I soon learned that this was not uncommon. If alive, most men were so ripped apart by the war, and so shaken by the instability of the nation, that they could not muster up the emotional strength to truly be fathers and take care of their families. His mother was in another village far away. In this Liberia, one of the only ways that a woman could provide for herself and her children was to have a boyfriend. It normally went like this: if she would give her boyfriend sex, he would help provide for her, and this meant that she and her children might not starve. You can see the cycle. This would inevitably lead to more children to feed. Saye's mom now had several other children she needed to care for, and Saye had been left in the wake of it all. Due to the reality that boyfriends rarely stuck around long, Saye's mom was most likely working at finding a new one and simply trying to survive.

Saye had been left with Grandma, who was around 80 years old, and this meant he basically fended for himself. He was known as the beggar child. He would go from hut to hut and even find his way to nearby villages, sometimes miles away, trying to find someone who would take pity on him and give him some rice or banana. Now I understood why he was so drawn to the white lady who was visibly "fat and greasy"—what they call you if you look healthy. It was my honor to be "taken to" by him, knowing that whatever we do for the least, we do unto Jesus Himself. Without going into all the details of the story, I did what I could at that moment; I gave him the fruit I had, prayed for him, and then determined in my heart to go home and seek God for a long-term solution for this child.

> I WAS A 26-YEAR-OLD JESUS FREAK IN THE BACK WOODS OF LIBERIA WITH NO MISSION'S BASE, NO MONEY, NO INFRASTRUCTURE—JUST RAW GOD.

I had no idea what I was doing! I was a 26-year-old Jesus freak in the back woods of Liberia with no mission's base, no money, and no infrastructure—just raw God. Good thing God is enough. Through a series of amazing Divine encounters over the next 48 hours, I discovered a malnutrition unit at a nearby Methodist hospital. The unit had nurses who would work (for about $5) to rehabilitate children like Saye. They were doing amazing work. However, they were so busy in the unit caring for the children that they rarely had time to go into the villages and find others who were in need. I was thrilled with gratitude at the privilege of being the missing link for both the hospital staff and children like Saye.

On the next hospital day, not only was I able to bring Saye, but two other desperate children I had found in that same village as well! After only a couple weeks they were all restored to strength. One was an 8-month-old baby, Baby Kou, who looked the size of a newborn. If I am remembering correctly, her mother died at birth. Because of this, she was left with her elderly grandparents, who were feeding her rice water (foamy water at the top of a pot when you boil rice). When we found her, she was on the verge of death. I clearly remember her grandmother handing her to me saying, "If you don't do something, she will die." No pressure. Ahhh, what a privilege to be the hands and feet of Jesus. By the end of my time in Liberia—7 months—I had the joy of helping many more children receive rehabilitation treatment and medicine, and many of them started attending school. It was amazing to watch God break into their worlds and rescue them time and time again.

51

THE KINGS OF THE EARTH WILL BOW

Not long after this, during a time of prayer in my modest cement-walled missionary room, I began to meditate on and pray into Psalm 72. This time of prayer put a whole other spin on my Liberian experience, and like Psalm 89:14, it marked me. Looking back, I can see that the revelation I received through this Scripture was a shaping motivation for much of what we are doing today in Canada as we seek to influence the leaders of the nation to do justice and love mercy (see Mic. 6:8).

> THIS KING DEFENDED THE AFFLICTED AND SAVED THE CHILDREN OF THE NEEDY. HE WOULD CRUSH THE OPPRESSOR...HIS RULE WOULD BE REFRESHING TO THE PEOPLE...

Psalm 72 is a prayer of David for his son, Solomon, who was about to succeed him as the king of Israel. It was also a Messianic psalm, meaning it was a prophetic psalm regarding Jesus and how He would rule in His eternal Kingdom. The psalm speaks of a king who would be endowed with the Lord's justice and with the Lord's righteousness so that he could judge the people, specifically the afflicted, in righteous ways.

This King defended the afflicted and saved the children of the needy. He would crush the oppressor and would have an everlasting Kingdom—this is how we know it was not only a prayer of David for Solomon but also a Messianic psalm speaking of the reign of Christ. His rule would be refreshing to the people and in His days those who were righteous would prosper. There would be prosperity in the land, and His rule would extend from sea to sea and from the river to the ends of the earth. And then it goes on to say,

> Yes, all kings shall fall down before Him; all nations shall serve Him. For He will deliver the needy when he cries, the poor also, and him who has no helper. He will spare the poor and needy, and will save the souls of the needy. He will redeem their life from oppression and violence; and precious shall be their blood in His sight (Psalm 72:11-14).

IN HIS BIGNESS AND IN HIS MASSIVE AUTHORITY, HE SEES AND HEARS AND ACTS TO DELIVER THOSE WHO COULD NEVER PAY HIM BACK.

This King is awesome! He is strong, yet kind. Just, yet merciful. In His massive power, strength, and dominion, He chooses to deliver the needy—even though He doesn't have to; He is the King and can do what He wants! He chooses to reach out to the afflicted who have no one to help; He chooses to save the needy from death, oppression, and violence, and specifically He chooses to defend the children of the needy (see Ps. 72:4). He does all of this because their blood is precious in His sight.

Oh, how could you not love a King like this! As I meditated on all this, I began to fall more and more in love with Jesus and His ways. In His bigness and in His massive authority, He sees, hears, and acts to deliver those who could never pay Him back. This is so like God. Next I began to meditate specifically on verse 11 where it says that the kings of the earth will bow down before Him and serve Him. Let me say it again, in case you did not fully catch that: *the kings of the earth will bow down before Him and serve Him.* Think about that. I sure did and still do.

CAN YOU IMAGINE A WORLD WHERE THE KINGS OF THE EARTH, WHERE THE KINGS AND LEADERS OF NA-TIONS…REGIONS, CITIES, AND TOWNS WERE ALL BOW-ING DOWN TO JESUS AND WALKING IN HIS WAYS?…THE DEATH AND THE DESTRUCTION AND THE STARVATION THAT DAILY KNOCKED AT MY DOOR IN LIBERIA WERE ALL BECAUSE KINGS WERE NOT BOWING TO JESUS NOR WALKING IN HIS WAYS.

Can you imagine a world where the kings of the earth, where the kings and leaders of nations, where the kings and leaders of regions, cities, and towns were all bowing down to Jesus and walking in His ways? Truly bowing down, and truly walking in His ways? Not just men or women talking Christian lingo for political advantage, but men and women who live it?

I don't understand all of the back room politics that led to the crisis in Liberia, but I do know that the death and the destruction and the starvation that daily knocked on my door were all because kings were not bowing to Jesus nor walking in His ways. Even though they may have professed His name, perhaps because it was culturally and even politically beneficial for them, they were not authentically bowing their lives to Him. They were serving many other things. They served pride. They served riches. They served the opinions of others. They served political power. They served personal glory. Sound like anyone you know? Maybe lucifer? (Sorry to state the obvious so bluntly.)

A NATION LAY IN RUINS AND A PEOPLE WAS DEVASTATED ALL BECAUSE KINGS WERE SERVING THE WRONG LORDS.

The Liberian rulers refused to bow to Jesus and His ways. How do I know this? Easy. According to Psalm 72, Jesus' ruler has regard for the poor, needy, and afflicted who cry out. Not so here. I didn't need to know the history of Liberia or the personal credos of those in authority—the fruit was all around me. A nation lay in ruins and a people was devastated all because kings were serving the wrong lords. The lords they served—pride, power, riches, and the like—apparently had very little regard for little ones like Saye. It brought right home to me the reality that the little boy in my arms and his daily struggle to survive was all because kings refused to bow to Jesus and His ways. At that moment, I was struck with this revelation: *we can spend our whole lives picking up orphans, one at a time, and this would be both noble and deeply rewarding, but if we can touch the heart of kings, we can liberate a nation. In a moment, we could liberate a multitude of Sayes, Baby Kous, and the sea of men, women, and children who stand with them.*

IF WE CAN TOUCH THE HEART OF KINGS, WE CAN LIBERATE A NATION.

It would have been very easy, believe it or not, for me to stay in Liberia forever. I remember the night before I left Ganta, the town where I was serving. Two of "my boys," Cheema and Torch, slept over that night. I don't know exactly what it feels like to be a mother, as I am not one in the natural yet, but I am confident that I have a close idea. These two and a handful of other Liberian children had become like my own. During my time in Liberia, we were inseparable. They went with me everywhere. I can say with total honesty that leaving them was the hardest thing, emotionally, I have ever done in my life. I have never wept so hard for love as when I sat on my floor with my head pressed up against the wall, watching them sleep for the last time. *It was hard.* I still cry when I think about them, and am weeping even now as I type.

It would not have been courageous to stay in war-torn, poverty-plagued Liberia. It would have been the easiest thing. What took courage was to return home, out of obedience to the call of God, and to begin to walk a step at a time toward influencing the most powerful political leaders of my nation. Unpredictable Liberian pre-teens with semi-automatic weapons were a delight to me. First world politicians and people of influence were terrifying. They were foreign creatures altogether. But God was taking my perspective to a whole other horizon. He was lifting my eyes to see something that has the power to shift the reality of multitudes. I might never hold another orphan in my arms, but what if I gave my life to have the honor of playing a *small* part in changing the world for multitudes of needy, helpless, and voiceless children? What about a big part? If I was going to sacrifice and leave my Liberian children, it was for something *big*. As I heard a street kid say once, "Go big or go home." Well, I was going home and it was time to go big too—big for my God and big for these ones who had captured my heart.

55

IF TOUCHING THE HEART OF A KING COULD TRULY LIBERATE A NATION, THEN I THINK IT IS ONLY REASONABLE AND SANE THAT WE, AS LOVERS OF CHRIST, WOULD BE INTERESTED IN DOING THAT.

As I meditated on the revelation of Psalm 72, about the kings of the earth bowing, God was injecting a core DNA into my spiritual make-up. He was imparting an intuitive knowing that not only had He called us to touch the lowliest of society, but He had called us to impact the hearts of kings as well. It is God's will that they lay foundations of righteousness and justice that will be the landing pad for His rule and thereby bring freedom to the oppressed, weak, and vulnerable. If this is true, which I clearly believe it is, then I am totally "in." If touching the heart of a king could truly liberate a nation, then I think it is only reasonable and sane that we, as lovers of Christ, would be interested in that.

56

CHAPTER 3

Dream: You Are the Salt of the Earth

You are the salt of the earth; but if the salt loses its flavor, how shall it be seasoned? It is then good for nothing but to be thrown out and trampled underfoot by men (Matthew 5:13).

Recently on a trip to Israel, I had a powerful dream that drove home the truths that: (1) God has called us to disciple nations and (2) God has called us to work at establishing righteousness and justice in the earth. In the dream, I was ministering at a conference that a good friend of mine was hosting. While preparing, I felt the power of God begin to come upon me in a very tangible way. I specifically felt His presence on my hands, and I could feel it with increasing intensity. When I looked down at my hands, I saw little clear crystals beginning to form. I knew that it was salt in its pure form, before it goes through a commercial process. It was pure, raw chunks of salt. In the dream, as I looked at it, I knew intuitively that it was salt from Heaven. It was something my Father in Heaven was giving me! It was so cool!

Many in the room, my friend included, began to gather around, and we all looked in wonder and childlike excitement at what was happening. My friend ran his hand over mine and took all the salt that had accumulated. He then cupped it in his hand and formed it into a ball about the size of a golf ball. He looked at the salt ball inquisitively and walked off. In the dream, I was initially annoyed that he would take my salt and leave—but I quickly got over it, somehow knowing that there would soon be more. Sure enough, immediately more salt began to form on my hands, and I continued to rejoice in my heart at the wonder of God and His ways. I then awoke abruptly, knowing that it was a "God dream" and that the Lord had an intention in His heart to reveal something powerful to me through it. So I began to pray. Soon thereafter, my roommate returned from swimming with friends in the Dead Sea and said, "Faytene, look at these amazing balls of salt we found." In her hands was the exact thing I had seen in my dream: salt balls! God had my full attention now, and I was even more eager to hear what He had to say.

As I prayed, three Scriptures rushed into my mind. I was thankful for this because I wholeheartedly believe that all revelation must be confirmed by the Word of God. The Scriptures were Matthew 5:13, Hebrews 11:33, and Revelation 19:8. As I dug into them, and brought them before the Lord in prayer, a powerful revelation began to unfold before me. In the rest of this short chapter, I want to take you on a journey and invite you to consider what I learned through them and through the dream.

> LIKE SALT SPRINKLED OVER A PIECE OF MEAT, WE ARE CALLED TO BE EVERYWHERE, AND IN EVERYTHING, MAKING THE WORLD A BETTER PLACE.

Matthew 5:13 says,

> *You are the salt of the earth; but if the salt loses its flavor, how shall it be seasoned? It is then good for nothing but to be thrown out and trampled underfoot by men.*

Modern dictionaries define salt as a mineral used for preserving food, as well as a seasoning. Along with this, it is used to cure. *Matthew Henry's Complete Commentary on the Whole Bible* speaks of this text saying that, "Christians…are the salt of the earth. If they be as they should be they are *as good salt,* [pure], and small, and broken into many grains, but very useful and necessary…."

Matthew 5 is declaring that, as believers in Christ, it is our calling to be the preserving agents of our world. Like salt sprinkled over a piece of meat, we are called to be everywhere, and in everything, making the world a better place—tasty—and bringing truth that will preserve it from destructive patterns and influences—decay.

> THE ABILITY TO DO THIS WOULD NOT COME FROM OUR OWN STRENGTH, GOOD IDEAS, GOOD INTENTIONS, OR ABILITY TO "FIGURE OUT" SOLUTIONS WITH OUR CARNAL MINDS.

In the dream, the salt was directly from Heaven, not something that I got from earth. I want to highlight that the Lord was clearly saying He is the One who will pour out an anointing from Heaven on His children to be the salt of the earth. The aspect of Him being the source is so important for us to catch. The ability to be the salt does not come from our own strength, good ideas, good intentions, or ability to "figure out" solutions with our carnal minds. Our ability, like Daniel in the Old Testament, to interpret dreams and have solutions full of wisdom, will be supernaturally endowed upon us by His empowering grace.

We cannot be the salt of the earth without God's help, but at the same time, we have a great responsibility to receive what He has given us. Jesus ripped the veil between earth and Heaven when He died on the Cross. As ones who have received Him as Savior, we now have access to what we need from that realm, even while still on earth. With access comes responsibility. Matthew 5:13 seems to say that if we do not activate our saltiness in the earth then we are good for nothing! That is intense. I don't know about you, but when I see Jesus face to face, after I cross into eternity once and for all, I want Him to look at me and say, "Well done, good and faithful servant," not, "Hey, nice to finally see you here, Good For Nothing."

We are called to use what He gives us as an offering of love and worship to Him. As I thought of the dream in light of Matthew 5:13, I had a sense that God was pouring out a fresh empowerment to be the salt of the earth. I pondered in my heart, wondering if an anointing like this could shift nations and topple social Goliaths. I then began to think of Hebrews 11:33.

Hebrews 11:33 has become an anthem in my spirit. It is found at the end of what is often called by Bible teachers the *great hall of faith*. Hebrews 11 begins by saying, "Now faith is the substance of things hoped for, the evidence of things not seen. For by it the elders obtained a good testimony" (Heb. 11:1-2). It goes on to boast of the elders of the faith, including Abel, Enoch, Noah, Abraham, Sarah, Isaac, Jacob, Joseph, Moses, Gideon, Barak, Samson, Jephthah, and others who walked in amazing faith in their generation. The awesome celebration of their lives leads right into Hebrews 11:33.

> "...THROUGH FAITH SUBDUED KINGDOMS, WORKED RIGHTEOUSNESS, OBTAINED PROMISES, [AND] STOPPED THE MOUTHS OF LIONS."

After the description of these awesome heroes of the faith, Hebrews 11:33 says that they, "...through faith subdued kingdoms, worked righteousness, obtained promises, [and] stopped the mouths of lions." The chapter then goes on in verse 34 to say that these ones, "quenched the violence of fire, escaped the edge of the sword, out of weakness were made strong, became valiant in battle, turned to flight the armies of aliens" and so on. This text is phenomenal.

As I meditated on this text, in light of the dream, the portion that said, "by faith they subdued kingdoms [and] worked righteousness," was highlighted to me like techno color! I knew the Lord was speaking. The word *worked* in the Greek is the word *ergazomai*, which means to labor, work out, cause to exist, or to produce. This blew my mind! These heroes of the faith, in their generation, had lived lives in such a way as to actually create righteousness and cause righteousness to exist! Amazing.

> WORKED (ERGAZOMAI): TO LABOR, WORK OUT, CAUSE TO EXIST, OR TO PRODUCE.

I believe that the reason the salt in my dream was on my hands is because the anointing He was pouring out was not only to think righteously, though that is part of it, or to talk righteously, though that is part of it, or to walk righteously, though that is part of it, but the anointing He was pouring out from Heaven was an anointing to actually create and impart righteousness in the earth! It was an anointing to work it into the earth, like you would work oil into a person's shoulders when giving a shoulder rub. It was an anointing to literally massage, or work, righteousness into our regions, cities, nations, cultural, spheres—everything!

Think about it; when you feed a needy person, you create righteous satisfaction in their life. You have created it. When you are a voice for the voiceless and they are protected because of it, you create safety and security in their world. When you break down a wall of disunity between people groups, you create reconciliation in the earth. You create it! You bring it into reality. You change the face of the earth, literally. God is the Creator, and we are made in His image. We, in His anointing, are called to create too; create righteousness and goodness. This is phenomenal. After having the penny drop on this, I was getting more and more excited and flipped eagerly to Revelation 19:8.

...THE ANOINTING HE WAS POURING OUT FROM HEAVEN WAS AN ANOINTING TO ACTUALLY CREATE AND IMPART RIGHTEOUSNESS IN THE EARTH.

In order to get the full impact of Revelation 19:8 and what the Lord was showing to me about the dream, I will begin quoting at the beginning of chapter 19,

After these things I heard a loud voice of a great multitude in heaven, saying, "Alleluia! Salvation and glory and honor and power belong to the Lord our God! For true and righteous are His judgments, because He has judged the great harlot who corrupted the earth with her fornication; and He has avenged on her the blood of His servants shed by her." Again they said, "Alleluia! Her smoke rises up forever and ever!" And the twenty-four elders and the four living creatures fell down and worshiped God who sat on the throne, saying, "Amen! Alleluia!" Then a voice came from the throne, saying, "Praise our God, all you His servants and those who fear Him, both small and great!" And I heard, as it were, the voice of a great multitude, as the sound of many waters and as the sound of mighty thunderings, saying, "Alleluia! For the Lord God Omnipotent reigns! Let us be glad and rejoice and give Him glory, for the marriage of the Lamb has come, and His wife has made herself ready." And to her it was granted to be arrayed in fine linen, clean and bright, for the fine linen is the righteous acts of the saints. Then he said to me, "Write: 'Blessed are those who are called to the marriage supper of the Lamb!'" And he said to me, "These are the true sayings of God." And I fell at his feet to worship him. But he said to me, "See that you do not do that!

*I am your fellow servant, and of your brethren who have the
testimony of Jesus. Worship God! For the testimony of Jesus is
the spirit of prophecy"* (Revelation 19:1-10).

This entire Scripture is so amazing. It reveals God in all of His awesomeness. He is good and kind, but He is also serious and holy, and He
will judge unrighteousness in the earth. This reality is so clear and intense in this Scripture. I believe it was Thomas Jefferson, the third president of the United States and a political philosopher, who said, "If God
is just I tremble for my country because His justice can only be stayed for
so long." He was a wise philosopher and an intuitive politician. God is
just, and God is merciful. We not should trivialize either one of these attributes of who He is.

Moreover, there is amazing news revealed in verse 8. In the midst of
the end-time judgments being released against corruption, harlotry, and violence against His servants, there is a company in the earth that will emerge
in stunning beauty. This company is, and will forever be known as, the Bride
of Christ. There will be a great and awesome wedding feast on the day
when Jesus returns for the second time, and there will be a Bride—His
Church made up of Jews and Gentiles—who has made Herself ready. This
Bride, it says, will be granted a beautiful garment that is clean, bright, and
totally out of this world (literally). This garment is made of white linen,
otherwise known as the righteous acts of the saints.

62

IT SAYS THE GARMENTS WE WEAR WILL BE THE RIGHT-
EOUS ACTS OF THE SAINTS!

I don't know about you, but meditating on this text in the context of
my dream led me into a major "Selah" moment. *Selah* means stop, pause, and
think about it. I was, and still am, quite stunned by it. Scripture does not say
that the garment we will wear on that great and awesome day of the return
of Christ will be the garment of unity, though He will have a unified and
functional Bride; or the gifts of the spirit, though He will have a Bride who
knows His spirit well; or our big ministries, budgets, or church buildings,
though these are all weapons to advance His Kingdom mightily in this age.
It says that the garment we will wear will be the righteous acts of the saints!
Acts of the saints!

You mean we are actually expected to *do something* to prepare for our wedding? Reality check: what bride doesn't do something (many things!) to prepare for her wedding day? Just ask any bride—there is a lot of preparation that goes into the big day. It doesn't just "happen."

You mean to tell me the seal of our salvation is reflected in how we live our lives? You mean salvation is not just about passive grace that forgives me of my sins and eases my guilt, but that there is more? You mean to tell me that *the preparation of the Bride of Christ for the return of Jesus is directly related to our righteous acts in the earth?* Oh my. That is what it says. However, I had never once in my life heard a teacher or preacher put it this way. Wow.

I am not preaching salvation by works—stay with me. What this text seems to be revealing is that the ones who are truly saved, the ones who are truly forgiven, the Church that is truly washed clean by the atoning sacrifice of Jesus will arise and clothe herself with a response to that grace-filled forgiveness. That response is doing righteous acts. My historical intuition tells me that some of the greatest preachers our world has ever seen (Charles Finney, John Wesley, Leonard Ravenhill, and the like) are likely sitting in the great cloud of witnesses, and they are loving this chapter.

63

> ...THE ONES WHO ARE TRULY FORGIVEN, THE CHURCH
> THAT IS TRULY WASHED CLEAN, WILL ARISE AND
> CLOTHE HERSELF WITH A RESPONSE...THAT RESPONSE
> IS DOING RIGHTEOUS ACTS.

Jesus' blood cleanses us; we are made new. As we are made new, His Spirit transforms us into His likeness. As we are transformed into His likeness, we do what He would do—righteous acts in the earth. It all comes out of a place of love and worship for the Lover of our soul, Jesus Christ. It is a response of love, and it is our end-time mandate. We are called to work righteousness into the earth. Not only is it our calling and destiny, but it will be the very thing we wear as a garment on our wedding day! The anointing He is pouring out on His children to "work righteousness" is necessary for His Bride to come forth beautified and prepared for His return.

I don't know about you, but I am really looking forward to the day He returns to His creation as promised. No one knows the time or the hour, but we are exhorted by Scripture to be alert and to be ready as though it could be today. This revelation invokes in me a desire. Just like brides in the earthly realm, who pour themselves out to be ready for their "big day"—not because they have to but because they are passionate—I want to be ready. I want to be prepared, and Revelation 19 says the indication of our preparation will be the type of garment we are wearing.

> AS WE ARE TRANSFORMED INTO HIS LIKENESS, WE DO WHAT HE WOULD DO…THIS IS OUR END-TIME DESTINY.

He will have a Bride who has a beautiful garment—she will be stunningly gorgeous, the best creation has ever seen.

CHAPTER 4

Does Righteousness
Exalt a Nation?

Righteousness exalts a nation, but sin is a reproach to any
people (Proverbs 14:34).

A PEARL OF WISDOM: HEARING IN STEREO

In conversations I have had with awesome leaders regarding the transformation of nations into God's intended destiny, I have noticed that many
points of view and perspectives can come up.

Some say, "If you want to transform a nation, you need to focus on
the harvest and bringing people into the Kingdom. If enough people
get saved in a nation, that nation will be changed. Jesus was not a politician; He was a preacher." Those who gravitate to this truth exclusively
often have a deeply evangelistic motivation that has been given by
God—and they are right! When enough people get impacted by the
power of God and His manifest reality, it is just a matter of time until
that nation is completely rocked from the inside out. I believe true revival will always lead to reformation and transformation.

Most of our contemporary Western world and cultural systems are a
direct product of someone's ideology. If the individuals steering the systems of our nations have been enraptured with love for God and a revelation of eternity, they will create structures that are very different from the
ones that are consumed with selfish motives or humanistic persuasion. The
ones who have a revelation of eternity are more motivated to behave as
though their actions do have eternal consequence. Those who don't have a
revelation of eternity will simply be governed by the "now" temptations of
power, prestige, riches, and the like instead of the truth that one day they
will need to give an account for how they conducted themselves. Revelation

governs our ideology, and our ideology governs our behavior. If you get enough "good behaving" people making decisions for a nation, it is only a matter of time until that nation will be transformed for the better.

Others say, "If you want a nation to be changed, all you have to do is discern what the Lord is saying and then prophesy it into the atmosphere of the nation and it will land and shift nations into their destiny." Those who see national transformation through this lens are the prophets. They are the ones who have received a God-given prophetic lens on life and they see the world through it—and they too are right! On many occasions, I have personally witnessed when a seasoned cluster of believers, or a seasoned individual, issued a God-inspired decree—through prayer—over a community or a nation and the impact is so powerful that we have read about the effects in the regional or national newspapers the next day! It is real. Any wise and spiritually astute community leader will be asking spirit-filled believers around them to pray and decree prophetic words of life over their jurisdiction in faith. This type of spiritual activity does shift things for sure.

There are others who say, "Sister, you need to discern all the roots of the nation that are ungodly and get the Church together and repent through identificational prayer, remove the stones in the highway, and prepare the way for Jesus through national holiness; then that nation will be changed." It would seem that those who gravitate toward this vein have a deeply pastoral heart and motivation, pursuing inner-healing for a nation—these ones also are right!

Scripture is clear—we must repent and turn from our wicked ways if we want God to heal our land (see 2 Chron. 7:14). By the end of these types of discussions, the eager and aspiring nation-changer for God might find herself thoroughly confused and unsure of where to start, what angle to take, or who to believe.

...WE ALL TEND TO SEE THE WORLD THROUGH OUR LENS, GIFT MIX, OR CALLING.

A very wise spiritual mother in my life, Stacey Campbell, once said, "Very few people in the Body of Christ have the maturity to hear in stereo." When she said this, a penny dropped for me. We all see the world through our own lens, gift mix, or calling. Another senior pastor, who did much mitigation and reconciliation with churches experiencing inner-strife with leadership, shared with me that "the main reason for most church splits is because people see things differently, from different perspectives, but they do not discern that both perspectives are correct, given by God, and meant to complement one another." Even if we are all looking at the same dice, depending on the angle we have, we may see a different number.

> MATURE BELIEVERS HAVE THE ABILITY TO HEAR
> DIFFERENT STREAMS OF THOUGHT AND PERSPECTIVES
> AND KNOW THEY CAN ALL BE TRUE AT ONCE.

Mature believers have the ability to hear different streams of thought and perspective and know that they can all be true at once. Here are a couple of examples where the Bible speaks "in stereo." Jesus was 100 percent God, right? (See John 1:1.) But was He 100 percent man too? (See Philippians 2:7.) Of course. He was both 100 percent man and 100 percent God at the same time. It seems impossible, but it is true. Salvation is free, right? (See Romans 6:23.) But to follow Jesus will cost you everything, right? (See Matthew 16:24.) They are both true, and they are both essential revelations God has called us to embrace and walk in. It sounds schizophrenic to the logical mind, but it works in God's economy. I have heard it said, "If God is so small that I can figure Him out from front to back, then He is not God." There is a seed of wisdom in that. God's ways are above our ways, and once we get to the other side of eternity, we will see clearly some of these things which are a mystery to us now.

I wanted to share Stacey's word about "hearing in stereo" upfront because, in this chapter, I am going to present another "angle" of revelation for how to impact and transform nations. However, I also want to be clear and say that I believe we need it all! I am committed to hearing *and* walking in stereo. We need to tenaciously go after souls, we need to prophesy into our nations with bold faith, we need to repent and remove the ungodly roots in our nations, and we need to be mature children of God who, like the fathers of old, "…through faith subdued kingdoms, [and] worked righteousness…" (Heb. 11:33) in their generation to the glory of God. We need a people who will stop moaning about or "discerning" what is wrong and who will simply rise up in love to fight against the injustices and perversion of our age.

I believe we are in an hour when all the gift mixes need to take their place with bold faith and run wholeheartedly. I am not you, and you are not me. You need to be you. I need to be me. We are the Body of Christ, and we all need to be faithful in our individual functions, the eye being the eye, the ear the ear, and the mouth the mouth—each of us functioning at full capacity, loving, encouraging, and cheering one another on because we understand that there is a bigger picture we are creating together.

I BELIEVE WE NEED IT ALL! WE ARE THE BODY OF CHRIST, AND WE ALL NEED TO BE FAITHFUL IN OUR INDIVIDUAL FUNCTIONS.

In this season of my life and ministry, for many of the reasons already expounded on in this book, God has deposited a deep conviction in me of the importance of influencing national policy—meaning politics. Yes, I just said the "P" word. If you have not detected it already, God's interest in this arena has become, to me, undeniable. As a matter of fact, the more I have thought about God and government, the more I have realized that we are hard pressed to find a single book of the Bible that does not talk about government, rulers, kings, administration (whatever you want to call it) in some form. You would be very stretched to form a solid theological argument that, as Christians, we should not be interested in who governs our nations. You actually have to be a very selective reader to not see government throughout the Word of God.

A few clear examples: Leviticus, Judges, First Kings, Second Kings…get the picture? It is overt in many of the names of the various books of the Bible, not to mention throughout the content of them. Even Song of Songs, the gooey intimacy book of the Bible, talks about Solomon's kingly grace. I love how God makes it so easy and straightforward for us. I believe Scripture is clear: God is keenly interested in who runs our nations and how they run them. However, I want to be upfront and let you know that I did not always buy into the statement I just made.

WE ARE HARD PRESSED TO FIND A SINGLE BOOK OF
THE BIBLE THAT DOES NOT TALK ABOUT GOVERNMENT.

Even though I became a Christian in 1995, it was not until between 2003 and 2005 that the Lord began to overtly shake me up about all this and to bring clarity to what He was asking me to do practically. It was really during this period that He began to lay a mandate on me to raise up a movement in my nation to impact the political leaders of the land face to face. It was to be a movement that would fight for God's pre-ordained purposes in this nation, not from an exclusively evangelistic, prophetic, or pastoral perspective, but from a reformation perspective. He began to speak to my heart things like, "Faytene, where is the voice of righteousness and justice coming from your generation in this nation?" Or, "Faytene, who is the main influence in this nation? Who is discipling this nation?" I have learned that, when God asks you a question, it is usually because He is about to put His finger on something. He was pointing out a missing link in my nation, particularly when it came to the younger generation, and He was starting to put a fire in my bones to be one of those who would help fill in the gap. He was provoking me to create a movement, a salt-movement, in my garden of Canada and in my moment of history.

69

WHEN GOD ASKS YOU A QUESTION, IT IS USUALLY
BECAUSE HE IS ABOUT TO PUT HIS FINGER ON
SOMETHING. HE WAS POINTING OUT A MISSING LINK
IN MY NATION.

TRADITIONAL MARRIAGE IN CRISIS

In 2005, our nation hit a crisis zone regarding the traditional definition of marriage. The leaders in the nation at the time were working hard to change the age-old definition of marriage from a legal covenant between a man and a woman to a legal covenant between two persons (meaning a man and a man, or a woman and a woman, man and dog, woman and fish—I am being a bit cheeky here, but it is the reality of what these definitions could eventually mean). The action our government was taking at this window in our national history was incredibly bold and, ironically, not celebrated by the majority of Canadians at the time—according to many major polls. Yet those in favor of it still persisted in pushing the legislation in our Parliament.

THE ACTION OUR GOVERNMENT WAS TAKING AT THIS WINDOW IN OUR NATIONAL HISTORY WAS INCREDIBLY BOLD AND, IRONICALLY, NOT CELEBRATED BY THE MA-JORITY OF CANADIANS AT THE TIME.

I hit a destiny "breaker switch moment" that year when I heard a report from a reliable source telling me of an encounter that a group of senior pastors had with our Prime Minister at the time, Paul Martin.

I HIT A DESTINY "BREAKER SWITCH MOMENT"...

A group of senior pastors from the region where I lived in Vancouver, British Columbia, had traveled to the nation's capitol earlier that year to discuss the issue of reforming the traditional definition of marriage with the prime minister. I am told that, as they met with him, they asked, "Prime Minister, why is it that you and your government are pushing so aggressively to put this socially liberal agenda through the House of Commons? It is clear that this is a controversial social issue in Canada and that many are not in agreement. Why are you pushing so hard and being so aggressive?" Pushing, they were. These politicians, who were elected to represent Canadians, seemed abnormally motivated to pass this legislation in spite of a very large national outcry against it. They even extended Parliament that summer, and cut short debate in the Senate—which is supposed to be the chamber of "slow second thought"—in order to ram the legislation through. It was all very surreal.

I want to pause for a moment here and apologize to the nations of the earth for my nation, Canada, which has set such a strong socially liberal example when it comes to this important issue. I am deeply sorry for the ripple effect this has already had on some of you in your nations when those with similar agendas—to dismantle the traditional definition of marriage—point to Canada as a good example. I believe we have been anything but a good example on this issue. With whatever sphere of grace and authority I have as a national leader, I wholeheartedly apologize to you right now through these pages. Please continue to pray for us as we seek for solutions and strategy on how to bring restoration to the biblical definition of marriage in Canada.

Back to the story. In response to the question from these pastors, the Prime Minister said, "Well, first of all, we are not doing anything that mainline Church denominations have not already clearly endorsed," speaking of the Anglican Church of Canada who had *some* key leaders at the time who were also pushing hard for same sex unions. "Second," he said, "we believe this is a 'human rights' issue." Wow, that was revealing. Though I believe in protecting the oppressed, voiceless, and vulnerable, when I look at how human rights legislation has been applied in the borders of my nation in the past years, I have to raise an eyebrow to it.

One extreme example occurred when a man named John Sharp was allowed, by a Provincial Supreme Court, to possess child pornography on the basis of what they called "artistic merit" and his "right" therefore to possess it. This is pure whack. We currently have a climate in Canada where pastors have been fined for teaching the Bible, where doctors who are not willing to perform or give referrals for abortions, because it goes against their conscience, are being threatened with the possibility of being taken before human rights tribunals, and where a prominent college campus has appointed "conversation facilitators" to shut down any conversations between students that reflect what they deem to be "improper thought"—all this in the name of protecting "human rights." One has to look at these things and ask, *Who decides whose rights are the ones to protect and whose are the ones to bulldoze?*

This is human rights advocacy at its worst. As I have observed this in my nation, I am now at the point where I think it is time to stop emphasizing our human rights and to start emphasizing our human responsibilities. I believe it was Tommy Tenney who said, "If you teach a child their rights, you breed a selfish, self-focused person. If you teach a child their responsibilities, you breed a responsible citizen."[1] I am getting more and more excited about the latter all the time.

I AM NOW AT THE POINT WHERE I THINK IT IS TIME TO STOP TALKING ABOUT OUR HUMAN *RIGHTS* AND TO START TALKING ABOUT OUR HUMAN *RESPONSIBILITIES*.

If all that I just shared is not enough, I was also shocked by the statement Prime Minister Martin made about this legislation being a human rights issue because sexual rights are nowhere in our Candian Charter of Rights and Freedom—though religious rights very clearly are. Moreover, the entire Charter begins with a preamble that says, "Whereas Canada is founded upon principles that recognize the supremacy of God...." I did not see the supremacy of God being considered *at all* by this government even though it is clearly printed in the Charter. Even if a few Christian leaders seemed to be endorsing, and pushing for, the redefinition of marriage, that voice was extremist.

If they really wanted to know what the majority of Christians in Canada were saying about this issue, a survey of the denominations would have sufficed. If every Christian denomination across the nation was asked about their view of this topic, the socially liberal voice of a few would have, almost certainly, been drowned out. Democracy was not truly being considered in this decision, it would seem. However, though both of these reasons given by the Prime Minister were, in my opinion, not valid, the primary statement that provoked me to action was still to come out of his mouth. The "breaker switch" flip in my heart came with his next reason.

"Third," I am told that Prime Minister Martin said, "we believe this legislation is representing the voice of the younger generation. If it does not go through in the current Parliament, it will go through eventually. We might as well just get it over with." When I heard this, my eyes almost popped out of my head! If I were a cartoon, steam would have been blasting out of my ears. I thought, *The younger generation! What?!* At that time, I still considered myself part of that younger generation.

Prime Minister Martin and I were definitely not singing the same tune! With all due respect, he was not *at all* representing my view nor the view of thousands of other young Canadians. Immediately I thought of the many mass Christian gatherings that take place in my nation every year. One of them was attracting 15,000-20,000 youth and young adults who were totally on fire for God and totally in love with Jesus. I thought, *How could Prime Minister Martin not be aware of these young people and their views?* Then the obvious occurred to me—*because we had not been telling him.* We had been silent, disengaged, and we had not shown up at the platforms of national influence to share our voices.

If Prime Minister Martin did not know about this mass demographic of young people in our nation, it was our fault.

> IF PRIME MINISTER MARTIN DID NOT KNOW ABOUT THIS MASS DEMOGRAPHIC OF YOUNG PEOPLE IN OUR NATION, IT WAS OUR FAULT.

Like most Western nations, Canada is a democracy. In a democracy, every voice has a responsibility to show up at the table of national dialogue. It seemed that our voice had not been showing up—at least not in a way that was forceful enough that it could not be ignored. I am sure there was the odd "peep" from the odd politically-oriented socially conservative young person, but those peeps were apparently not registering. It was becoming clear that a mobilization of this voice was in order.

After hearing of the Prime Minister's comments, a prophecy that Cindy Jacobs[2] had released over my nation in 2004 came back to me. In this prophecy she said [I am paraphrasing from memory], "It is going to be the younger generation that is going to begin to rise up and address the government leaders of our nation. They will say, 'This is not who we are, and we don't believe in it that way,' and they will begin to be a voice for marriage and family values to impact this nation and the leaders of this nation…."

> SOMETIMES YOU JUST HAVE TO RISE UP AND STEP INTO DESTINY BY FAITH.

I was tired of just hearing prophecies about the younger generation at this point—I had heard many of them. This time, a conviction was beginning to rise in me that the days of hearing a prophetic word, rejoicing in it, and doing nothing were over. Sometimes you just have to rise up and step into destiny by faith. I was nailed with conviction—the type of conviction that inevitably leads to action. What it was all supposed to look like was not yet clear in my mind, but I was definitely nailed.

GUILTY AS CHARGED: DISENGAGEMENT

True confessions: at this point in 2005, though I understood the revelation that the Lord had given me in Liberia about the kings of the earth bowing to Jesus and His ways, actually influencing them practically was still *nowhere* on my radar. I know it sounds loony, but this is so typical sometimes. It is one thing to think something is important; it is another thing to actually live like it is.

> IT IS ONE THING TO THINK SOMETHING IS IMPORTANT; IT IS ANOTHER THING TO ACTUALLY LIVE LIKE IT IS.
>
> "DO YOU THINK, IF YOU WERE ALIVE AT THE TIME OF WILBERFORCE, THAT YOU WOULD HAVE BEEN A PART OF HIS MOVEMENT TO ABOLISH THE SLAVE TRADE?"

A couple who are my good friends were recently having a conversation while driving home from seeing the movie *Amazing Grace*. For those of you who have not seen it, it is a powerful movie about William Wilberforce and his political movement to abolish the global slave trade that was being perpetuated by Great Britain just over 200 years ago. It is an awesome historical story of conviction, good vs. evil, long-term perseverance, struggle, failure, and eventual victory. As they drove home, my friend asked her husband, "Do you think, if you were alive at the time of Wilberforce, that you would have been a part of his movement to abolish the slave trade?" My friend searched his heart in desire to give an answer that had integrity and said, "I would like to think so, but in reality, what am I doing right now about the injustices that are around me, like abortion?" *Selah*.

If the truth be known, up to that point in 2005, though I had been a Christian for ten years already, in that time I had not voted in any municipal, provincial, or federal election. Even though I had a heart to change my world, I didn't realize the importance of faithfully accessing the tools of democracy right in front of me to change my nation. I didn't think voting had much consequence or that my vote would make a difference. Even if I had, I didn't know whom to vote for and was too focused on Jesus to take the time to find it out—not considering that Jesus was quite interested in my nation and who would rule over it. It also did not occur to me that I might encounter His presence in a very intimate way as I took time to explore things He cared about, like who would be the future leader of this nation that the Word clearly says He is asking for (see Ps. 2). My journey with the Lord has proven, time and time again, that you will find Jesus in places you least expect. (I found Him in a Tim Horton's ladies' room once, but that is a story for another book.)

> EVEN THOUGH I HAD A HEART TO CHANGE MY WORLD, I DIDN'T REALIZE THE IMPORTANT TOOLS OF DEMOCRACY WERE RIGHT IN FRONT OF ME TO CHANGE MY NATION.

I don't remember political responsibility ever being talked about at church, and I don't remember any of my friends ever talking about it either—I am not saying they didn't, I just don't remember it. It was nowhere on the radar, even though I loved God and I loved my nation. Knowing what I know now, this bewilders me, and speaks so loudly of the enemy's efforts to draw the Body of Christ into a state of slumber, deception, and paralysis, thereby causing us to be somewhat insignificant influences in our nations. We sit back and criticize the changing of laws, enjoying our nice roads and freedoms, but we do nothing to salt our world with His righteousness. Ouch. But it's true, or at least it was in my case.

> ...SPEAKS SO LOUDLY OF THE ENEMY'S EFFORTS TO DRAW THE BODY OF CHRIST INTO A STATE OF SLUMBER, DECEPTION, AND PARALYSIS, THEREBY CAUSING US TO BE SOMEWHAT INSIGNIFICANT INFLUENCES IN OUR NATIONS.

Because of my historical lack of "getting it" when the Lord began to ask me to put aside total focus on mercy missions work—though I will always have an element of focus there—and begin to raise up a movement of grass-roots political reformation in my nation, I needed to be convinced. I needed to be convinced that this was from the Word of God and that this somehow would matter in eternity. Though many dots had already been connected, at that point in my journey, there were still a couple I was wrestling with. It was not enough to be convicted, passionate, or reminded of a prophecy like Cindy Jacob's—I wanted to understand this from the Word of God. So, let's go there.

CHOICE OF LEADERS

HAVING A RIGHTEOUS RULER AFFECTED THE LAND, THEIR FOREIGN RELATIONS, THEIR ECONOMICS, THEIR HEALTH, THEIR FERTILITY, AND MUCH, MUCH MORE. IT AFFECTED THE HEAVENS OVER THEM.

Throughout the Books of Kings, Chronicles, and Judges you can see how righteous, or unrighteous, leadership affected a nation. When those in authority were acting in line with God's nature as a righteous and just king, the entire nation would receive the blessings of the Lord. Conversely, when they did not rule in this way, the people and the land did not enjoy the blessings of the Lord in the same way. This wasn't simply about the Israelites being happy because they had a nice guy for a ruler. Having a righteous ruler affected the land, their foreign relations, their economics, their health, their fertility, and much, much more. It affected the heavens over them. Why? Because, as I talked about in Chapter 2, when they were walking in right alignment with Heaven's revealed blueprint for righteousness and justice, this created a landing pad for the presence of God. And when the presence of God was with them, it affected everything. God spoke to His people Israel at the inception of their nationhood that this was a spiritual law that could not be evaded.

In Deuteronomy 28, the Lord outlined to Moses both the blessings the people of Israel would invoke upon themselves as a nation if they walked obediently in covenant with God and the curses that would fall upon them if they did not. Following is a chart that outlines both. If this does not put the fear of the Lord in us regarding the importance of righteous rulers, I don't know what will!

Note: Feel free to scan this chart, part of the reason I chose to literally type out all the blessings and curses was for *visual impact*.

BLESSINGS

- exalted above all nations
- blessed in the country and in the city
- fruit of their body blessed
- produce of the ground blessed
- herds and cattle blessed and their offspring blessed
- blessed coming in and going out
- enemies defeated seven ways
- storehouse blessed
- blessed in the land the Lord would give
- all nations would see them and fear (respect/reverence)
- blessed with the treasure of Heaven
- the work of their hands blessed
- lend but not borrow
- would be the head and not the tail, above and not beneath

CURSES

- cursed in the city and country
- basket and kneading bowl cursed
- fruit of their body cursed
- cursed with confusion
- herds and cattle cursed, and their offspring also cursed
- the Lord would rebuke everything that they set their hand to until they are completely destroyed and they perish quickly
- cursed with plague that would cling to them until they are consumed from the land they are to possess

- consumed by fever

- consumed by sword

- consumed with scorching

- consumed with mildew

- the heavens shut up and the skies would rain down
  powder and dust until they are destroyed

  defeated by their enemies

- would become troublesome to the kingdoms of the
  earth because they are dispossessed

- would be defeated before their enemies and they
  would flee seven ways before them

- their carcasses would be food for all the birds
  of the air and the beasts of the earth

- stricken with the boils of Egypt, with tumors, with the scab,
  with the itch from which they could not be healed

- the Lord would strike them with madness and blindness

- they would grope at noonday, as a blind
  man gropes in the darkness

- they would not prosper

- they would only be oppressed and plundered
  continually and no one would save them

- they would betroth a wife but another man shall lie with her

  they shall build a house but not dwell in it

- they shall plant a vineyard but shall not gather its grapes

- their sons and daughters would be given to another people,
  and their eyes shall look and ail with longing for
  them all day long

- there shall be no strength in their hand

- a nation whom they have not known shall eat the fruit of
  their land and the produce of their labor

- they shall be only oppressed and crushed continually

- they shall be driven mad because of the sight which their eyes see

- the Lord will strike them in the knees and on the legs with severe boils which cannot be healed, and from the sole of their foot to the top of their head

- the Lord will bring them and the king whom they set over themselves to a nation which neither they nor their fathers have known, and there they shall serve other gods made of wood and stone

- they would become an astonishment, a proverb, and a by word among all the nations where the Lord would drive them

- they would carry much seed out to the field but gather little in, for the locust shall consume it

- they shall plant vineyards and tend them, but shall neither drink of the wine nor gather the grapes, for the worms shall eat them

- they shall have olive trees throughout all their territory but shall not anoint themselves with oil, for the olives shall drop off

- the alien who is among them shall rise higher and higher above them and they shall come down lower and lower

- the foreigner shall lend to them but they shall not lend to him

- the foreigner shall be the head, and they shall be the tail

- all these curses shall come upon them and pursue and over take them, until they are destroyed

- they shall serve their enemies whom the Lord will send against them, in hunger, in thirst, in nakedness, and in need of everything; and He will put a yoke of iron on their neck until He has destroyed them

- the Lord will bring a nation against them from afar, from the ends of the earth as swift as the eagle flies, a nation whose language they will not understand, a nation fierce in counte nance, which does not respect the elderly nor show favor to the young; they shall eat the increase of their livestock and the produce of their land until they are destroyed; they shall not leave them grain or new wine or oil, of the increase of their cattle or the offspring of their flocks until they have destroyed them; they shall besiege them at their gates until their high and fortified wall, in which they trust, come down throughout all the land; and they shall besiege them at all the gates throughout all the land which the Lord their God has given them

- they shall eat the fruit of their own body, the flesh of their sons and daughters whom the Lord their God has given them

- the sensitive and very refined man among them would be hostile toward his brother, wife of his bosom, and the rest of his children whom he leaves behind, so that he will not give any of them the flesh of his children who he will eat, because he has nothing left in the siege and desperate straights in which their enemy would distress them at many gates

- the Lord would bring them and their descendants extraordinary plagues, great and prolonged plagues until they are destroyed

- they shall be left few in number, whereas they were as the stars of the heaven in multitude

- the Lord will rejoice over them to destroy them and bring them to nothing

- they shall be plucked off the land which they go to possess

- the Lord will scatter them among the peoples, from one end of the earth to the other and there they shall serve other gods, which neither they nor their fathers have known— wood and stone

- they shall find no rest, nor shall the sole of their foot have a resting place, but there the Lord would give them a trembling heart, failing eyes, and anguish of soul

- their life shall hang in doubt before them, they shall fear day and night and have no assurance of life

- in the morning they shall say, "Oh that it were evening!" And at the evening they shall say, "Oh that it were morning!" because of the fear which terrifies their heart, and because of the sight which their eyes see

- the Lord will take them back to Egypt in ships, by the way of which He said to them, "You shall never see it again." And there they shall be offered for sale to their enemies as male and female slaves but no one will buy them

In summary, God was saying that if they walked in obedience to Him as a nation, their economics, national security, land production, livestock production, and global reputation would all be blessed and there would be an open Heaven over their land! I cannot think of a nation on the planet that would not be excited about this. Actually, it is what they all hope for and strive for. Conversely, God was saying that if they walked in disobedience, God Himself would contend against them and would shut up the heavens over the nation. We need to think about this. We need to think about this seriously. The harvest was affected, their production was affected, and their lives in every aspect were radically affected.

81

IF THEY WALKED IN DISOBEDIENCE, GOD HIMSELF WOULD CONTEND AGAINST THEM AND SHUT UP THE HEAVENS OVER THE NATION.

When I started seeing words like *harvest* and *open Heaven* in these promises, I began to get even more excited about the idea of righteous kings making righteous decisions to lead nations. In a New Testament context, *harvest* clearly speaks of souls. Jesus taught this in Luke 4 and other places. It is also clearly demonstrated in Revelation 14, where John is prophesying about the great in-gathering of souls at the end of the age, which He calls the harvest of the earth. Could it be that the blessing that will come upon a nation that keeps covenant with God on the national level will not only be a physical harvest—though it will be that—but that it will be a spiritual harvest of souls as well? I will explore this a bit more in the next chapter—stay with me.

Throughout the history of Israel God has kept His Word. He is the ultimate promise keeper—whether in times of rest, war, the exile to Babylon, or the current Diaspora, whether or not they were walking in righteousness before the Lord directly impacted their national experience. Furthermore, though Deuteronomy 28 was written to Israel specifically, I believe the New Testament gives us ample indication that the same laws are applied to any nation that either does or does not walk in the ways of the Lord. This is one of the reasons why the apostle Paul exhorted his spiritual son Timothy in First Timothy 2:1-4 saying,

> *Therefore I exhort first of all that supplications, prayers, intercessions, and giving of thanks be made for all men, for kings and all who are in authority, that we may lead quiet and peaceable lives in all godliness and reverence. For this is good and acceptable in the sight of God our Savior, who desires all men to be saved and come to the knowledge of the truth.*

This Scripture draws a direct link between praying for our leaders, living peaceful lives, the release of salvation, and pleasing God. If that is not the blessing of God being released, I don't know what is! This was good advice that a good spiritual father was giving to his son. I believe the apostle Paul was giving Timothy this advice because he understood the principles we have been discussing.

HE IS RAISING UP A PEOPLE WHO UNDERSTAND THAT RIGHTEOUSNESS MATTERS—THAT JUSTICE MATTERS.

On a micro-scale, the Lord was teaching me this principle as I served at NeighbourLink (the journey described in Chapter 2). Acts of righteousness and justice equal the blessing of God and creation of a dwelling place for Him. On a macro-scale, we are now contending for the full outpouring of the blessings, which come from righteousness, into the nations of the earth. God is raising up a people who understand all that I have been sharing with you.

He is raising up a people who understand that righteousness matters—that justice matters. They understand that unjust bloodshed on the land of a nation, through things like abortion, locks up the heavens and restrains the harvest in that nation (see Deut. 28:23). This new breed of reformers understands that the nation who cares for its refugees, orphans, and elderly will attract His blessing and that the nation that does not will invoke His judgment. They understand that dishonoring the Lord's divine order in sexual relations causes His face to be turned from that nation as He is forced by His own spiritual laws to rebuke all we set our hands to (see Deut. 28:20). In this hour of history, God is raising up a people who understand that righteousness and justice are the foundation of His throne. Because of this, who rules over our nations and how they rule should be of urgent interest to us. In my own nation of Canada, the principles I have been speaking of have proven abundantly true. Let me give you a few very strong illustrations of these laws in action.

GOOD GOVERNMENT AND GOOD DOLLAR?

Near the end of 1987, the Supreme Court of Canada was looking at a case dealing with the leading abortion doctor in our nation, Henry Morgentaler. By January 1988, the Supreme Court ruled on this case and acquitted him of all charges of abortion, even though he had been practicing them illegally. This ruling served to strike down all of Canada's abortion laws as unconstitutional. Since that moment, there have been no functional laws restricting abortion in Canada—none. It has been open season on the womb for a solid 20 years. This one case has led to the unjust bloodshed of anywhere from 2.5 to 4 million unborn Canadians.

At almost the exact same time that this law was being overturned, we hit a major national recession. As a young girl, I can remember my parents speaking about it at the dinner table; it affected almost every Canadian. The economic drop was so instant and steep that the media named the trigger day "Black Monday." For clarity's sake, Black Monday was a global crash; however, Canada was easily swept into its effect, seemingly completely unprotected by God's favor at that time.

Is it a coincidence that this court case and Canada's economic recession paralleled within the same four-month window? Maybe, but I doubt it. It seems to me like a spiritual law kicked in and the heavens of blessing were shut over our nation because of our mass bloodguilt. Millions of babies in my generation have been killed because of this one decree in 1988. Heaven saw, and Heaven responded.

In the summer of 2008, we had a similar experience. On July 1, 2008, this same abortionist was honored with the highest civilian honor of the nation, The Order of Canada. My team and I were chilled as we watched national television that night. The broadcast had a clip of Mr. Morgentaler accepting the award with great boasting and pride, basically saying, "It's about time." The arrogance was stunning. It was common knowledge, and even national news at that time, that millions of Canadians in no way considered him a national hero. The very next news story that same night reported a massive market crash in Toronto that same day. Coincidence? Maybe, but I doubt it.[3] Our team keeps the news video that aired that night on our computers as a reminder of how real these "coincidences" seem to be.

A few months later, in September 2008, the U.S. economic crisis hit. In spite of the economic trauma that our closest trade partner was experiencing, Canada was relatively unaffected. Our Prime Minster encouraged Canadians during that time, saying that we would weather the economic storm, and repeatedly cited an international study, which assessed Canada's economy as one of the strongest in the world. The Prime Minister seemed to be correct. Our dollar was managing well, in spite of the shaking to the south and in other nations. It was managing well, that is, until the day that Henry Morgentaler actually received his award of honor on October 10, 2008. On that very day, the Canadian dollar plummeted to an 84 cent low, and as of the writing of this book, it has not yet rebounded. Coincidence? Maybe, but again, I doubt it.

Furthermore, not only did Canada's dollar plummet, but the Prime Minister's popularity and the stability of his government did as well. What is interesting is that, just weeks prior to this shaking, the same Prime Minister stated that he had no intention of bringing forth any legislation to protect the unborn in Canada. At that time, he revealed that he would force his cabinet to vote against any legislation brought forth by private Members or by the opposition parties that would re-open the debate on abortion. I don't believe he realized that, because of God's laws, his posture on this justice issue would have an impact, both on the economy and on his favor level in the nation. He did not discern the link between righteousness and blessing. Whether he and his advisors see it or not, the truth remains, and the economic and political graphs seem to reflect it.

On a more positive note of testimony, currently every province in my nation is in debt. Some are even in deep financial distress. All except one: Alberta. In recent history, Alberta has been the only province that has consistently stood for traditional family values, especially in reference to marriage. That province also funds biblical studies in their public schools, thereby overtly inviting God Himself into the life of one of their primary social systems and into the minds of young Canadians. Is it a coincidence that Alberta is the only province that is experiencing major economic blessing and the only one that is not in debt? Maybe, but I doubt it.

As I began to get more curious about these trends, I dug even deeper into our national history. I found that, in the early 1960s, the Canadian dollar also took a steep fall. Do you think it is coincidence that, at this same time, a floodgate of socially liberal agendas began to creep onto the scene? Over the next 40 years—from the mid '60s to just past the turn of the millennium—our federal government made several legislative moves that were directly opposed to biblical righteousness. They legalized sodomy, no fault divorce, public gambling, and abortion. In that same time period, though there were short periods of peaking, our dollar dropped from $1.05 to $.60 to the U.S. dollar! Was this a coincidence or God's laws in action? The following chart was taken from CBC online.

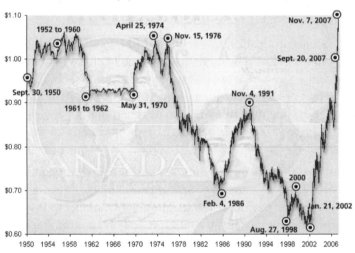

A history of the Canadian dollar since 1950
What's behind the loonie's many ups and downs?

In the window from January 2006 to early 2008, Canada saw the dollar soar back up to a record-breaking $1.14 peak. On January 23, 2006, we elected the first practicing Christian Prime Minister and the most socially conservative government that we have had in decades. It was not a "Christian government" but was filled with men and women who had a reverence for God and understood that He called them to be salt and light in their generation. They understood that they had a responsibility before God, not just before Canadians. They had a burning motivation to leave the nation better than they found it.

WAS THE RISE IN THE DOLLAR BECAUSE OF GOOD ECONOMICS OR BECAUSE OF THE BLESSING OF GOD BEING POURED OUT IN RESPONSE TO RIGHTEOUSNESS?

These leaders worked hard to enact laws to protect our youth from sexual predators, crack down on crime, apologized for historical injustices done to the indigenous peoples of Canada, and alleviated tax burdens on the common Canadian. I am not saying they were perfect, but they did some amazing stuff in that time period! Was the rise in the dollar because of good economics or because of the blessing of God being poured out in response to some of these legislative decisions? I am sure you can guess what my opinion is. My take on all this is simple and biblical: righteousness exalts a nation (see Prov. 14:34).

In conclusion to all this, I would just like to say: if we call ourselves lovers of God, we should be more than motivated out of that love for Him to labor for the things that are on His heart. Righteousness and justice are the foundation of His throne for a reason; they are important to Him. If we love Him, they should be important to us too. If our dollar gets blessed in the process, hooray! However, it is just a by-product of a nation that is truly after His heart.

If all you care about is economics and the environment, then vote, support, and encourage the man or woman who will fight for godly values—your vote will pay off. It is a temporal motivation, but it will get you what you want. However, if you could care less about economics, the environment, and the like, if all you care about is pleasing God's heart, then vote, support, and encourage the man or woman who will fight for godly values. It will bring pleasure to His heart because His heart burns for righteousness.

Endnotes
1. More about Tommy Tenney at www.tommytenney.com.
2. Cindy Jacobs is the founder of Generals of Intercession and an internationally recognized prophetess. Visit www.generals.org.
3. The good news is that the granting of this award to Mr. Morgentaler has awakened a massive sleeping giant in my nation. Many who have not thought about abortion in years are now being very vocal against it. Yeah God.

CHAPTER 5

Righteous Leadership and Open Heavens

The Lord will open the heavens, the storehouse of His bounty,
to send rain on your land in season and to bless all the work of
your hands… (Deuteronomy 28:12 NIV).

Before I close the first section of this book—in which I have been attempting to unpack the "reasons" we need to arise and impact our nations—and before we enter into the next section—which will be primarily about key principles the Lord has taught our team over the past years—I want to take a risk. I want to explore a few questions that have been burning in my heart and are, perhaps, a little "out of the box." I talked about them, at a surface level, in the last chapter. Perhaps they have been burning in your heart too. Here they are:

What does contending for national righteousness and justice have to do with *souls*?

Does it have anything to do with souls?

Does any of this stuff have an echo in eternity on that level?

Because God is real, eternity is real, and because God is the best thing that has ever happened to me, and billions of others, the "soul" factor has always been a nagging one for me. If I am going to give my life for something, I want it to echo in eternity with the fruit of souls. I want to say at the onset of this chapter, however, that I am still very much exploring these questions theologically and in prayer. I don't come to this discussion professing to be an expert with perfectly distilled answers, but a fellow seeker with a couple of ideas. I invite you to read these next pages with a pondering heart. Let's dream together.

Could it be that national righteousness could really lead to an open Heaven effect that affects the ingathering of souls? Conversely, could it be that national unrighteousness locks up the heavens in a way that people's ears are stopped and hearts hardened to the very One who loves them and is calling them by name, Jesus Christ? I don't know for certain, but I am becoming more and more convinced.

IS THERE AN ECHO IN ETERNITY?

I can think of nothing more valuable to God than the soul of a human being. I, like many of you, do nothing halfway. When I hear the Lord say something to my heart, I give everything I have in response. There is no half-heartedness in my "yes" to God. This is the way He has made me.

Moreover, my desire has always been to live a life of *maximum Kingdom impact.* I made this my prayer early on in my Christian walk, saying to the Lord,

I want to live a life of maximum Kingdom impact. I want to pour my life into the thing that is going to bring You the most reward in eternity. I want to give my life, full on, for what matters most. Help me to live my life with maximum Kingdom impact, and guide me to know what that is.

At a foundational level, I believe there is nothing that beckons more of God's affection than the eternal condition of a person's soul. This is why He gave the most precious thing that He had for it—*His son, Jesus.* At the most basic and simplistic level, this is the good news: He gave His one and only Son to redeem humankind. This is the Gospel.

At my core, I am not sure if I am more of a reformer or a revivalist-evangelist with a primary passion for souls. I am told William Wilberforce had a similar wrestle, so I am comforted to know I am in good company as I grapple with the *how does politics affect eternity* question. At times I have lived in an intense inner-tension because *my* heart so burns for the harvest yet, in this season, God has called me to pour most of my time and resources into addressing social justice issues, calling the Church to do the same, and leading young people to meet with federal politicians. Because of this, over the last several years, I have come to a few personal vision crisis points (just ask any of my advisors!).

Having just laid bare my inner-tensions before you, I want to add the disclaimer that I believe the way to live a life of maximum Kingdom impact is to simply live a life of daily, obedient, submission to the will of the Father—no matter what it is. God does not need to justify Himself about why He asks us to pour ourselves into a certain thing. He is God, we are not, and Father knows best; so sometimes we simply need to obey His call, even if we do not understand the entire picture up front. So that is my little "in stereo" disclaimer about what I am going to share with you. Even if I had no guarantee that a soul would be saved through righteous reformation—though I am increasingly convinced that many will be, and in reality, we see many come to the Lord through our ministry on a regular basis (thank You, God!)—I would still have said, "Yes" to pouring my life into it if I knew the Lord asked me to. Father knows best.

RIGHTEOUS LEADERSHIP AND OPEN HEAVENS

Proverbs 29:2 paraphrased says, "When the righteous are in authority, the people rejoice; but when the wicked rule, the people mourn." This Scripture indicates that, when righteous men or women are in authority, the people will rejoice and be glad. Why? Well, let me answer by saying something that may sound bold, but is very easily backed up in reality. I believe that the people will rejoice not only because righteous authorities will make good choices for them that will cause them to be prosperous and have a cozy life, but I believe it is deeper than that. I believe there is a principle in the spirit that righteous and just decisions, which more often than not are made by righteous and just people in authority, create a spiritual reality over the areas of their jurisdiction.

> I BELIEVE THERE IS A PRINCIPLE IN THE SPIRIT THAT RIGHTEOUS AND JUST DECISIONS, WHICH MORE OFTEN THAN NOT ARE MADE BY RIGHTEOUS AND JUST RULERS, CREATE A SPIRITUAL REALITY OVER THE AREAS OF THEIR JURISDICTION.

To illustrate practically, have you ever been to a region or nation where the leaders allow blatant sexual exploitation of children, where there is no restraint on violence or on hard and destructive drug use in the open streets? What is the atmosphere in that area? Is it inviting, nice, cozy, and light—the kind of place where you want to take your family and throw down a blanket for a wholesome picnic? Or is the atmosphere icky, dark, eerie, slimy, or even flat-out terrifying?

What is allowed to take place in an area affects the atmosphere. This is common sense because we constantly experience it in a variety of ways, whether for good or for evil. As a person who worked on the deep inner-city streets of one of the most crime-ridden neighborhoods in North America for more than eight years, I know this reality well. Conversely, it is the place where God is honored and His ways lifted up where He feels at home and rests His head. The result: where God's presence is dwelling, people get saved.

WHAT IS ALLOWED TO TAKE PLACE IN AN AREA AFFECTS THE ATMOSPHERE.

I am not suggesting that Holy Spirit does not break in and touch people in the midst of gross spiritual darkness. Actually, He does it all the time. Just talk to the drunk who got saved by the voice of God drawing him as he hit bottom in the back alley or the drug addict who met God in the midst of her lowest low. But what we are after is seeing nations brought to the feet of Jesus. We are hungry for mass harvest, not just for one or two coming into the Kingdom.

The Lord clearly told us His desire is that *none* would perish (see Matt. 18:13-14). When there is an open Heaven in the atmosphere corporately, people are drawn to Him whether or not they are in crisis. Where the Holy Spirit is totally welcome, He will hang out and draw people to Jesus. I have seen more people get sovereignly saved at our mass prayer gatherings, where the Glory of God falls and shifts the atmosphere, drawing people to Him, than in any other context. It is what He does when He comes.

When Holy Spirit is present He starts knocking on hearts, asking for entrance. Following is a tangible example of a community I visited that was experiencing this kind of God atmosphere, not just at a gathering or at a prayer event, but in a brooding and resting reality.

Open Heavens in the Arctic

Over the last few years, I have had the incredible privilege of making several trips to the very northern regions of the Canadian Arctic. If you have watched the *Transformation II* documentary produced by the Sentinel Group,[1] you will know that this region of the earth has experienced an amazing move of God. I visited the communities and fellowshipped with the believers who were in the room at the very time when a supernatural wind filled it and literally shook the entire place. The move in the north is authentic and has transformed entire communities.

One community I visited, Wakeham Bay, had experienced this sovereign move of God firsthand. Late one night after a service, I stood in the yard of the house where I was staying and soaked in the atmosphere. It was still, calm, and so peaceful. The presence of God was so tangible, even in the streets. There was no fear of someone walking by at this late hour who might rob or attack me—like you feel in some cities in southern Canada—it was pure God atmosphere. This is my theory: I believe without a shadow of a doubt that anyone who did not know Jesus personally and who came into that atmosphere would begin to have thoughts of God, and I believe they would very soon after surrender themselves to Him. In this type of atmosphere, living for God just makes sense, and the revelation of who He is so easy to receive.

The mayor of the town is a spirit-filled believer in Jesus Christ. She leads and stewards the town as a ministry to the Lord and faithfully gives herself in it, seeking to only do what would bring pleasure to His heart.

I thought, *What would happen to the atmosphere in that town if a wicked mayor was set into place and began to do things that grieved Holy Spirit?* Well, let me ask you this: have you ever been in a church service where Holy Spirit is so heavy and thick and then, all of a sudden, someone leading the service does something in the flesh or says something out of selfish ambition or someone walks in with an attitude of disunity? Have you noticed how the presence of God can lift at times like that—especially if that person has a place of authority in the service? The Holy Spirit is grieved. Have you ever noticed how easy it is to push Him away? He is strong, but He is also sensitive.

In the same way, it is my opinion that if a wicked person was given the position of mayor and that person began to execute their wickedness, it would not be long before Holy Spirit would be so grieved that He might just leave. The atmosphere would be shifted, and that would affect the people—no doubt. Let's return for a moment to Deuteronomy 28.

Deuteronomy 28:12 says to the nation that walks in His ways, "The Lord will open the heavens, the storehouse of His bounty, to send rain on [their] land in season and to bless all the work of [their] hands…" (NIV). As discussed in the last chapter, this is indeed speaking of natural blessings and natural economics—but what about the spiritual principles that these words represent? What is an open Heaven spiritually? What is His bounty? In a spiritual sense, what is His rain? What is our land? What is the work of our hands? These terms: *open Heaven, rain,* and *land* are all common nouns used by Charismatic preachers worldwide when preaching on and expounding spiritual principles. Actually, as preachers, we use these words much more in a spiritual sense than in a physical sense.

A quick study of the phrase *open Heaven(s)* revealed the following Scripture references:

- Deuteronomy 28:12—the Scripture you just read.

- Malachi 3:10—speaking of the financial (natural) blessing the Lord will pour out when we do not withhold our tithe.

- John 1:51—when Jesus is explaining the spiritual open Heaven over His life.

- Revelation 4:1—when the apostle John saw a spiritual door open in Heaven and heard a voice saying "Come up here!"

HEAVENS (SHAMAYIM): THE HEAVENS, SKY, OR ATMOSPHERE
OPEN (PATHACH): TO BE THROWN OPEN, FREED, AND LET LOOSE

Scripture clearly shows us that the open Heaven is not just about the natural realm, though it affects it. There is such a thing as a spiritual open Heaven as well. This is precisely what is being talked about in John 1:51 and in Revelation 4:1. As Christians, our inheritance in Christ is an open Heaven because Jesus constantly lives under one (see John 1:51) and He is in us! That means an open Heaven—no barrier between us and God—is to be our daily reality.

This is why it is so powerful when we walk into Parliament and into parliamentarians' offices. We bring the open Heaven with us everywhere we go because we bring Jesus! As we carry this open Heaven reality into situations, we have the power to shift atmospheres! As we shift the atmospheres in places of influence and bring the influence of the Lord there through His reality in us, we have the potential to bring that same atmosphere shift over entire nations. What do I mean exactly? Let me explain: when a group of people, who are filled with the presence and power of God and who walk in the reality of the open Heaven in us through Christ, walks into a parliamentarian's office, the atmosphere there will inevitably shift. When the atmosphere shifts, he or she just may begin to think "God thoughts" and agree with "God ways." Those "God thoughts" just might lead them to make "God-type" decisions. Those God-type decisions just may influence the atmosphere and reality for entire nations. This mass atmosphere shift could mean that many more people will be open to receiving the truth of who Jesus is—and this can just keep going and going. This is about shifting the atmosphere of our nations. Meditating on this potential is so exciting to me. Let's keep dreaming more on this front.

...THE ATMOSPHERE OVER OUR NATIONS WILL BE THROWN OPEN AND FREED!

In Deuteronomy 28:12, the Hebrew word for *heavens* is the word *shamayim*, which means the heavens, sky, or atmosphere. The Hebrew word for *open* is the word *pathach*, which means to be thrown open, freed, and let loose. Oh my goodness. This is amazing. So what this Scripture is suggesting is that the promise of Deuteronomy 28:12—for the nation that walks in alignment with Jesus, His heart, and His ways—is that the atmosphere over our nations will be thrown open and freed! It sounds like mass eviction of the demonic realm. I can think of a few streets in my nation that could use some of that big time. It also sounds like *revival* to me! Where the atmosphere of God is, there you will find revival. There you will find people giving their lives to Jesus.

The open Heaven is the place of revelation and connection to God. What is the spirit of revelation for? According to Revelation 19:10, it is to draw us to Jesus. The starting point of a relationship with Jesus is salvation. There you will find transformation. There you will find restoration and perhaps even reformation. I am getting more and more excited about this national righteousness stuff all the time! The blessing that will come upon the nation that walks in the ways of the Lord will not only be natural, but this blessing will affect the spiritual atmosphere as well. Not only do we know this intuitively through our experience, but it is very clearly outlined in the Word. This is too good. Let's unpack a few more words from Deuteronomy 28:12: *rain, land, bounty,* and *work of our hands*.

RAIN (MATAR): RAIN, HEAVY RAIN.
LAND (ERETS): EARTH, COUNTRY, TERRITORY, DISTRICT, OR PEOPLE OF THAT LAND.
BOUNTY (OWTSAR): TREASURE, STOREHOUSE, TREASURY, ARMORY, OR PLACE OF GOD'S WEAPONRY.
WORK (MAASEH): UNDERTAKING, PURSUIT, AND THAT WHICH YOU PRODUCE.

The Hebrew word for *rain* is *matar* and simply means rain, but it suggests a heavy rain. The Hebrew word for *land* is *erets*, which means earth, country, territory, district, or people of that land. Hmmm. That is interesting. So this is saying that God will pour out a blessing on the people of our land and that it is not a "normal" blessing, but it is a heavy one; it is a heavy rain, a *big* outpouring! As already mentioned, I cannot think of a better blessing that could come upon any people than the very presence of God—the presence of God that draws people to the knowledge of His Son, Jesus.

The Hebrew word for *bounty* is the word *owtsar*, which means treasure, storehouse, treasury, armory, and the place of God's weaponry. Finally, the Hebrew word for *work*, as in the work of our hands, is *maaseh*, which means undertaking, pursuit, and that which you produce. When this open Heaven comes, it will affect everything.

In a New Testament context, what is our land and work? Easy answer: it is the advancement of the Gospel of Jesus Christ and the advancement of His Kingdom. When Jesus told His disciples to pray for laborers for the harvest, He was speaking of those who would go forth to preach the Gospel of salvation with signs and wonders following and to make disciples—even of nations (see Matt. 28 and the discussion in Chapter 1). When speaking of God's treasure and weaponry in a New Testament context, we are normally referring to tools and gifts that the Lord gives us to get the job done. They are the gifts of the Spirit, the empowerment of the Spirit, and the grace of the Spirit to share the message of saving grace and impart His fragrance everywhere He sends us. This is really amazing.

Since national righteousness opens up the heavens of blessings in the physical realm in a way that affects everything in our nations—economics, land, health, etc.—could it be that there is a link to an open Heaven in the spiritual realm as well? Could it be that the nation whose atmosphere is flung open wide and freed up will also experience an outpouring of spiritual blessing and a revelation atmosphere that will result in multitudes coming to the saving knowledge of Jesus Christ? Just like you can see more clearly in a room that is smokeless (than in one that is filled with smoke), in the same way, is it possible that the unsaved will see more clearly when the spiritual atmospheres in our nations are cleared up? I don't know for sure; I am just exploring here, but the thought excites me.

The bottom line is: we have nothing to lose by dreaming with these Scriptures and thoughts. The Lord has already called us to be the salt of the earth and to contend for righteousness. It is just amazing and awesome to think that this contending could lead to the liberation of a multitude and the release of mass harvest. It is amazing for me to think that it is possible that our reformation efforts will not only bring remedy to physical needs—like for my orphans in Liberia—but to the needs of the spiritually impoverished as well. If this is true, it is all together phenomenal!

Note: for a sneak peak on why I am increasingly convinced there is something to this chapter, skip to the end of Chapter 9 and read the prophecy by Stacey Campbell called, "I See Sickles."

Endnote

1. Find out more about the Sentinel Group and this powerful documentary at www .sentinelgroup.org.

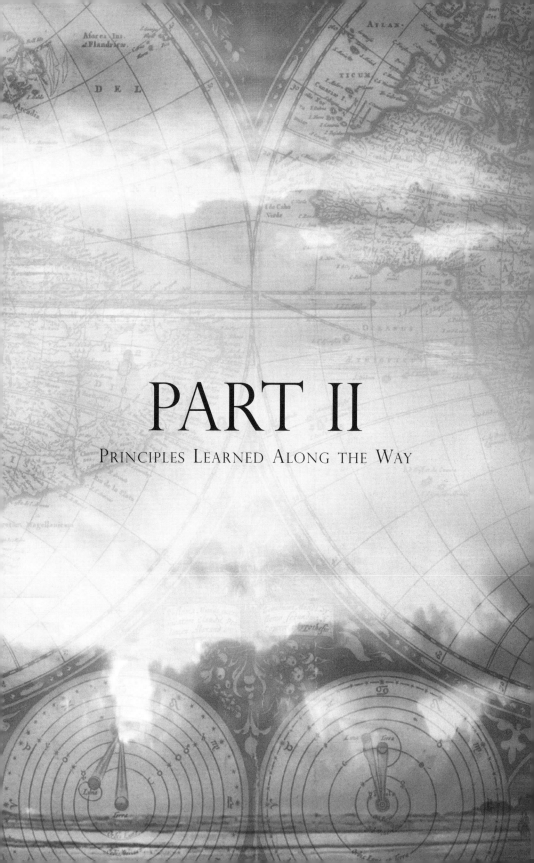

PART II

Principles Learned Along the Way

CHAPTER 6

Ultimate Intercession

...[hanging on the Cross] *He said, "It is finished!" And bowing His head, He gave up His spirit* (John 19:30).

In the spring of 2007, I had the opportunity to speak to the Canadian Justice Committee regarding Bill C-22. If passed, the law would raise the age of sexual consent from 14 to 16 years of age. I want to say upfront that appearing before this committee was one of the most intense spiritual confrontations I had experienced to date. I was representing the MY Canada Association,[1] one of the non-profit organizations for which I provide leadership. We were one of five groups that were addressing the Justice Committee that day. Three of the groups were radically socially liberal and were totally opposed to this bill to protect the youth of our nation from sexual predators. Not only were they against the bill, they were actually lobbying to add an amendment to it that would lower the age of consent for anal sex. It was clear from the beginning that this was going to be a clash, likely a head-to-head clash, three, maybe four, heads to one.

...APPEARING BEFORE THIS JUSTICE COMMITTEE WAS ONE OF THE MOST INTENSE SPIRITUAL CONFRONTATIONS I HAD EXPERIENCED TO DATE.

To address the committee, the Lord arranged the most phenomenal co-witness to go with me—Donny. Donny was a young man who had been exploited as a boy-child prostitute on the streets of Vancouver and represented the demographic that this legislation would work to protect. The Word of God says that we overcome by the blood of the Lamb—meaning the authority of the finished work of the Cross—and the word of our testimony—what the Lord saved us from. Understanding this, we knew our most potent tool would not be our ability to quote facts or put together tight sociological arguments. We knew that our most effective strategy would be to go in the assurance that Jesus was with us and that we, particularly Donny, had a testimony to share.

Donny stunned the parliamentary committee with his personal testimony of being used by older men in the street life of the Vancouver sex trade. It was raw, real, and irrefutable. You could have heard a pin drop. As a matter of fact, Members of Parliament are still speaking about how much of an impact his testimony had on them that day. As we shared, it was easy to see that the words were going deep into their hearts—sometimes silence is loud. Even the most socially liberal Members of Parliament were being convinced of the need to support this legislation.

> WE KNEW THAT OUR MOST EFFECTIVE STRATEGY WOULD BE TO GO IN THE ASSURANCE THAT JESUS WAS WITH US AND THAT WE, PARTICULARLY DONNY, HAD A TESTIMONY TO SHARE.

At the end of the testimony, there was a time of questions and a quasi-debate between all the groups. It was at this point when the battle began to rage. The gay rights and left-winged lobbyists who surrounded us were intimidating, articulate, and aggressive as they tried to convince the committee members of their view in spite of Donny's testimony and other common sense arguments that were presented. The Lord gave Donny and me great grace to stand our ground, however, and to tactfully answer questions with strong counterpoints. I am so thankful for the encouragement of the Word of God for these very scenarios. Jesus told us in Luke 21:12-15:

> …*You will be brought before kings and rulers for My name's sake. But it will turn out for you as an occasion for testimony. Therefore settle it in your hearts not to meditate beforehand on what you will answer; for I will give you a mouth and wisdom which all your adversaries will not be able to contradict or resist.*

It was amazing that, though we were grossly outnumbered among the witnesses and aggressively opposed, God seemed to fill our mouths every time we opened them. The final opinion of the committee was seemingly in our favor.

In spite of the apparent committee meeting victory, as I walked out of the Parliamentary building, I was shaken to the core in my spirit. It took me a good three or four hours to get back to myself, both spiritually and emotionally. It felt as if a 12-ton truck had just run me over. It was clear that what we came up against in that room was not just a "little debate" but the opposition of powers and principalities that drive ungodly agenda in nations (see Eph. 6:12).

CUT THE EYELID SO I CAN SEE

Let me try and give you an idea of what it felt like. Have you ever seen the movie *Rocky*? It came out in 1976 and was about a club fighter who makes his way to the world heavyweight championship for boxing. There is one scene in the championship fight when, after several rounds of intense beatings, Rocky goes to his corner for a round break. His face is severely beaten, so much so that one of his eyes is swollen shut. His coach looks at him with concern and essentially asks Rocky if he wants to continue or not. Rocky looks up at the coach and says, "Cut me, Mic!," meaning, cut open my eye. In an awesome act of 1970s-movie gore, the coach cuts his swollen eyelid and blood and water gush all over the place. After the eye is cut, he could open it again, see straight, and keep fighting. He then gets back in the ring and goes on to win the championship. It is an amazing scene of courage, cost, and victory.

103

No matter how hard the confrontation is, if you show up and keep standing when I send you, you will win.

Let's just say that, after a few rounds of being pounded on by our opponents before the Justice Committee, I could relate to that scene in Rocky! I was somewhat stunned through the beating and was trying to regain my bearings so I could see straight and keep my fight up. In that moment, I could hear Holy Spirit saying to me, "Cut the eye, Faytene; cut your eye, keep going, and keep fighting no matter how hard the confrontation is. If you show up and keep standing when I send you, you will win." There is a cost to changing nations; don't be fooled. Just because you have taken a punch does not mean you have lost; actually, victory may be just around the corner. It was for Rocky, and it was for us.

WHILE GOOD MEN SLEEP, NATIONS ARE LOST

That night I went home and thought about sending an e-mail out to our organizational membership list of 4,000 plus asking them to back us up by contacting the members of the Justice Committee and expressing their support for C-22. Though we had done well in the committee, I knew the fight was not yet won, and we just might need to go a few more rounds until we won the "championship." In all honesty, however, I was exhausted, and by the time the day was done—we had other meetings that day too— all I wanted to do was go back to my house and rest my head on a pillow. I *really* wanted to go to sleep. Back at my home office, in total exhaustion, I pondered whether or not to take the needed hour or more to format the e-mail and mobilize our "troops" across the nation to be a voice for this key bill at this key time. Did I mention I was *really* exhausted and *really* wanted to go to sleep?

While sitting there, Holy Spirit packed me another wallop and this phrase came into my spirit, "While good men sleep, nations are lost." Stunned by the penetrating power of what I had just heard, I pondered the words again: *while good men sleep, nations are lost*. In moments like that, I often think of Hebrews 12:4, from the chapter right after the one about the heroes of the faith that subdued nations and worked righteousness (see Chapter 3). Hebrews 12:4 says, basically, "[get over yourself!] You have not yet resisted to bloodshed, striving against sin…." You need to persevere.

There was another time this same message was driven into me from another angle. It was during a meeting I was at where a highly respected Member of Parliament was addressing a group of Christian leaders. It was a smaller networking meeting for key leaders, and this man had been invited to speak to us and challenge us—and that he did. Just prior to his sharing, we had gone around the table and each one of us had shared who our national heroes were. Many of the obvious names came to the table. Names of renowned Christian church leaders, political leaders, and historical leaders all rolled off the tongues as people shared.

The last person to share was the Member of Parliament who was scheduled to address us. He said that his hero was the man who had worked and succeeded in changing the definition of marriage. There was a gasp in the room, dodging eyes all around, and you could have heard a pin drop! We could not believe that this Member of Parliament, a very respected, socially conservative leader in our nation, said that the "Father of Same-Sex Marriage" in Canada was his hero! I have to admit, I was one of the shocked ones. I did not know what to think. He went on to explain,

> When this Member of Parliament stood up in the House of Commons over a decade ago and announced his legislation, we all laughed at him. We told him it would never happen, and we told one another it would never happen. He was not daunted. He continued and continued and continued until—well—here we are today. He has proven us all wrong. I have a deep amount of respect for this man, not because of what he did but because he did not give up fighting for what he believed in, even when everyone was telling him he was crazy.

With echoes of this moment in my spirit, and what the Holy Spirit had just spoken to me, I was at the point of no-return. God knows how to speak my language and cause me to lose sleep. I pushed myself up to the computer keyboard, buckled down, and somehow mustered up the strength and focus to get the e-mail out to call the nation to action.

The next morning, I went to my computer to clear out some work before we attacked another day of meetings on Parliament Hill. About five e-mails had come to my inbox as a direct result of the e-mail I had sent out the night before. I opened the e-mails and each one said something along the lines of, "Faytene, we read your testimony of speaking to the committee regarding raising the age of consent. We are so glad that there is a young person like you taking a stand for righteousness. We want you to know that we are praying for you." I scrolled through these e-mails, which I know were meant to be an encouragement, and I thought with exasperation, *You want me to know that you are praying for me?!?* I know I should have been thankful, but honestly, all I wanted to do was throw the computer—pardon the blunt honesty.

105

Praying for me!? *Praying* for me was not the point of the e-mail. The point of the e-mail was to get people to back us up in a very hands-on way. All I thought was, *People, get off your butts and back us up. Do something! There is a time for action, and this is it. There are countless lives of young Canadians who will be protected if we get this bill passed.* Recognizing the edge in my attitude, I immediately began to repent of my judgmental thoughts and guarded my heart. I knew well enough by this point that the easiest way to get stunted in your calling and destiny is to become cynical, critical, dishonoring, and judgmental. I repented and declared thankfulness for those who had responded in prayer while still hoping that the multitudes would flex their muscles a bit in a hands-on way.

As we were scheduled to meet with more parliamentarians that day, I got up from my desk and headed back to Parliament, carrying this experience on my mind and pondering it in my heart. As I walked on Parliament Hill, I thought, *God, talk to me about this, please.* Holy Spirit consoled me that there were many who had read my request, took it seriously, and e-mailed the committee, only they did not let me know (and that is OK; I am learning I can hear by the Spirit on this stuff). Then He spoke to my spirit in a soft but strong tone a phrase I will never forget. He said, "Faytene, if Jesus would have stopped in the Garden of Gethsemane, you would all be going to hell." If Jesus had stopped at Gethsemane, we would all be going to hell! Once again, His words hit me with a force—like a sack of cement. I understood the message immediately.

ULTIMATE INTERCESSION

The Garden of Gethsemane was the place of intercession Jesus went to before He confronted death on the Cross. It was in God's divine order that He went to Gethsemane first. It was essential. After all, He only did what He saw His Father doing, so we can be confident He was walking in divine order. I actually believe that the main battle in the spirit realm happened here in the place of prayer. The Garden of Gethsemane was the place where powers and principalities were shaken and where Jesus settled His will to the will of the Father once and for all. The Cross was secured in Gethsemane when Jesus spoke the words of complete surrender. These words often echo in my soul, "...O My Father, if it is possible, let this cup pass from Me; nevertheless, not as I will, but as You will" (Matt. 26:39). I believe it was this moment of settling and these hours of intercession that gave Jesus the strength to walk through what He was about to walk through for us: brutal beatings, massive humiliation, and ultimately one of the most painful deaths known to humankind—crucifixion on a cross.

> IT WAS IN GOD'S DIVINE ORDER THAT JESUS WENT TO GETHSEMANE FIRST. IT WAS ESSENTIAL.

Gethsemane was an awesome power encounter that secured the victory of the Cross, but Jesus still had to actually go to the Cross. It was not enough for Him to pray; He had to take His intercession into the place of action. Think about it. *The greatest act of intercession that all of creation ever witnessed was **not** a prayer. It was an action*—the action of a real Man who had consecrated His will to the will of the Father. It was a real Man with real nails going through real flesh and His real body being beaten with real whips and hanging on a real cross. His crucifixion was very hands-on in absolutely every way.

> THE GREATEST ACT OF INTERCESSION THE WORLD EVER WITNESSED WAS *NOT* A PRAYER. IT WAS AN ACTION.

I believe there is a false teaching in the Church today suggesting that intercession is unilaterally expressed through prayer or that the most powerful form of intercession is prayer. Intercession, plainly defined, means to stand in the gap or to make up the difference. When Jesus was on the cross with the nails being rammed through His hands and feet for us, and the thorns were pressed into His skull, this was the

107

most powerful act of standing in the gap that the earth had ever seen—and will ever see.

In this one act, He was creating a bridge out of hell and eternal damnation into Heaven and eternal life with the Father. It was extremely "practical." He lived His intercession; He is His intercession. He did not simply pray His intercession. He became intercession for us. I am overwhelmed when I meditate on the reality that the redemption of humanity and creation was hanging in the grip of the obedience of one Man, Jesus Christ. I am so thankful He was obedient. I am so thankful that He did not stop at the place of prayer in the Garden of Gethsemane and that He went to the Cross in obedient love for you and me.

The Cross was the will of the Father. He had to allow the lashes of whips, He had to let the nails go through His hands, and He had to let the spear pierce His side. This act of intercession was the Father's ultimate will in complete manifestation. Are you hearing me? I don't mean to be cheeky by asking this. I only wish I could express the magnitude of how loud this is in my spirit. God is looking for a landing pad in the earth. That landing pad is lives laid down in total obedience, no matter what the cost.

As we sat in that committee room testifying in the midst of brutal pressures from forces, both natural and spiritual, pressing in on us, we were standing in the gap for a mass of young people who were being sexually exploited. Where their voice could not reach, our voice was reaching for them. We were standing in the gap between the oppressed and the ones who had the power to make righteous legislation that could change their world forever.

> HE LIVED HIS INTERCESSION; HE IS HIS
> INTERCESSION...HE BECAME INTERCESSION FOR US.

I honor the praying intercessors of my nation and the nations of the earth. I honor the prayer movements and prayer giants God has given as gifts to the earth, but I want to say this one more time—prayer is only one form of intercession. We need to break the backs of the powers and principalities that have bound up our nations by using the spiritual weapons God has given us of prayer and fasting. But then we need to take it further.

We need to crucify our will to the will of the Father and actually act out our commitment to see righteousness and justice established in our nations.

We need to get out of our Gardens of Gethsemane and go to our crosses to secure the victory. It is only then that we can truly echo the words of Jesus saying, "It is finished" (John 19:30). This style of sacrificial action, coming from a place of total consecration to the Father's will, is key if we truly are going to see our nations restored to God's ways. I can hear some of you saying, "Well, my job is to stay in the Garden…others will go to the Cross." Well, all I have to say to that is, Jesus told us to be like Him, and He did both.

WE NEED TO BREAK THE BACKS OF POWERS AND PRIN-CIPALITIES THAT HAVE BOUND UP OUR NATIONS BY USING THE SPIRITUAL WEAPONS OF PRAYER AND FAST-ING. BUT THEN WE NEED TO TAKE IT FURTHER. WE NEED TO GET OUT OF OUR GARDENS OF GETHSEMANE AND GO TO OUR CROSSES TO SECURE THE VICTORY.

109

My tone in writing these words is not harsh or critical. I am simply passionate for the fullness. This is one of the reasons why, over the last years, we have worked to not only build up a movement of action, but also a mass movement of prayer through TheCRY's[2] mass prayer and fasting gatherings. In everything we do, we must prepare the way in prayer. We just can't stop there. Let's take up our cross and follow in the ways of our King.

Endnotes
1. For more information about MY Canada, visit www.4mycanada.ca.
2. To find out more about TheCRY, visit www.thecry.ca.

CHAPTER 7

Consecration That Shifts Nations

*"This is Jacob, **the generation** of those who seek Him, who seek Your face"* (Psalm 24:6).

The issue of radical consecration to the will of the Father is essential for seeing our nations turn back to God and the fullness of His dominion manifested in the earth. It was lack of consecration to the will of the Father that caused Adam and Eve to lose their keys of authority in the Garden of Eden. It was total consecration to the will of the Father that caused Jesus, the Second Adam, to win it back. It is continued consecration to the will of the Father, by those of us who are alive in the earth now, that will cause nations to be redeemed from destruction, restored to righteousness, and truly discipled for His Glory.

I believe we are living in the era of human history when God, by His Spirit, is seeking to bring forth a manifestation of these mature sons and daughters who, like Jesus, will live lives that are wholehearted demonstrations of consecration. Their lives will scream out, "Not my will but Yours be done!" The apostle Paul teaches us that all of creation is waiting for these ones to come forth.

Romans 8:18-21 says,

> *For I consider that the sufferings of this present time are not worthy to be compared with the glory which shall be revealed in us. For the earnest expectation of the creation eagerly waits for the revealing of the sons of God. For the creation was subjected to futility, not willingly, but because of Him who subjected it in hope; because the creation itself also will be delivered from the bondage of corruption into the glorious liberty of the children of God.*

The phrase *revealing of the sons* is made up of the Greek words *apokalupsis* and *huios*. These words together mean the disclosing, making bare, causing to be made visible, manifestation, or the appearing of the off-spring, descendants, dependants, followers of, pupils of, or those in the likeness, nature and image of God. The King James Version New Testament Greek Lexicon goes on to say that the sons of God are, "…those who in character and life resemble God, [and they are] those who are governed by the Spirit of God…." All of creation is eagerly waiting for the Church of Jesus Christ to walk in this level of maturity.

I believe all of creation is groaning and waiting because they know something! They know that when these ones begin to appear *en masse*, they will walk in the original mandate given to Adam and Eve and the commission to disciple nations. They will begin to walk in dominion stewardship of the earth, subduing the darkness and sin that causes corruption and decay and cultivating life and goodness. Their very presence in the earth will cause curses to be broken off of nations and the dominion of God to be made manifest. But it all begins when these ones, like Jesus, bow in radical consecration to the will of the Father.

112

REVEALING (APOKALUPSIS) AND SONS (HUIOS): TOGETHER MEAN THE DISCLOSING, MAKING BARE, CAUSING TO BE MADE VISIBLE, MANIFESTATION, OR THE APPEARING OF THE OFFSPRING, DESCENDANTS, DEPEN-DANTS, FOLLOWERS OF, PUPILS OF, OR THOSE IN THE LIKENESS, NATURE, AND IMAGE OF GOD.

I am talking about something much deeper than praying a prayer of salvation and dedication to God. I am talking about a lifestyle of total, sold out abandon to the will and ways of the Father so that even creation will look at us and say, "They are ones who resemble God in the earth and are completely governed by His spirit." One of the great reformers and conse-crated ones in the history books of my nation, Louis Riel, summed this up well when he said, "My life belongs to God: let Him do what He wishes with it."[1] This same reformer also said, "The spirit of God affects us where He wishes and to the extent that suits Him."[2] The two seem to go hand in hand: total consecration and total surrender to, even consumption by, the will of the Father in Heaven.

> THEY ARE ONES WHO RESEMBLE GOD IN THE EARTH AND ARE COMPLETELY GOVERNED BY HIS SPIRIT.

SIGNS IN THE SKY: A GENERATION MARKED "X"

I will never forget the first sermon I preached after giving leadership to my first mass prayer gathering, TheCRY 2006. For those of you who may not be aware, TheCRY in my nation of Canada is very similar to The-Call[3] led by Lou Engle in the United States of America. TheCRY is a mass assembly of prayer and fasting. We only do a CRY when the Lord clearly says, but when we hear His voice telling us to, we hold nothing back. We lay down our lives in the months leading up to TheCRY in order to call the entire nation, young and old, to come and contend for His purposes in Canada. On the day of a CRY, as a nation, we come and stand together with one voice contending for massive shifts on a variety of moral and legislative fronts. Each CRY has been incredibly powerful in its own way. We have seen much tangible fruit from these gatherings and often stunning answers to prayer, both in the nation and in the younger generation at large. To give you a full understanding of why my first message after TheCRY was so impactful, I offer some background information for this particular CRY.

Many elements go into planning a mass prayer event like TheCRY, held on Parliament Hill. As petty as it sounds, one of these elements is designing an event t-shirt. We wanted to design a shirt that would be a statement of sorts for the movement—not so much an entrepreneurial initiative, but a statement. Because of this, we wanted something that first of all had meaning before the Lord, and then would also have meaning for the people. Because one of God's names is Creator, and He is the most creative Guy in the universe—and because TheCRY was hopefully His idea not just ours, I thought I would ask Him what He wanted on the shirt.

As I prayed into it, I received a very vivid picture in my mind of a person in a t-shirt with an X on it. I then heard the Lord say,

113

I am going to mark many in your generation on that day. I am going to mark, with a mark of consecration all those who are willing to give themselves wholeheartedly for My purpose in Canada. They will arise with such a depth of consecration to Me and My purposes in Canada, that it will change this nation and impact the nations of the earth. Put the X on the t-shirt as a statement in the heavenlies. I am marking this generation.

I HEARD THE LORD SAY, "I AM GOING TO MARK MANY IN YOUR GENERATION ON THAT DAY."

That was all I needed to hear! I designed the t-shirt and continued on with other things that were still before us to prepare for the day.

Several weeks after the t-shirt revelation, I received an e-mail from a lady who had been praying on our 24/7 Prayer Siege to End Abortion,[4] a prayer initiative we lead whose whole focus is praying for the ending of abortion. She said that during her time of prayer she felt a very strong leading to go to and pray into Ezekiel chapter 9. The Lord then spoke to her to e-mail it to me; she had a sense it would mean something to me. This is what it says in Ezekiel 9:3-4:

> ...And He called to the man clothed with linen, who had the writer's inkhorn at his side; and the Lord said to him, "Go through the midst of the city, through the midst of Jerusalem, **and put a mark** on the foreheads of the men who sigh and cry over all the abominations that are done within it.

Mean something to me!? Did it ever! "...Put a *mark* on the foreheads of the men who sigh and *cry*..." You could not get much more accurate than that! The Lord was speaking. His eyes were looking to and fro for those whose hearts were wholeheartedly devoted to Him—those who would cry out for the nation to be redeemed and restored. The theme about wholehearted consecration only intensified as the day grew closer. One of the other Scriptures that became very alive to us was Psalm 24.

A CONSECRATED GENERATION WITH AUTHORITY TO SPEAK TO THE GATES OF OUR NATIONS

Psalm 24 is a psalm of David and is very powerful. In my assessment, it can be broken down into three main parts. The first part, verses 1 and 2, is a description of the Lord's awesomeness in creating and ruling over the earth. This part declares that, "The earth is the Lord's, and all its fullness…." I love this Scripture; you get such a sense of the magnitude of God's authority and power as you read it.

The second part, verses 3 to 6, describes a generation who will be given access to the Hill of the Lord. They are those who have clean hands and a pure heart, who will not lift up their souls to any idol, and who will not lie. They are described as a Jacob generation. They are a radical generation of purity that will seek the face of God. This part ends with, "Selah," thereby exhorting us to stop and think about what we have just read.

The third part, verses 7 to 10, is a strong decree that I often hear prayed and declared in Christian prayer settings. These verses declare to the gates (of both Heaven and earth I believe) to be opened up, or lifted up, to let God come in! In these Scriptures, God is described as the Lord of Hosts, which means Leader of the Battle, and as the King of Glory. These verses hold in them an intense command for the Lord to be welcomed into the earth in both His power and glory.

I believe there is no coincidence in Scripture. There is no coincidence to the three main themes of Psalm 24: God's dominion in the earth, a consecrated and pure generation, and an authoritative decree that opens gates of glory. I believe they are absolutely connected in principal, just as they are in this text. The earth is the Lord's—period, end of story. He made the earth and He is coming back for it. In the interim, He is going to cause a generation to emerge that, with the DNA of Psalm 24:3-6—radical purity, consecration, and hunger for God—will emerge with an incredible voice of authority.

Their authority is going to stem from the two things that come before it in this chapter: the revelation of God's Lordship over the earth and the entire consecration of their lives—I mean entirely given to Jesus Christ. The voices of those who function out of these two places will have the authority to speak to the gates of cities, nations, and I believe, the earth. When these voices decree it, there will be authority to call forth the Lord of Hosts to wage war against injustice and the King of Glory to take His rightful place of honor. The following is the visual of this in biblical context.

> THEIR AUTHORITY IS GOING TO STEM FROM THE TWO THINGS...: THE REVELATION OF GOD'S LORDSHIP OVER THE EARTH AND THE ENTIRE CONSECRATION OF THEIR LIVES.

Literally and historically, this psalm is speaking of the walled city of Jerusalem. The city of Jerusalem had gates where things came in and went out and each gate had gatekeepers. When the person in authority gave the command to shut the gate, it was shut. When the person in authority gave the command to open the gate, it was opened. If a person did not have authority in that city, it did not matter how much he kicked, screamed, and put up a fuss, the guy manning the gate would not open it or close it. There were only certain people in the city who had the authority to declare that the gate to that city be opened or closed. When they spoke, things happened. If others without authority spoke, things did not happen.

God is raising up a generation whose voice is going to be recognized in the heavenlies, even if their names are not known on earth. They will declare to the gates of our nations, both in the natural systems and in the spiritual realms, and gates will be opened. They will declare to unrighteous gates to be shut, and they will be shut. When they speak, mountains in the spirit realm will be moved.

> GOD IS RAISING UP A GENERATION WHOSE VOICE IS GOING TO BE RECOGNIZED IN THE HEAVENLIES, EVEN IF THEIR NAMES ARE NOT KNOWN ON EARTH.... WHEN THEY SPEAK, MOUNTAINS IN THE SPIRIT REALM WILL BE MOVED.

The reality that some voices have weight in the spirit and others do not is totally verified by Scripture. Do you remember the time in Acts 19 when some itinerant Jewish exorcist tried to cast out demons in the name of Jesus? Acts 19:15-16 tells us,

> And the evil spirit answered and said, "Jesus I know, and Paul I know; but who are you?" Then the man in whom the evil spirit was leaped on them, and overpowered them, and prevailed against them....

This Scripture clearly shows us that talking the talk does not mean you have authority in the heavenlies. These exorcists were not consecrated to God or commissioned by Him to do His work. Because of this, they had no authority at all and got a good beating as a result of pretending otherwise. God is raising up a generation that, on the foundation of His dominion in the earth and out of the place of radical consecration to Him, are going to have the authority to arise and speak to the gates of nations.

All this was becoming so alive to me as we prepared for TheCRY. So much so that we produced a video completely dedicated to Psalm 24 and played it, with Parliament as the backdrop, on the actual day. As I already shared, while we prepared for TheCRY, this word about consecration just continued to develop in our spirits. However, if the truth be known, this word was one that had pierced my own heart several years prior in a season when God radically confronted me on the issue of consecration.

THE SWORD WILL TOUCH YOUR OWN HEART FIRST

When I became a full-blooded Christian in 1995, my life was turned upside down—or perhaps I should say right side up. Prior to this, I had a general belief in God but lived a life full of moral compromise void of true encounter and true relationship with Jesus. I heard someone say once, "Just because you sit in a garage does not make you a car. Just because you go to a church building does not make you a Christian." This is absolutely true. Though I believed in God, I was not in relationship with Him and had no assurance that I would go to Heaven if I died.

In 1995, when I accepted Jesus as my Lord, Redeemer, and Savior, so many things that had been out of alignment in my life straightened out in an instant. The things I had been running to for fulfillment—immoral relationships, earthly success, alcohol, and so forth—fell off of me as I received the washing of the Holy Spirit. It was awesome. Everything I had been searching for—love, peace, joy, forgiveness, hope, contentment—came rushing into my inner-person like an awesome waterfall. I am so thankful to say that it has never left. I received immediate freedom from many things that I had struggled with for years. Well, everything except one thing: an eating disorder that had haunted me since the age of 14.

> EVEN THOUGH ON THE OUTSIDE I LOOKED LIKE I HAD IT ALL TOGETHER, ON THE INSIDE I WAS OUT OF CONTROL, AND I KNEW IT.

Bulimia was the one thing that kicked my butt. I likely had one of the worst cases of bulimia you've ever heard about. This inner-beast ruled my life for years. My entire day would be planned around eating and purging—sometimes from morning to night continuously. Even though on the outside I looked like I had it all together, on the inside I was out of control, and I knew it. I don't know why God does things the way He does, why He delivers us from some things immediately while other things we have to wrestle down. Looking back, I have to say a couple of things: (1) God is faithful and (2) it would seem that He wanted to use this bondage issue to teach me some things about authority, faith, and specifically consecration.

From the time I asked Jesus to be my Savior, I began to seek Him with all my heart for deliverance from bulimia. I went forward for prayer whenever it was offered at my church. I met with my pastor to receive prayer ministry and counseling. I sought the Lord in my own prayer times and eventually began to seek professionals who could help me. I went to counselors in my home city and drove hours to others recommended by friends. I really wanted to be free.

I began to understand that there were things in my emotional life that were driving me to food for comfort, and this drive came from things in my past that many people wrestle with—rejection, insecurity, self-hate. I worked hard. I forgave everyone I knew to forgive, everyone who had ever rejected me or made me feel less than treasured. I repented for believing lies about myself. I had deliverance from demonic things that had gained entrance to my life through sins I had committed prior to coming to Christ. I did everything I knew to do. Yet after having dealt with my inner-emotional issues and after having received the spiritual deliverance I needed, the eating disorder still had an ugly grip in the day-to-day reality of my life.

> IN THIS STATE OF HOPE DEFERRED, PART OF ME SIMPLY GAVE UP AND BELIEVED THE LIE THAT I MIGHT NEVER BE FREE.

Proverbs 13:12 (NIV) says, "Hope deferred makes the heart sick, but a longing fulfilled is a tree of life." The truth was, my hope had been deferred. I had done everything I knew to do to get free, I thought, and yet still this beast ruled me on the inside. I felt like I was losing. In this state of hope deferred, part of me simply gave up and submitted to the lie that I might never be free. It did not occur to me that I already was free (see Gal. 5:1) and that all I needed to do was simply submit to that truth and begin living like it. I had lost my fight. My fight became limp on the inside of me, and I thought, *I guess I will just live the best Christian life I can and accept the fact that I am a screw up in this area of my life.*

One thing that was really confusing was that, although I was in willful disobedience in the sin of gluttony—that is what bulimia is—the Lord was still using me and I was growing in the gifts of the Holy Spirit. I could prophesy. I could hear God. I could lay hands on the sick and see them healed. I could preach and teach and lead worship. Even though I knew I was living a sinful life, God still seemed to be using me at a certain level. With the combination of hope deferred and what seemed to be spiritual growth in my gifts, I simply gave up. I wanted to be free but was blind as to how to get there. After several months of living in this state, God confronted me head on.

THE LIE OF ESAU

One night when I was sleeping, totally minding my own business (likely snoring my head off), God broke into my world in the form of a prophetic dream. In the dream, a well-known prophetic minister was standing in front of me and began to prophesy over me with a very intense level of authority. She prophesied into my destiny and gift mix. In the dream, she began to go through the ministry gifts outlined in Scripture and, one by one, told me all of the gifts that I was not. Sometimes the enemy of true destiny is running after *good* things that are not *God* things.

> SOMETIMES THE ENEMY OF TRUE DESTINY IS RUNNING AFTER *GOOD* THINGS THAT ARE NOT *GOD* THINGS.

As a young woman of zeal with my whole life and destiny in front of me and a level of anointing already functioning in my life, I had received prophetic words from people in every direction imaginable. Pick a destiny, and I likely had a prophetic word for it! Some of them were truly words from God; others were simply things people were saying to me out of their own perception or desires for me. We call these words "soulish prophecies" because they originate from the soul of a man or woman, not from the Spirit of God. In the dream, this prophetess was breaking these soulish prophetic words, and the confusion they broke off of me and setting me back in proper alignment. She then began to prophesy into my destiny and gift mix. When she proclaimed what I truly was, the power of God hit me in a way and with a level of authority that I have rarely felt. It was like someone had taken my finger and put it into a 440-volt electrical outlet—the power of God was so charged. I felt as if lightning was going up and down my body. The intensity was so great in the dream that it shook me out of my sleep. I was jolted upright in my bed. I somehow catapulted onto my knees and was screaming my head off—whether audible or inner, I still do not know. I am sure it was quite the sight, and I will be asking for the re-play on this scene when I get to Heaven!

120

> YOU HAVE BELIEVED THE LIE OF ESAU. YOU HAVE BE-LIEVED THE LIE THAT YOU CAN HAVE YOUR STEW AND YOUR BIRTHRIGHT TOO.

I then heard the Lord say, "Faytene, this *is* your destiny. I have brought your destiny before you tonight in this dream, but you have believed the lie of Esau. You have believed the lie that you can have your stew and your birthright too. This is a lie. Tonight you need to choose one or the other: your idol of gluttony [food] or your destiny."

The fear of the Lord hit me in power, and in that instant, I understood the cost of my lifestyle of compromise and sin; for perhaps the first time, I saw clearly that this was what it was. In order to relay the full impact of all this, let me unpack the Esau story a little.

The story of Esau is found in the Book of Genesis. Esau was the oldest son of Isaac and Rebecca. Scripture tells us that, "…Esau was a skillful hunter and a man of the field but [his little brother] Jacob was a mild man, dwelling in tents" (Gen. 25:27). One day Jacob was hanging out in the tent cooking stew when Esau came in famished with hunger. He was weary after working in the field and was consumed with his hunger pains. Genesis 25:30-33 says that he looked at his brother and said,

> …"Please feed me with that same red stew, for I am weary."…But Jacob said, "Sell me your birthright as of this day." And Esau said, "Look, I am about to die; so what is this birthright to me?" So he swore to him, and sold his birthright to Jacob.

Esau was weary. He was in a time of inner-weakness where his fleshly hunger was screaming out to the extent that he was convinced he was about to die. Clearly he was being a tad bit melodramatic. Esau must have been a healthy, muscular man. He was nowhere near dying from starvation in that moment. He was simply a hungry young man with hunger pains that were affecting his self-control.

It can be said of Esau that he was lacking in fear of the Lord as well. Deuteronomy 21 teaches us that, according to Old Testament law, a double portion of inheritance was due the firstborn son. Esau knew this. He knew that his birthright was a double portion of his father's inheritance and that to faithfully steward it was both a privilege and responsibility before God. Perhaps what he was doing, when he agreed to surrender his birthright to his little brother, did not really register with him. Perhaps he thought it was a joke or that what his brother was proposing would never really happen. Perhaps he just missed the obvious—that this was serious.

Perhaps he did not know the Lord's promise to Abraham, that Abraham's descendants would be as the stars of the sky and the sands of the sea and that in him all the nations of the earth would be blessed. Perhaps he forgot that, as the firstborn son of Isaac, he was in this direct line of blessing. Perhaps he really thought he was going to die. Perhaps Esau thought

121

he could somehow get away with it, that he could fulfill the lusts of his weak flesh and still walk in his divine inheritance as the firstborn son of Isaac. If this was in the subconscious of his mind while having this conversation with his stew-holding brother, he was wrong. It is sobering to think that, in one moment of compromise, he lost so much.

> PERHAPS ESAU THOUGHT HE COULD SOMEHOW GET AWAY WITH IT, THAT HE COULD FULFILL THE LUSTS OF HIS WEAK FLESH AND STILL WALK IN HIS DIVINE INHERITANCE.

What he lost in this moment of compromise materialized two chapters later in Genesis 27 when Jacob received the blessing of the first-born from Isaac. The fruit of Esau's sell-out is reflected throughout of the rest of Scripture. In Genesis 50:24 it says, "And Joseph said to his brethren, 'I am dying; but God will surely visit you, and bring you out of this land to the land of which He swore to Abraham, to Isaac, and to Jacob.'" Did you catch that? Scripture does not speak of the promise He gave to Abraham, Isaac, and Esau, even though Esau, as firstborn son, was the rightful heir. No, Scripture says here, and throughout the rest of the Bible, that God is the God of Abraham, Isaac, and Jacob. Esau's name was struck out of the Messianic lineage, and through this moment of compromise, the promise was re-directed to his younger brother Jacob. This is chilling.

This one transaction in a desert tent, when Esau traded his inheritance for short-term satisfaction, rewrote the rest of the Bible! All of this was ultimately fulfilled when the promised Messiah, Jesus Christ, indeed came through the lineage of Jacob. The ramifications of this one transaction are mind-blowing and sobering, and they will echo through eternity. Even the Book of Revelation tells us that the gates of the new city of Jerusalem will be made of the 12 tribes of Jacob (Israel), not Esau.

> I DID NOT YET UNDERSTAND THAT WHEN THE BIBLE SPEAKS OF GRACE IT IS NOT THE GRACE TO KEEP SINNING.

Grace

The Lord was warning me through the dream encounter that, if I persisted in my sin and compromise, my very destiny was in jeopardy. Because I had heard so much teaching about God's grace, I can remember being a little confused by this. I said to the Lord, "God, what about Your grace? What about Your unconditional forgiveness?" I did not yet understand that when the Bible speaks of grace it is not the grace to keep sinning. When the Bible speaks of grace, it is the grace to be forgiven, repent, turn from our wicked ways, and walk in righteousness by His grace. Furthermore, I did not see the obvious: forgiveness is for those who repent, not those who do not. To repent does not just mean to say you are sorry; that is confession, not repentance. To repent means to turn from your sin and walk the other way. Scripture is clear that, if we persist in our sins, we will be given over to them (see Rom. 1:24). Whatever we submit to will rule us. This is what happened to me. Now was the time to use my own will to submit to something new—to the truth that I was free—and to walk in it.

The Lord then spoke to my heart in response to my honest question about grace and said, "Faytene, I love you deeply and My gifts and callings are irrevocable. This is why you find yourself still operating in the gifts of My Spirit at a level. But if I were to release you into the fullness of what I have called you to, with this level of compromise in your life, it would just be a matter of time until the enemy would use it against you at such a level that it would destroy you."

123

I have heard psychologists say that some people are motivated away from pain while others are motivated toward reward. I must be one of those people who are motivated toward reward, because as soon as the Lord showed me so clearly what the eating disorder was costing—my destiny—it was finished. I was done with it. Caput! I did not need any more inner healing; I did not need any more deliverance; I did not need anyone else to baby me and pray for me.

What I simply needed was to stop sinning.

Unfortunately, we have seen time and time again when sin and compromise are not dealt with and it ends up destroying leaders in the Body of Christ and wounding multitudes around them. Sin is so dangerous. I am so thankful that the Lord drilled this revelation into me early in my Christian walk. I prayed often as a new believer, "God, if You need to slow me down in order to build a foundation for me to stand on in later years, do it! I want to be an oak tree in the spirit that has deep roots and the character to withstand the tests of time—not a tree that looks big but whose roots are shallow and is easily uprooted by wind storms because of it." I pray He continues to deal with me like this in any and every way I need it! I love the rebuke and holiness of God. It is so life-giving.

A NEW PAGE

I SIMPLY NEEDED TO RISE UP IN MY IDENTITY AND AUTHORITY IN CHRIST AND STAND FIRM.

It is amazing; after I crossed this line of personal consecration, everything began to change. It took me a few months of wrestling down temptations and old mindsets and of picking myself up when I stumbled, but after that season, I never went back to my stew of compromise. When the temptations would come, I would simply recognize the truth that I was free; I would rebuke them as lying thoughts and feelings and command them to go back to the pit of hell. They always left instantly when I addressed them in this way. They have ceased to return. I did not need an anti-depressant pill. I simply needed to rise up in my identity and authority in Christ and stand firm. The only power the enemy has over our inner lives is the power to deceive. If he can convince us that we are not totally free in Jesus, then he will seduce us into acting like it, and we will soon find ourselves bound in his kingdom of sin.[5]

As I shut the door on this lifestyle of compromise and threw myself into the arms of Jesus in radical consecration, the doors of revelation began to open over my life—wait a second, this sounds like Deuteronomy 28:12 in action (see Chapter 5!). It was after this moment of consecration when He began to give me keys and insight into the spiritual destiny and current state of my nation of Canada. He began to give me national insight and revelation that led to my first published book, *Stand on Guard*.[6] This book became a self-distributed best-seller, is in the hands of almost every federal parliamentarian in my nation, and has been accepted into the Parliamentary Library of Canada. I am told by an eye-witness that it even sits on the shelf directly behind our Prime Minister's desk.

As I stepped out of the darkness of compromise into the light of consecration, I began a journey of accelerated growth and favor so that now I am at the tip of the spearhead for one of the main movements in my nation. It is humbling and scary to think about. God is serious when He says things like what He said to the nation of Israel before they stepped into their Promised Land, "Consecrate yourself for tomorrow I will do amazing things in your midst" (Josh. 3:5 NIV). At the beginning of this chapter, I told you that I would never forget the first sermon I preached after The-CRY in 2006—I haven't forgotten to finish my explanation of this story [smile]. So with all these things in mind, let's get to it.

SIGNS IN THE SKY: X MARKS THE SPOT

I was preaching in a small town in British Columbia, Canada, at one of those awesome backwoods camp meetings. The meeting was in an outdoor tent, and prior to the meeting, I joined with the leaders of the camp outside the tent to pray for the night. We pressed in together and invited the Lord to come in power that night to speak to the hearts of all those gathered. Due to the fact that it was only a few days after TheCRY 2006, I had not had much time to prepare—all my focus had been on this mega prayer event we just completed on Parliament Hill.

As I prepared my heart in the little time I had, I asked the Lord what He wanted me to share with those gathered. He comforted me and said,

"SHARE WITH THEM WHAT I HAVE TOLD YOU ABOUT A GENERATION THAT I AM RAISING UP THAT WILL BE MARKED WITH A SPIRIT OF RADICAL CONSECRATION...."

Share with them what I have been speaking to you: Psalm 24. Tell them what I have told you about a generation that I am raising up that will be marked with a spirit of radical consecration, a generation that will be totally possessed with My heart, totally given over to the will of the Father, and tell them that I am about to pour out an authority on them that will shift this nation back to Me in accordance with My pre-ordained purposes.

That was easy. I lived and breathed this message.

We closed the prayer time, and I began to walk toward the tent where I would be preaching. All of a sudden, something incredible caught my eye! I looked up in the clear blue sky and could hardly believe what I saw. In the sky was a massive, I mean *massive,* X. It had come out of nowhere. We had heard no airplanes that could have left a jet stream in that shape, and there had been nothing there just minutes prior. It was the only thing in the sky. You could not miss it. What blew me away even more is that it looked exactly like the X I had seen in the vision when I was praying about what to put on the t-shirt for TheCRY. I laughed and thought to myself, *Wow, that is one of the best sermon confirmations I have ever seen.*

ALL OF A SUDDEN, SOMETHING INCREDIBLE CAUGHT MY EYE!

I went into the tent and preached my heart out, mosquitoes and all. To this day, this word about consecration has never left me. I believe it is a plumb line revelation. Our God is a God of grace, of course. This is why He sent Jesus. But He is also looking for the mature sons of God to be manifested. He is looking for the generation that will be so given over to His will and ways that He can trust them with the keys to nations. They are a generation motivated out of love for God and His love for the world. They are possessed with a spirit—and His name is *Holy Spirit.* Because they are possessed with this Spirit, they are just that, Holy, and they are wholly given over for His purposes in the earth.

CONSECRATION IS THE AUTHENTIC FRUIT OF A LIFE CONSUMED IN WORSHIP.

In Romans 12, the apostle Paul tells us that this is nothing to boast about, this is our reasonable response to Him for all that He has done for us. I pray that we would truly hear, heed, and respond to this awesome call. I pray that God will find in us a generation that is entirely given over to His will. It is simple, but it is not easy. Otherwise everyone would be doing it. Consecration is the authentic fruit of a life consumed in worship. Let's arise together and lay down our lives in total worship of our God. Since I could never say it better than the Bible, I will finish this chapter there:

> *I beseech you therefore, brethren, by the mercies of God, that you present your bodies a living sacrifice, holy, acceptable to God, which is your reasonable service* (Romans 12:1).

Mark me, Jesus.

Endnotes

1. Faytene Kryskow, *Stand On Guard* (Credo Publishing, 2005), 131.
2. *Stand On Guard,* 132.
3. To find out more about TheCall visit www.thecall.com.
4. To find out more about the 24/7 Prayer Siege 4 Life visit www.bound4life.ca.
5. Very often when I share about the struggle I had with bulimia, I get e-mails from others who are currently in this battle. Because of this, I have put my testimony on DVD in hope that it will impart faith and deliverance to those seeking it. You can get this resource at www.faytene.ca. Bless you as you come into freedom.
6. *Stand On Guard* is a prophetic call and research on the righteous foundations and righteous covenants Canada was founded on. You can get it at www.faytene.ca.

CHAPTER 8

The Voice
Prepares the Way

He said: "'I am the voice of one crying in the wilderness: Make straight the way of the Lord,' as the prophet Isaiah said" (John 1:23).

Consistently over these past years the Lord has spoken this phrase to my spirit, "I am looking for a voice. I am looking for a voice of righteousness and justice that will go forth in this nation to prepare the way for My Kingdom to come." This is nothing new. From the dawn of creation to the coming of our King Jesus, God has always used voice to create reality.

Genesis 1:1-3 says,

> *In the beginning God created the heavens and the earth. The earth was without form, and void; and darkness was on the face of the deep. And the Spirit of God was hovering over the face of the waters.* **Then God said,** *"Let there be light"; and there was light.*

God said! At the foundation of creation, God knew what He wanted to create and began to create it. Step 1: open mouth and speak.

SAID (AMAR)—TO SAY, TO COMMAND, OR TO TELL.

The word *said* in the Hebrew is the word *amar,* which can be translated as, to command, or to tell. When God wanted to get the creation ball rolling, He simply rose up and said it!

GOD RELEASED HIS VOICE, AND HIS VOICE
CREATED REALITY.

One might wonder why He didn't do it a different way. Why didn't Scripture say something like: "Then God picked up His tool belt and went to work," or "Then God knelt down and started to shape the waters," or "Then God shooed the darkness away"? It doesn't say any of these things. It says, *"Then God said* [commanded or told]...." God released His voice, and His voice created reality. This spiritual law is repeated multiple times throughout Genesis, and it is echoed throughout the whole of Scripture. Proverbs 18:21 says, "Death and life are in the power of the tongue...." James also teaches us that our words are so powerful that they can set entire forests aflame (see James 3:1-5). Life, death, and forest fires! That is intense power.

One of the most awesome Old Testament examples of the power of our voices is found in Ezekiel 37, the well-known chapter regarding the valley of dry bones. The first part of this Scripture explains the dialogue between the Lord and Ezekiel.

> *He asked me, "Son of man, can these bones live?" I said, "O Sovereign Lord, You alone know." Then He said to me, "Prophesy to these bones and **say to them,** 'Dry bones, hear the word of the Lord! This is what the Sovereign Lord says to these bones: I will make breath enter you, and you will come to life. I will attach tendons to you and make flesh come upon you and cover you with skin; I will put breath in you, and you will come to life. Then you will know that I am the Lord.'" So I prophesied as I was commanded. And as I was prophesying, there was a noise, a rattling sound, and the bones came together, bone to bone* (Ezekiel 37:3-7 NIV).

IN HIS DETERMINATION, THE LORD SENT A MAN WITH
THE MOST POWERFUL CREATIVE TOOL IN THE UNIVERSE:
A VOICE FILLED WITH THE POWER OF THE SPIRIT.

In this encounter, the Lord took the prophet Ezekiel and set him in the middle of what looked like an impossible situation. To the natural eye, it was obvious: the situation was desperate; it was a valley of very dry human bones. In spite of the obvious scenario of death and demise, the Lord had a plan to bring forth strength and victory out of the destitute situation. In His determination, the Lord sent a man with the most powerful creative tool in the universe, a voice filled with the power of the Spirit. In the midst of this valley of dry bones, the Lord commanded the prophet Ezekiel to release his voice and prophesy. At first the bones began to assemble, and tendons and flesh appeared, but there was no life yet in them. The Lord commanded Ezekiel to prophesy again. Life then filled the bodies and they stood to their feet in strength. Verse 10 tells us, "….they came to life and stood up on their feet—a vast army."

PROPHESY (NABA)—TO BE UNDER THE INFLUENCE OF THE DIVINE.

The word *says* in verse 4 when the Lord says, "Prophesy to these bones and *say* to them…" is the word *amar* again—the exact same word that I cited from Genesis chapter 1 when the Lord *spoke* creation into reality. The word *prophesy* is the Hebrew word *naba*, and it means to be under the influence of the Divine. So what the Lord was saying to Ezekiel was (this is my personal amplified version), "I am going to come upon you with My divine Spirit, with the Spirit of prophesy, it is the very same Spirit that created the earth and the heavens. It is *My essence*. I am going to come upon you with My Spirit, and I want you, under the inspiration of My Spirit, to command these bones to arise. When you do this, they will arise and they will be a mighty army."

That is the power in the voice! It is not fantasy or hypothetical thinking. This is how the universe works. Let me give you another solid example of this principle in action. This time it is in the New Testament, and it is demonstrated through one of my favorite Bible characters: John the Baptist.

Matthew 3:3 quotes Isaiah 40:3 when describing John the Baptist, declaring he was "The voice of one crying in the wilderness: "Prepare the way of the Lord; Make straight in the desert a highway for our God." When

Scripture introduces us to John the Baptist's ministry, it actually describes him as *being a voice*, not just as having a voice. It was his calling to prepare the way for Jesus. Father God, in His divine order and wisdom, commissioned John as a *voice*. God did not commission him to build a manger where Jesus was going to be born; He did not commission John to go gather all of the disciples so they could be ready and raring to go when Jesus arrived on the scene. The Lord did not tell John the Baptist to go get all the sandals ready that Jesus was going to need for His ministry in the earth, although this might have made sense knowing from Scripture that Jesus did a lot of walking. No. When the Lord needed someone to prepare the way for the Messiah to come, he called a man to be a *voice* proclaiming His coming and calling people to ready their hearts through repentance.

FATHER GOD, IN HIS DIVINE ORDER AND WISDOM, COMMISSIONED JOHN AS A *VOICE*.

I believe that, as a voice in the earthly realm, John actually prepared a highway in the spirit realm for the manifestation of God incarnate, that is, Jesus Christ. Scripture tells us that, "…the worlds were framed by the Word of God, so that the things which are seen were not made of things which are visible" (Heb. 11:3). Job 22:28 also explains this reality, teaching us that, when we are in proper alignment with God's heart, "[We] will also declare a thing, and it will be established for [us]…."

Our words, when inspired by the Spirit of God, have the power to create structures in the spirit realm. What we see in the physical realm hangs upon that framing. Just like the outside of a house—paneling, brick, whatever—cannot hold up without the unseen framing, in the same way, the physical world is first framed by God's word in the spirit. Another Scripture that reveals this is Amos 3:7, which says, "Surely the Lord God does nothing, unless He reveals His secret to His servants the prophets."

There is a divine order that says that before God moves in the earth, He first moves through His voices in the earth. Before something is manifested in fullness, a voice must declare it. The connection between the Holy Spirit-inspired voice and what is manifested in the natural realm is evident throughout Scripture. Paul even taught, in Ephesians 2:20, that the prophets were one of the key ingredients to laying the foundation for the household of God—otherwise known as the Church. You cannot get away from it. I believe it is because of this unavoidable Kingdom principle that, before Jesus came, John had to manifest. When John arrived on the scene, he had a focused mission: *be a voice; prepare the way.*

> OUR WORDS, WHEN INSPIRED BY THE SPIRIT OF GOD, HAVE THE POWER TO CREATE STRUCTURES IN THE SPIRIT REALM. WHAT WE SEE IN THE PHYSICAL REALM HANGS UPON THAT FRAMING.

In Matthew 3:3, the word *voice* in the Greek is the word *phone*, which means sound or uttered words. The word *crying* is the Greek word *boao*, which means to raise a cry, to speak with a high and strong voice, or to implore. John knew that the greatest thing he would ever do would be to stand in the midst of a desert and raise a cry declaring that the Messiah was about to come, that people should repent and make themselves ready. It is possible that, whether a single person came out to hear or not, whether a single person listened to what John had to say or not, whether a single person responded in his heart or not, John would still have accomplished his mission. I believe he was not only preaching to people, but to powers and principalities. He was building a structure in the spirit realm for the very Word of God Himself, Jesus Christ, to manifest. It is totally amazing when you really meditate on it. What an honor John had. If Jesus was a Boeing 747, John's words were the landing strip.

133

> VOICE (PHONE)—A SOUND OR UTTERED WORDS
> CRYING (BOAO)—TO RAISE A CRY, SPEAK WITH A HIGH AND STRONG VOICE, OR TO IMPLORE

In 2005, just before we launched out to lead our first team of young adults to address the senior political leaders of our nation on issues of righteousness and justice, the Lord revealed the principle that I have just outlined for you as one of the plumb lines we were to apply: the voice prepares the way. He said, "Faytene, My ways are the same yesterday, today, and forever—I have always used a voice to prepare the way, and I am going to do it again." Like He sought out John the Baptist in the desert and Ezekiel in the valley of dry bones, God is looking for a voice in the earth today. I believe He is looking for a voice of righteousness and justice that will prepare the way for Jesus again. This voice will be abandoned to the will of the Father and full of His inspiration, and this voice will not hold back. When we speak, reality will be created. When we speak justly, justice will be created. When we speak righteously, righteousness will be made manifested in the earth. Righteousness will be created.

Edmund Burke summed this up well in his famous quote, "All that is necessary for evil to succeed is that good men do nothing." Perhaps with this in mind, one might say, "All that is necessary for unrighteousness to prevail is for the righteous to keep their mouths shut."

GOD IS LOOKING FOR A VOICE IN THE EARTH TODAY. WHEN WE SPEAK, REALITY WILL BE CREATED.

GOD PUMPS UP THE VOLUME

In late August 2005, we arrived with our first team of young adults at the Parliament of Canada to do just this: be a voice. For ten days we traveled more than 3,000 miles, mostly by car, and were finally at our destination: the capitol of Canada. During the ten days, we had stopped in eight cities, met with over 30 political leaders, hosted prayer rallies on the steps of five of our provincial legislative buildings, hosted six city-wide rallies in churches, and had been featured in regional and national media eight times. It was an intense schedule, and it was intensely fruitful. The team of young adults was amazing, and the nation was being shaken as they were sharing their voice in the tone of honor, love, truth, and power with national leaders and national media. The nation was taking notice, and it was exciting to see God back us up as we stepped out of our comfort zones in a big way.

The entire way the Lord was encouraging us, "Be a voice to your political leaders and nation, but also challenge the Christian community to do the same. Prophesy to the dry bones of your generation. Call them to rise up."

I KNEW BEYOND A SHADOW OF A DOUBT THAT THIS
WAS NOT JUST A NICE GIFT, BUT THAT IT HAD STRONG
SPIRITUAL SIGNIFICANCE AS WELL.

Earlier that year, during a powerful time of prayer with some friends, one of them felt a leading from the Lord to give me his shofar. It was one of those really nice ones, about 3 feet long or so with beautiful texture and color. Knowing how expensive shofars are, I was very humbled by the gift. However, I have to confess that I did not see myself as a shofar-blowing Christian. I had never had a shofar and had no idea how to blow one. When my friend laid it in my hands, however, the power of God hit me with incredible force, and I hit the ground as though a 2-ton truck had fallen on me. The weight of what was released at the granting of this gift was quite stunning. After this experience, I knew beyond a shadow of a doubt that this was not just a nice gift, but that it had strong spiritual significance as well. With the gift had come an impartation. It felt like a commissioning. I chuckled to myself and thought, *Well, I guess now is the time to learn how to blow one of these things.*

That shofar and I became pretty good friends over the next months. I blew it in my office, in my kitchen, in my living room, while driving in friends' cars—anywhere. I am sure I was quite annoying. That's OK. I was practicing. It was no surprise to me when I felt the direction of the Lord to take the shofar with me on our trip across the nation that summer to address political leaders.

On the last day, our team was to be at the Parliament of Canada for meetings. We decided to take one last prayer walk through the Parliamentary buildings. That morning, I had felt to do one of those "weird Christian" things. I sensed the Lord telling me to take my shofar and blow it inside the Parliamentary buildings, specifically in the Peace Tower. For those of you who are not familiar with the Parliament of Canada, the Peace Tower looks similar to Big Ben in Britain and is the centerpiece of all of our Parliamentary buildings.

I always thought people who did stuff like that were a little strange; you know what I mean. I thought, *God, are You crazy!?* Then I realized that this was an idiotic question. God specializes in the paranormal. Good thing. In the post-911 North American context, getting the shofar past security, not to mention actually blowing it in the Peace Tower, was going to take a

135

miracle! Security on Parliament was tight, and anything that looked as though it could be used as a weapon might quickly be confiscated. A 3-foot ram's horn with a sharp end would likely raise an eyebrow or two. Regardless, the idea would not leave my mind, so I went for it! The Lord gives and takes away. The Lord gave me the shofar, and I figured, if He allowed the security to take it away, that was His prerogative. What a ride.

> I FELT THE LORD TELLING ME I WAS TO TAKE MY SHO-FAR AND BLOW IT INSIDE THE PARLIAMENTARY BUILD-INGS…I THOUGHT, *GOD, ARE YOU CRAZY?!*

In faith, I approached the front of the security line with my shofar in hand. All week long, as we had been going in and out of this security point, the guards were quite stern and stone-faced with us. This time, for some reason, their countenance was totally different. First, they were smiling. This was a new thing. Second, they all seemed to be in a very light-hearted mood. The weekend was close at hand, and they were showing it! The main guard at the door looked at me and the group of young adults trailing in behind me and, with a smiley greeting, said, "Hey, hey, party at the Peace Tower!" I looked back at him, quite shocked, and sheepishly said, "Uh, yah, party at the Peace Tower." Then he pointed at my shofar and said, "What is that thing you have?"

I responded and said, "It's my horn." Before I had time to think twice about it, my mouth got ahead of my brain, and I blurted out, "Do you want me to prove it?" He looked back at me, shrugged, and said, "Yah, sure prove it!" We all know what that means. The only way to prove a horn (shofar) is to blow it!

> "IT'S MY HORN." BEFORE I HAD TIME TO THINK TWICE ABOUT IT, MY MOUTH GOT AHEAD OF MY BRAIN, AND I BLURTED OUT, "DO YOU WANT ME TO PROVE IT?"

OK wait a second; I need to explain something here: *this was huge in spiritual terms!* The security to the main Parliamentary buildings was right at the base of the Peace Tower. This is in the center of the Parliament buildings and is the visual centerpiece of Parliament. When people think of the Parliament of Canada, this Peace Tower is what comes to their mind. Furthermore, the Peace Tower has deep meaning to me personally. Pretty much every vision that I have ever had, in which the Lord spoke to me about reclaiming the righteous foundations of Canada, has in some way included the base of the Peace Tower.

In my spirit, I knew the base of the Peace Tower represented the foundations of the nation, specifically the righteous ones. For a full explanation of all this, I refer you to my book, *Stand On Guard.* So the Peace Tower of Canada represents the epicenter of national political influence, and to me the base of it represented the righteous covenant that our Founders had with the Lord.

> I KNEW THE BASE OF THE PEACE TOWER REPRESENTED THE FOUNDATIONS OF THE NATION, SPECIFICALLY THE RIGHTEOUS ONES.

Further, it is widely accepted in the Body of Christ that shofars symbolically represent the voice of the Lord. During the desert wanderings, shofars were used to communicate when the Lord was telling the nation of Israel to move locations or when He was calling them to rally for war. They were also used to signal key appointed feasts when the Lord was calling His people to gather. This imagery is carried throughout the New Testament as well (see 1 Cor. 15, Rev., etc.). So here is the picture: we are standing at the epicenter of national political power, at the place that represents the foundations of our nation, and we are about to release the *voice* of the Lord. Oh my goodness; this is not a small thing. If what I have been saying about the power of our voice is true, then this was a recipe for a national shaking.

> IT IS WIDELY ACCEPTED IN THE BODY OF CHRIST THAT A SHOFAR SYMBOLICALLY REPRESENTS THE VOICE OF THE LORD.

Back to the story.

Knowing all this, and knowing that I might never get another chance to blow the shofar in the base of the Peace Tower, I did the only reasonable thing. I let it rip! I put the shofar up to my mouth, and with all the faith and oxygen in me, I blew it as loud, as strong, and as long as I could. It was wild. After the last ounce of breath was out of me, I lowered the shofar and looked at the security guard who had given me the go ahead. His eyes were as big as Frisbees! He was stunned, and not only him but all the other security guards as well. I could tell by the looks on their faces that they did not know whether to throw me down and put hand-cuffs on me or to laugh at my naïve boldness.

In a soft tone, I looked at the guard and said, "Are you the head guy here?" He said, "No." To which I responded, "Oh, sorry, I thought you were in charge." Meaning: I thought you had the authority to let me do that. Well, the main authority in Heaven had clearly ordained it! One guard broke the silence by bursting into laughter, and soon the whole place was roaring in hysterics. Realizing that it may have been an oversight on their part, they allowed me through the security line—horn and all. We were off the hook, and the mission was accomplished!

I COULD TELL BY THE LOOKS ON THEIR FACES THAT THEY DID NOT KNOW WHETHER TO THROW ME DOWN AND PUT HAND-CUFFS ON ME OR TO LAUGH...

We did a short tour of the Peace Tower, prayed some more in the Parliament buildings, and then went back outside to find some of our team who had been on the parliamentary grounds filming. As we walked out the door, one of our team who had been on the lawn came running up to me, laughing with excitement, and asked, "Where were you when you blew the shofar?"

"You heard it? How in the world did you hear it? We were in the basement of the Peace Tower where security is." I was amazed. I had been with these guys all week, staying at the National House of Prayer,[1] which is a 20-bedroom dormitory facility. Whenever I wanted to get the team to come to the meeting room, I would blow the shofar to get their attention—but they would not hear it. The dormitory area was much smaller than the distance from the Peace Tower Basement to the parliamentary lawn! I thought, *How in the world did these guys hear the shofar this time?* My friend looked back at me and said, "Are you kidding? Who didn't hear it?! We were on the other side of the lawn of Parliament, and we heard it loud and clear. Everyone heard it! I thought for sure you were up on the very top of the Peace Tower blowing it." We laughed hysterically in amazement.

> I AM ABOUT TO GIVE YOU ACCESS TO PLACES THAT ONLY I CAN GET YOU INTO, AND I AM GOING TO AMPLIFY YOUR VOICE.

The fact that the entire Parliament could have heard the blasting sound means one of two things: either the Peace Tower engineering has an incredible ability to amplify sound and I just happened to blow the shofar in the right direction, or it was a supernatural amplification. Either way, it was a miracle because, even if there is a natural, architectural explanation, I was not aware of it and, therefore, had no clue what direction to aim. I believe that this whole experience was not only an assignment from God, but a prophecy. I believe that God was speaking through this experience and saying:

> This is what I am about to do with the Church in this nation. I am about to give you favor and access to places that only I could get you into, and I am going to amplify your voice. It is time for the voice of My Bride to be heard again in this nation. Let it rip, I am going to amplify your efforts. All you need to do is show up in faith and obedience to what I tell you to do.

THE NATION SHAKES

What is even more amazing than the testimony of how the Lord got us past the Peace Tower security and how the sound supernaturally projected across the Parliamentary grounds is what began to take place afterward. A few weeks later, when our parliamentarians came back from their summer break, the national political scene began to shake. The political party in office at the time was incredibly socially liberal. They had been in power for over a decade and in that time had reinforced many anti-biblical notions and pieces of legislation—the most notable was the legalization of

139

same-sex marriage. In early November of that year, only weeks after our shofar-blowing miracle, deep corruption in the governing party was verified and exposed to the nation at large. In a matter of months, the entire Parliament was turned upside down. This climaxed on November 29, 2005, when, through a non-confidence vote, the government was defeated by the opposition parties. The result was that we were thrust unexpectedly into our next national election, three years premature. In a matter of weeks, the entire government had collapsed. Chilling.

> IN A MATTER OF MONTHS, THE ENTIRE PARLIAMENT WAS TURNED UPSIDE DOWN.

I want to make something clear, however; I am not attributing the fall of the corrupt and immoral government unilaterally to our rag tag group of young adults who had stirred things up in the nation that summer or to me blowing a horn in the Peace Tower. (I realize I may sound like a bit of a nut cake, even as I share this testimony, but I want to re-emphasize that my primary purpose in sharing is to illustrate a principle: the power of God's voice.) To try to take that kind of credit would be incredibly arrogant and would disregard the effect of the many other Christian groups who had also been mobilizing in prayer and action leading up to the fall of the government.

On the other hand, I believe that, when God prompts us to do something and we obey, mountains are moved in the spirit realm. Like in the days when they marched around the wall of Jericho seven times, blew the trumpets, and the walls came crashing down, God still moves today in wild ways. I would insult God with unbelief if I did not have faith that our obedience that summer played a role in triggering one of the most drastic political shifts that our nation has seen in recent history. God is looking for a people. He is looking for a voice, and when we show up in faith and obedience, He shows up in power. It is the system of the Divine.

VOICE BOX OF THE NATION

When the ballots were counted on January 23, 2006, the change of the guard was made official. After 12 years of socially liberal rule, Canadians elected a new government made up of many Members of Parliament that held fast to socially conservative and biblical values on a variety of fronts. The leader of this party has been clear that he is a Christian. This admission was actually a really big deal. In my nation, where secular media is in the habit of demonizing anyone who professes faith in Christ, to admit such a thing would be thought of by some as political suicide. Where prayer in the former government was mocked and even shut down at key times, like at the September 11 Memorial service after the World Trade Center collapsed, this leader has finished every national address over these past years with the words, "God bless Canada." That is wise behavior. Our nations could use a little more of the blessing of God.

> WHERE PRAYER IN THE FORMER GOVERNMENT WAS MOCKED AND EVEN SHUT DOWN AT KEY TIMES...THIS [NEW] LEADER HAS FINISHED EVERY NATIONAL ADDRESS OVER THE PAST YEARS WITH THE WORDS, "GOD BLESS CANADA."

I am not endorsing a political party by sharing these things. Our team works with and supports strong morally-oriented men and women, no matter what political party they belong to. If someone stands for what we stand for, we get behind them, regardless of their political affiliation. Just this week, we aligned with someone who, in the past, was a strong political opponent. We aligned because they are bringing forth an amazing bill regarding the issue of human trafficking, and we want to support it. What I am trying to say is that this behavior point of our Prime Minister—blessing our nation—has been one of the most awesome blasts of fresh air my generation has ever experienced! I hope all future prime ministers, from whichever party, catch the wave and see the power of those three words. Honestly. Along with this, our sources also indicate that over 40 percent of Members of Parliament sitting in this Parliament (surveying all parties) profess to be born-again believers in Jesus Christ. For a nation that has been defiled to the core by an anti-God agenda for decades, this is a miracle. It is a resurrection and a return to moral sanity on many fronts.

IF SOMEONE STANDS FOR WHAT WE STAND FOR, WE GET BEHIND THEM, REGARDLESS OF THEIR POLITICAL AFFILIATION.

One of the promises that this new government had campaigned on was a free vote regarding whether or not to re-visit the same sex marriage legislation that had passed the spring prior. By the end of their first year as the governing party, a year and a half removed from the original legislative debate on the issue, they followed through on that promise. As a result, we found ourselves with a second chance to be a voice in defense of the traditional, biblical definition marriage. As I prepared to be part of this national dialogue, my memory rushed back to the spring of 2005 when this debate was at its apex the first time around. Many in Canada remember this spring well. We lost by a very slim margin. It was a rude wake-up call for those of us in the nation who hold fast to traditional values, and I believe it was a needed wake-up call.

That summer, just a couple weeks prior to the cross-Canada trip that I and other young adults embarked upon to address the leaders of our nation, I was at a national gathering and had the privilege of speaking with a woman who is a key political figure in our nation. She shared with me her experience in the House of Commons during the spring of 2005 when the traditional definition of marriage had been defeated. She said, "Faytene, if you would have been a Member of Parliament sitting in the House of Commons during the vote to redefine marriage, you would have seen that the public gallery was full of young people. About 70 to 80 percent of the gallery was young people." This should have been an encouraging report because only 25 percent of Canadians between the age of 18 and 25 years of age actually vote. As an age group, we have a reputation of being disengaged when it comes to shaping our nation in this particular sphere.

SHE WENT ON TO SAY, WITH TEARS NOW WELLING UP IN HER EYES, "WHEN THE MOTION TO PASS THIS LEGISLATION WAS APPROVED, THESE YOUNG PEOPLE ERUPTED IN A ROAR OF APPLAUSE AND JUBILATION."

She went on to say, with tears now welling up in her eyes, "When the motion to pass this legislation was approved, these young people erupted in a roar of applause and jubilation." She paused then said, "They were all young homosexual activists." A boulder of conviction dropped in my gut, and I was cut to the core. I felt like the biggest hypocrite on the planet. I was the one who had written the book regarding the importance of maintaining the traditional values our nation was founded on! I, like many other young people, had been at all the national prayer rallies declaring that we were rising up to "stand on guard," for Canada. I had said it, prayed it, sang it, declared it, bought the Canada t-shirt, and had even written a book on it—but I did not think to "show up" in the House of Commons the day that one of the oldest institutions known to humankind was under the threat of radical reformation in my Canada.

Not only was I convicted personally at the realization of this fact, but I was also convicted on behalf of my generation. I remembered all the times when I had been at youth conferences and sang with hundreds and sometimes thousands of other young people, "…I'm gonna be a history maker in this land…" and when we all walked away from the song and pretty much did nothing to prove those words true. The weight of the reality that it was people in my age group, not the older generation, in the public gallery declaring, "We don't want traditional marriage," hit me hard.

The memory of what our Prime Minister had said to older generation pastors from my area about their government thinking that they were representing the younger generation echoed in my mind.[2] We (I) had been so silent, and we (I) had been absent. I felt sick to my stomach, and all I could do was weep in the fear of the Lord for Canada and what we had just done as a generation.

NOT ONLY WAS I CONVICTED PERSONALLY BUT ALSO ON BEHALF OF MY GENERATION.

She went on to tell me that most of the Christian Members of Parliament took a long walk home that night. As she and her husband left the Peace Tower, a mass of young people were still jubilating on the front steps of our Parliamentary buildings. As the Members came out of the buildings, these young people hissed things like, "That is [so and so]. They are an evangelical." A couple of the Members of Parliament were even spat upon as they tried to make their way past the mob. Again I was convicted to the core. If only I had been there to at least take some spit for them, perhaps then my conscience would have at least been appeased.

My friend looked at me and said, "You know, Faytene, it doesn't take a lot to change a nation. It only takes a few people in the right places." In the midst of the conviction and deep fear of the Lord, faith filled my heart that, if we would simply show up to be a *voice*, God would show up. With all this in mind, as I looked square into the eyes of the second chance given us in 2006, I was determined to give this round everything I had. This time, nothing was going to stop me from showing up.

"IT DOESN'T TAKE A LOT TO CHANGE A NATION. IT ONLY TAKES A FEW PEOPLE IN THE RIGHT PLACES."

In the fall of 2006, I had moved to our nation's capitol, Ottawa, to establish an office for MY Canada there and to keep closer tabs on what was happening in Parliament. Throughout the fall, we worked hard to mobilize young people to meet with Members of Parliament. In these meetings, we implored them, for the sake of the next generation in Canada, to work and vote to preserve the traditional view of marriage, among other things. In early December 2006, when the second marriage vote came up, I was determined to do everything I knew to do.

HE LOOKED AT ME WITH A RAISED EYEBROW AND SAID, "ARE YOU AWARE OF THE PRESS GALLERY?"

The day prior to the vote, I was in the Center Block of our Parliament and bumped into an assistant whom I knew worked for a prominent Member. Knowing the power of the national media to influence both our Members of Parliament and Canadians in general, and knowing that they would be covering this vote as one of the leading national stories that week, I said to him, "I know you guys are likely going to be getting calls from the national media for statements to the press on the vote. If any of them want a statement from a group representing young people, *please* refer them to us."

He looked at me with a raised eyebrow and said, "Are you aware of the press gallery?" I looked at him and said, "Um, no. Talk to me!"

He explained, "There is a press gallery here in the Center Block where anyone, especially groups like yours, can go to get their opinion out to the press. A news alert will go out to all the national press notifying them that you will be there to make a statement. The cameras will be rolling and the press will likely show up to ask you questions, but even if they don't show up in person, the footage recorded in the gallery is often used for the evening national news anyway. You should book a time and make a statement."

I had never done anything like this but knew now was not the time to shrink back and hope someone else would do it. Actually, in times like this, I don't think there is ever a reason to shrink back. I am increasingly perplexed by how often we, as Christians, cower to intimidation and masquerade it by calling it wisdom. Sometimes I think that what we call wisdom is really just fear with make-up on. Fleshly "wisdom" might have said, "Faytene, leave it for the professionals," but faith said, "I don't see any professionals hanging around here right now, and there is a need. I can do all things through Christ who gives me strength. Here am I, Lord; send me." My friend gave me the contact information I needed, and as soon as I was back at my desk, I contacted the gallery to book my time. They confirmed that they could schedule me in the next morning, just a couple of hours prior to the vote. *Wow*, I thought, *it is that easy?*

145

SOMETIMES I THINK THAT WHAT WE CALL WISDOM IS REALLY JUST FEAR WITH MAKE-UP ON.

I went home that night and feverishly began to prepare what I would say in my statement and to enlist a band of intercessors to pray for me. The next morning, I went to the press gallery, backed by intercessors who came with me, and made my statement right after some of the most militant gay rights activists in the nation gave theirs—it was quite the contrast, I must say. The reporters barraged me, and I stuck to my key points. I simply reiterated, in different ways, "There are thousands of young people in the nation of Canada who are absolutely committed to the traditional view of marriage. This is who we are, and our voice is valid and growing…." It was intense.

> MORE THAN JUST A VOTE, THIS WAS WEIGHING DEEP IN MY CONSCIENCE, AND RIGHTLY SO. WHAT HAPPENED IN THIS VOTE WOULD AFFECT CANADA FOR GENERATIONS.

Throughout the entire week leading up to the vote, I had this brooding sense of doom in my spirit that we did not have the strength to win this second vote for marriage. In spite of this gut prophetic sense, for the sake of my conscience, I had to know that I had given it my best shot. I knew there would be a day, in eternity, when I would look Jesus face to face. I wanted to be able to look Him in the eyes and say, "Lord, I did all that I knew to do and in the strength that You gave me." I also knew there would be a day when my children or grandchildren would look me in the face and ask, "Grandma, what did you do when all this stuff was happening in Canada? Where were you?"

If we were going down as a nation on this moral battlefield, my hand was going to have to be pried off the sword at the end of it all. More than just a vote, this was weighing deep in my conscience, and rightly so. What happened with this vote would affect Canada for generations to come and would affect other nations in the earth as well as they considered the same debate. I could feel the magnitude of what was at stake deep in my bones.

After my statement to the public in the Press Gallery, I made my way to the House of Commons public gallery where the other young people had rallied a little over a year and a half earlier. I took my seat to pray with all the focus and faith I could find. The battle in the spirit was fierce. When the votes were finally cast, my prophetic gut sense proved true. Marriage fell again, this time by a significantly larger margin. We lost by more than 50 votes, as opposed to the one-vote margin previously.

> IT IS MUCH EASIER TO KEEP A GATE CLOSED THAN TO TRY AND CLOSE IT AFTER IT HAS BEEN OPENED.

They say that legislation is a mentor, and I suppose the large increase in the loss margin illustrates this. In a short year and a half, the moral mindset of the nation had changed so drastically that, all of a sudden, that which was a hot moral debate now seemed somewhat normative. This vote was a clear win for the gay agenda in more ways than one. For me, it was a huge eye opener to the reality that it is much easier to keep a gate closed than to try and close it after it has been opened. It is my belief, that the initial legislation from the spring of 2005 opened a door in the spirit realm over our nation and gave sodomistic strongholds greater leverage and greater access over the mindsets of the citizens of Canada—the theology of this, however, is the topic for another book.

If this is true, which I believe it is, this is all the more reason we need to pay attention and to be salt and light when the moral winds are at our back. Having said that, even when they aren't, we still stand for what we believe in. This is basic integrity. The story does not end there, however. Actually the most poignant "teachable moment" was still before me.

THE VOICE BOX OF THE NATIONS: MEDIA

After the vote failed, I and many others understandably left the House of Commons with a heavy spirit. I was alone now. The intercessors who had accompanied me for the press release had disappeared in the shuffle of the day's activity. It was just me, God, and the halls of Parliament. The natural agenda for the day was seemingly done, but I had a burning question in my heart, "Is there something more I can do, Lord? Before You, is there something more?" I was not striving; I was convicted and determined.

As far as I was (and am) concerned, the dialogue regarding the legal definition of marriage is not a dead one. There are no dead issues as long as they live in the hearts of people and those people are willing to act—prayerfully act is even better. The thought crossed my mind, *I wonder if I can make a post-vote statement to the press through the Press Gallery?* With nothing to lose except my fear, pride, and reputation (none of which we should hold fast to anyway), I made my way back to the Press Gallery to see what might come of it.

THERE ARE NO DEAD ISSUES AS LONG AS THEY LIVE IN THE HEARTS OF PEOPLE AND THOSE PEOPLE ARE WILL-ING TO ACT.

Interestingly, the last booking of the day was still open. There was a wonderful French Canadian man who was doing the scheduling, and even though it was too late to get a news feed to the reporters for them to be there for questioning, he agreed to let me present my statement in front of the cameras with the tapes rolling. If the reporters wanted the footage, they would come for it after the fact. I prayerfully gathered my thoughts together and stepped behind the podium microphone. I can't remember everything that came out of my mouth, but the last few words I remember vividly. With deep determination of spirit I looked into the national news cameras and decreed into them, "…this issue is not dead. It lives in the hearts of Canadians." You could feel the power of the decree and how important is was that these were the last words that day in the Peace Tower Press Gallery. Nothing of this magnitude is by chance. Sensing I had said all that God had put inside me for that moment, I stepped down from the platform.

DON'T YOU KNOW THIS IS THE MOST POWERFUL ROOM IN THE NATION? IF ANYONE WANTS TO CHANGE CANADA, THEY COME HERE FIRST…WHERE HAVE YOU BEEN FOR THE LAST THREE YEARS?

As the scheduler and I were both gathering our things to leave, he let out a deep sigh and said, "I am so glad this is over." A little confused by the statement, I prodded him, "What do you mean? Do you mean you are glad your day is over? Was it a rough day? Or do you mean you are glad the marriage vote is over?"

"I'm glad this marriage vote is over." Then he stopped, turned toward me, peered into my eyes, and while wagging his finger my direction, said something I will never forget. "They have been coming into this gallery for the last three years non-stop. They have been coming and coming and coming. Don't you know this is the most powerful room in the nation? If anyone wants to change Canada, they come here first. They have been coming, but hardly anyone who is saying what you are saying came. Where have you been for the last three years?"

I peered back at him, understanding fully, and replied, "Well, sir, I just found out about this place yesterday, but you can be sure you will be seeing me again."

That day I stumbled across one of the most powerful voice boxes of our nation. I want to say something. If we are the Bride of Christ, my friends, His Bride has a voice. It is time for us to show up in the voice boxes of our nations and use them wisely.

"Where have you been for the last three years?" still echoes through my spirit. I pray it will challenge you just as much. Sometimes we need to be challenged. The challenge is a winnable one, however—I know it. If we show up and speak with true, Spirit-led unction, we will win these and other moral battles that are staring us square in the eyes.

> THAT DAY I STUMBLED ACROSS ONE OF THE MOST POWERFUL VOICE BOXES OF OUR NATION. IF WE ARE THE BRIDE OF CHRIST, MY FRIENDS, HIS BRIDE HAS A VOICE.

149

THE FULLNESS OF THE VOICE OF A GENERATION

I would be very amiss in this chapter if I did not, at least in the final pages of it, take time to share with you a foundational revelation the Lord spoke to me regarding the voice of this generation in particular. What I am about to share with you, I believe, is a key revelation for those of us who have been born since the floodgates of abortion were opened against us in the 1960s and '70s.

> THIS IS THE SPIRIT OF YOUR GENERATION.... THEY ARE LOOKING FOR THEIR CAUSE.

In 2005, while at a national conference where thousands of Christians from across Canada had gathered for a time of seeking God on

Canada Day, I had a deeply impacting visionary encounter with God. It came in the form of two visions. In the first vision, I saw a map of my nation. It looked like a typographical map that you would see in a geography textbook. All over the map there were little black dots, and I knew they represented people in my generation. Some areas were more densely populated than others. These were the areas where natural population numbers were higher as well. I did not really know what the Lord was trying to speak to me, so I prayed for understanding. The more I looked at the vision, the more detail I saw until finally I could tell that the image was not static. The little black dots representing my generation in the nation were hovering and roaming a bit. Then the Lord said, "This is the spirit of your generation in Canada. They are looking for their cause."

Then I had another vision.

I saw the same map of Canada, only without the black dots. Out of the land, I saw faint incense rising to Heaven. Scripture teaches us that incense is representative of the prayers of the saints (see Rev. 5:8), so I knew that what I was seeing was intercession. Then I heard the Lord say, "One-third of your generation is already lifting their voice day and night, day and night, day and night saying, 'How long, O Lord? How long? How long until You avenge our unjust bloodshed?'" I knew that the Lord was not speaking about the prayers of the living, but that He was speaking about the unjust bloodshed of those in my generation whose lives had been terminated through abortion. Their blood was crying out to Heaven as a testimony against us, day and night.

> THEIR BLOOD WAS CRYING OUT TO HEAVEN AS A TESTIMONY AGAINST US, DAY AND NIGHT.

This is totally biblical. Actually, this revelation frames the Bible. We find it both in Genesis and in Revelation. When Cain attacked his brother Abel and killed him, the Lord spoke to Cain about the murder and said, "…What have you done? Listen! Your brother's blood cries out to me from the ground" (Gen. 4:10 NIV). In Revelation 6:9-10, we see this again when the apostle John describes a heavenly vision he had and says,

...I saw under the altar the souls of those who had been slain for the word of God and for the testimony which they held. And they cried with a loud voice, saying, "How long, O Lord, holy and true, until You judge and avenge our blood on those who dwell on the earth?"

THE LORD DESIRED TO BRING MERCY...FROM THAT MOMENT I WAS MARKED WITH THIS BURDEN.

This is what I was seeing in the vision. The blood of those who had been aborted, whose blood had been shed unjustly, was making intercession before the Lord. This injustice was crying out against us as a nation. It was incredibly intense. The Lord then went on to share with me the desire of His heart—even though the unjust blood was crying out as a testimony against us, the Lord desired to bring mercy, not judgment. I then saw the face of the Father in Heaven. He was turned to Canada with His hand cupped around His ear listening. He was listening, and He was longing for the fullness of the voice of our generation.

He said to me again,

Faytene, I want to hear your *voice*. One-third of your generation is already crying out to Me through their unjust bloodshed, but I am listening and I am longing to hear the fullness of the cry of your generation. Where are the other two-thirds of your generation who will lift their voices as well? Where is the voice of your generation that will cry out for mercy, establish justice, and prepare the way for My Son to be revealed in power in this land?

I WANT TO BE THE ANSWER TO THE FATHER'S LONGING TO HEAR OUR VOICE.

From that moment on, I was marked with this burden. When people ask me to explain in simplistic terms what I "do," which is such a hard question to answer, I often say, "I raise up a voice. I am working to raise up a voice in my generation that will speak to this nation in love, righteousness,

151

honor, and truth—a voice that will address the influencers in our nation—a voice that will call young lovers of God to become the influencers of today and tomorrow. A voice that will cry out for mercy to prevail. A voice that will cry out for His destiny—His dominion—to come in my Canada."

I don't know about you, but I want to be the answer to the Father's longing to hear our voice. I long to truly be part of that John the Baptist generation that will prepare the way for our King and His purposes in the earth. Since the Lord spoke these revelations to my heart, we have already seen Him do so much. However, I know we have only just begun. If we are truly the Bride of Christ, it is time for us to show up in the voice boxes of our nation and, like John the Baptist, lift our cry in the desert—prophesying until it becomes an oasis for our King.

Endnotes

1. To learn more about the National House of Prayer visit www.nhop.ca.
2. I share this story regarding Prime Minister Martin in Chapter 4.

CHAPTER 9

Legislating
in the Heavenlies

And I will give you the keys of the kingdom of heaven, and whatever you bind on earth will be bound in heaven, and whatever you loose on earth will be loosed in heaven (Matthew 16:19).

Again I say to you that if two of you agree on earth concerning anything that they ask, it will be done for them by My Father in heaven (Matthew 18:19).

I am a woman of action. It is my DNA. I can only sit in a church pew for so long before I start to get ants in my pants and need to get up and do something hands on to change my world. However, in this chapter, I want to take the opposite angle from what I said in the last one and emphasize the point that, *if we are contending for nations, we need to know that activism and action alone will not win the day.* We need to win the battle in the heavenlies first before we execute it in the earth. Many nation-shakers and history-makers of old demonstrated this principle with vividness. One of my favorites is Maria Woodworth-Etter.

ACTIVISM AND ACTION ALONE WILL NOT WIN THE DAY. WE NEED TO WIN THE BATTLE IN THE HEAVENLIES FIRST.

Maria would go into a community, lock herself in a room, and pray until she felt the breakthrough and release from the Lord. She would then go out into the streets and begin to preach the Gospel. Because she had broken open the spiritual realm in prayer, she would see multitudes come to Jesus and notable miracles break out all around her. There are numerous examples of other nation-shakers who functioned at this same level in their time.

There is no getting around it; if we are going to shake nations for Jesus, we need to shake the heavenlies first. Jesus taught us this clearly in Matthew 16:19 when He said, "And I will give you the keys of the kingdom of heaven, and whatever you bind on earth will be bound in heaven, and whatever you loose on earth will be loosed in heaven."

KEYS (KLICE): A KEY, KEEPER OF KEYS THAT HAVE THE POWER TO OPEN AND SHUT, AND POWER AND AUTHORITY OF VARIOUS KINDS.
BIND (DEO): TO FORBID, PROHIBIT, DECLARE TO BE ILLICIT, OR TO TIE UP.
LOOSE (LUO): TO SET SOMETHING FREE, DISSOLVE, DISASSEMBLE SOMETHING, OR LET SOMETHING GO.

The word *keys* in Matthew 16 is the Greek word *klice*, which means a key, the keeper of keys that have the power to open and shut, and it denotes power and authority of various kinds. The word *bind* is the Greek word *deo*, meaning to forbid, prohibit, declare to be illicit, or tie up. Lastly, the word *loose* in the Greek is the word *luo*, which means to set something free, dissolve, disassemble something, or let something go. So what Jesus is saying here, again, is that He has given us the power to decide what goes and what doesn't. When we, as His disciples standing in the earth-realm, forbid something in the name of Jesus, it is forbidden and disabled in the heavenlies. When we declare something is free, then it is free, and that reality is also activated in the heavenly realm. We have to realize the authority we have! It is mega.

Jesus, in Matthew 18:19, develops this further and says, "…I say to you that if two of you agree on earth concerning anything that they ask, it will be done for them by My Father in Heaven." There is great power in what we bind and loose in the earth, and there is great power in agreement. The word *agree* in Matthew 18 is the Greek word *sumphoneo*, which I am told is related to the English word *symphony*. That is so beautiful. What this Scripture is saying is that, when we come into one accord, into harmony like a sweet symphony in the earth regarding something, something will surely be given to us. It will be bound, it will be loosed—what we agree upon will be established. Amazing.

> AGREE (SUMPHONEO): TO AGREE TOGETHER, TO HARMONIZE, OR COME TO HARMONY (UNITY) WITH AN-OTHER.

I believe we have to seize this revelation. God has given us so much authority. When we agree, it is done. We need to take our place in prayer, decreeing into the earthly realm the advancement of the Kingdom of God, and then we must move out from that place into prayerful Kingdom-advancing action. If we don't do the work in prayer first, we may take a little ground, but not nearly the amount that we could have if we had prepared the way in prayer first. I want to be as effective as I possibly can this side of eternity so that we can bring Jesus the greatest reward possible. To walk this way is wisdom, and it is strategy.

VIMY RIDGE AND THE CREEPING BARRAGE

One of the best natural illustrations that I have seen of this principle happened during the Battle of Vimy Ridge in World War I. I am proud to say that my nation was at the forefront of this battle, which was considered a major turning point of the war. The following is a summary from Historica.ca that re-tells the intensity of what the Canadian troops were up against at the Battle of Vimy Ridge.

> Vimy Ridge was a formidable stronghold to breach. It was here that the Germans' heavily fortified Hindenburg Line met with their main trench lines leading north from Hill 70 near Arras, France. The German fortifications consisted of three layers of trenches, barbed wire and deep tunnels. The natural slope of the hill provided little cover for attacking Allied troops. French attempts to wrest control of the ridge throughout 1915 were rebuffed, resulting in some 150,000 French casualties. When the British army relieved French operations in March 1916, they were driven back before they could plan a major attack.

155

The crucial goal of the battle at Vimy Ridge was to break through the impenetrable German lines.[1]

AS THE AIR AMMUNITION HIT THE FIELD, IT CREATED A WALL OF SMOKE AND MUD. THE GROUND TROOPS WOULD ADVANCE BEHIND THE SMOKE SCREEN THAT HAD JUST BEEN KICKED UP BY THE BARRAGE.

The Canadians devised a brilliant strategy to take the ridge. It was an intense coordinated strike combining both air fire and ground troops as a tightly advancing front. They began early in the morning on April 9, 1917, with the air force loosing a barrage of gunfire in unison onto the field between the trenches where the Canadians had staked out the German front lines. As the air ammunition hit the field, it created a wall of smoke and mud. The ground troops would advance behind the smoke screen that had just been kicked up by the barrage. They kept approximately 300 yards behind it so that the Germans could not see them.

In perfect timing, the air force would then launch another barrage of ammunition in front of the foot soldiers, shielding them again so that they could continue to advance behind the cloud of smoke and mud that the ammunition had created. This continued until, to the surprise of the German front line, the Canadians were right on top of them. By that afternoon, two German front lines had been taken. By April 12, they had taken it all! It was said that, prior to this advance, success at Vimy had been measured in inches—this day it was measured in miles.

WHEN WE BEGIN TO EXERCISE OUR AUTHORITY IN PRAYER, IT RELEASES A BREAKTHROUGH SO THAT THE LABORERS CAN ADVANCE WITH SPEED AND FORCE— UNDETECTED BY THE ENEMY.

Just like the air force blinded the enemy so that the ground troops could advance virtually undetected, when we begin to exercise our authority in prayer, it releases a breakthrough so that the laborers can advance with speed and force, completely undetected by the enemy. Furthermore, when we release corporate prayers of agreement, just like the airplanes re-leased their ammunition all at the same time, a level of authority is released (see Matt. 18:19). When we function like this, our Father in Heaven will surely give us the victory.

One of the most significant personal encounters I have had with the Lord, to date, happened in the spring of 2006. Through this encounter the Lord drove the above principle home in my heart with an unshakable so-lidity.

IF YOU PRAY, YOU WILL WIN
IF YOU DON'T, YOU WON'T

We had just taken another team of young adults to Ottawa to meet with our federal officials. After an amazing week, the young adults had now gone back to their respective cities and regions, but I decided to stay in Ot-tawa a little longer to prepare for the upcoming CRY that summer. I was staying in the National House of Prayer along with a group from the small town of McLeannan, Alberta. This town is one of the only communities in Canada whose hospital board has decided that they will not allow abor-tions. Sensing it might be a divine appointment for all of us, one of the leaders of the National House of Prayer asked me to spend some time with them.

157

DURING OUR PRAYER TIME TOGETHER, THE SPIRIT OF GOD CAME INTO THE ROOM IN A VERY INTENSE WAY WITH A DEEP, DEEP BURDEN IN INTERCESSION.

At one point in the evening, we entered into a time of prayer for our nation. The team was intergenerational–several were older and about four were not yet 20 years old. During our prayer time together, the Spirit of God came into the room in a very intense way with a deep, deep, burden in intercession. There are times when God will do this. He will pour out a grace, burden, and strength to pray in a way that is totally supernatural. In these moments, God will often grant a deep revelation of His heart on an issue or for a region, people, etc. As you submit to and partner with the grace that He is pouring out, these times inevitably become very powerful and impacting. It was one of those kinds of times.[2]

> THEY WERE AGREEING IN PRAYER AND HONORING WHAT GOD WAS DOING WITH GREAT REVERENCE.

I was a little taken aback when the Lord began to move in this way because it was obvious that the burden to passionately cry out in prayer was being poured out more intensely on the younger ones in the room, not the older generation—who are most often the ones to lead in prayer in a group like this. What was coming out of these young people in prayer was not emotionalism. It was very holy, and you could feel the weight of the Lord's presence in a profound way.

Spontaneously and unorchestrated by anyone in the room, they began to cry out in prayer—specifically for the ending of abortion. We had not really even discussed the topic at that point so we all knew this was totally inspired by God, not by the power of suggestion. One of the young men, who was about 17 years of age, began to pray that God would save his generation just like He saved Moses in the basket from the decree of death that Pharaoh had issued. As he cried out, the other young people in the room mounted up with even greater intensity in prayer as well. It seemed that not only was there a more intense burden to pray being poured out on the young, but more grace and authority as well. I was impressed with the older generation's reaction. They were agreeing in prayer and honoring what God was doing with great reverence.

> IT WAS OBVIOUS THAT THE BURDEN TO PASSIONATELY CRY OUT IN PRAYER WAS BEING POURED MORE INTENSELY ON THE YOUNGER ONES.

I was in a kind of strange place though; I was feeling the burden of prayer that was on these youth, but at the same time, I was sensing some of what was going through the minds of the older generation. Sometimes I kick into the spiritual gift of word of knowledge (see 1 Cor. 12:8) without even realizing it, and I can hear what people are thinking. On a side note, this happened with Jesus many times when He discerned what people around Him were thinking. One example of this is Matthew 9:4, "But Jesus, knowing their thoughts, said, 'Why do you think evil in your hearts.'" The word of knowledge is a very real gift from Holy Spirit. This was one of those times when it was activated in me.

Often in prayer meetings like this, the Lord will give a burden to pray into a particular issue. Those present will lock together in agreement for that issue, and after a period of pressing in together, there will be a breakthrough. In this case, however, it did not seem to be happening this way. The more we prayed, the more and more intense it became, and there was no sense of a breakthrough coming, only a sustained and deeply mounting cry coming out of these young people for their generation. I could hear some of the seasoned ones beginning to think, *OK guys, it is time to wrap it up*, and, *Lord, give us the breakthrough.*

IN THAT MOMENT, I ENTERED INTO ONE OF THE MOST RIVETING PROPHETIC ZONES I HAVE EVER ENCOUNTERED.

In that moment, I entered into one of the most riveting prophetic zones I have ever encountered. It was like I was standing directly in the Lord's presence. He was awesome and strong and mighty. It was very much like what you read in the Books of Isaiah or Revelation when the writers describe the throne of God and the lightning and thunders that come forth from His throne. I was encountering the Lord in great power and great authority. It was His "lion" side, not His "lamb" side. Then the Lord spoke with a booming and thundering voice that I will never forget. He said,

> *Many are asking, when will it stop?*
> *When will this voice stop crying out?*
> *When will this burden lift? When will it lift?*
> *When can we get onto the next thing?*

Then, with even more authority, He said,

> *It will NOT lift.*
> *IT WILL NOT LIFT.*
> ***IT WILL NOT LIFT** until abortion is no more.*

I knew intuitively that the burden for seeing the end of abortion was nowhere near tapering down. As a matter of fact, it was the opposite. He showed me through this encounter that He is pouring out a sovereign move of His Spirit, especially among the youth, to pray until abortion is no more. They will not have to muster it up; it will land on them sovereignly. They will not have to work at it; it will be intensely undeniable—just as easily as they breathe oxygen, they will breathe this. It was as though He was saying that the younger generation had experienced the greatest amount of devastation because of the accrued numbers of abortions over the years, and because of this, they would have the deepest cry. Intense! But it makes sense. The Lord then addressed me directly and said,

> *If you do nothing else—nothing else—raise up a movement of those* [primarily in the younger generation] *who will pray 24/7 until abortion is no more. If the Church mobilizes in 24/7 prayer on this issue, you will see the end of abortion in your generation. If they don't, you won't.*

The call was clear and intense. Undeniable. I knew that, if we did not mobilize into 24/7 prayer on this issue, we would continue as we had in previous years as a nation: experiencing bite-sized victories at times, but not winning the battle. I also knew that the Lord was saying that we would be shocked at how quickly abortion would begin to be dismantled if we secured the "air force" in 24/7 prayer.

HER 10-YEAR-OLD SON HAD ENCOUNTERED JESUS, AND HE HAD TOLD HIM TO PRAY EVERY SINGLE DAY TO END ABORTION.

I was not surprised a couple of months later when I met a woman from Fort Saint John in British Columbia who told me that her 10-year-old son had encountered Jesus, and He had told him to pray every single day for the ending of abortion. Kids don't make that kind of thing up, and in our current culture, there are no voices in their worlds coaching them with pro-life messaging. If anything, the messages they are getting from most schools and media sources are aggressively pro-choice. His mother shared with me that she knew his encounter was real because it had seemingly come out of nowhere. This young boy was now praying every day faithfully for the ending of abortion. This was totally out of character—we all know most young boys would rather be playing video games than praying for something as intense as this. These encounters are more real than perhaps we realize. It seemed that he had not only gotten a revelation and assignment from Heaven but that the grace to pray had also been imparted through the encounter with Jesus. That is so powerful, and so real.

> SINCE I RECEIVED THIS INSIGHT, OTHERS IN DIFFERENT STREAMS IN THE BODY OF CHRIST HAVE RECEIVED THE EXACT SAME ONE!

It is amazing that since I received this insight, others in different streams in the Body of Christ have received the exact same one! We are currently working together in a coordinated movement to respond to the Lord. It is so exciting. Our piece of the strategy pie is that we have begun a virtual prayer wall where people can commit to praying for a minimum of 15 minutes a week to end abortion. Young and old from across the nation are participating, and as of the writing of this book, we are getting very close to seeing every slot filled![3] The air force of prayer is mounting. Also, since the launch of the 24/7 prayer siege for life, we have seen massive advances such as:

- The largest media outlet in our nation, CBC,[4] conducted an online Facebook[5] poll asking young Canadians what their number one wish was for Canada's 140th birthday. Out of 3,333 possible wishes that were posted and could be voted for, the number one wish of young Canadians was for the ending of abortion in Canada. This shocked the media—they had been proclaiming that the debate was over and that Canada was pro-choice. This poll proved them wrong, and because they had promised the nation that they would bring the poll results on Canada Day, they had to broadcast it on national news!

- The most recent national statistics on abortion show an overall decline in how many abortions are being done in Canada annually.

- There is a strong and mounting grassroots movement emerging, and in 2008, the largest nongovernmental event that took place on our Parliamentary grounds was a pro-life rally!

- We have had tabled the first winnable pro-life legislation that our nation has seen in decades!

Is this all just coincidence? No. To use the Vimy Ridge analogy again, the air force is being released effectively and in unison. Because of this, the ground troops are making strides! The best victories are still before us. I believe we are in one of the greatest national turnarounds on this issue that the Western world has seen.

WINDS, WAVES, AND SNOW OBEY HIM

With the work we are doing on Parliament Hill in Canada, we have seen this demonstrated time and time again. One such time happened in the spring of 2008 when our team was working diligently to see C-484 (the Unborn Victims of Crime Bill) passed into law in Canada. (Note: As of the writing of this book, this bill is still being debated, so I am going to share this testimony in present tense terms.)

IF PASSED, THIS BILL WILL ENSURE THAT WOMEN WHO CHOOSE TO KEEP THEIR BABY TO BIRTH WILL HAVE LEGAL PROTECTION FOR THAT CHILD.

If passed, this bill will ensure that a woman who chooses to keep her baby to birth will have legal protection for that child. Currently, because there are no laws on abortion in Canada, even a wanted child in the womb has no legal protection. To illustrate this, if a woman who is eight months pregnant is walking down the street and someone shoots her in the abdomen and the baby is killed, legally this crime is seen as an assault only against the woman. She would receive no compensation for the fact that her wanted unborn baby was harmed—the law does not recognize her loss in any way.

This is crazy—just ask anyone who has lost a baby to miscarriage. The loss of an unborn child is traumatic. In our opinion, C-484 is the most winnable bill protecting the unborn child that we have seen proposed in years. Because of this, we have determined to throw as much weight behind it as we can.

> IN OUR PRAYER TIMES, WE HAVE HAD A STRONG SENSE OF THE IMPORTANCE OF THIS PARTICULAR LEGISLATION.

Our team has worked diligently in very practical ways to be a strong voice of support for this bill. We have worked closely with MPs who are supporting it; we have met with many others in person, or we have called and e-mailed them. We have been publishing opinion articles in national and regional newspapers and speaking about the bill on radio talk shows. Finally, we have also been mobilizing Christians in our network to do the same by developing easy-to-use resources that enable them to be a voice in support of the bill. We have been working like ants utilizing the power of democracy to the maximum. Understanding the power of prayer, we have also been praying fervently for the bill. In our prayer times, we have had a strong sense of the importance of this particular piece of legislation, the very real battle in the spirit realm over it, and that we are gaining ground through working for it!

163

> WE ARE COMMITTING TO A THREE-DAY FAST TO PETITION THE HIGHER COURT OF HEAVEN TO ENSURE C-484 PASSES THE SECOND READING.

In the first week of March, word came to us that the bill was going to go for a second reading (which is about one-third of the way to being made legislation). In order to pass the bill, it has to pass through each reading stage, so this vote was crucial. As I came before the Lord asking Him to show me if we had already broken through and were going to win this vote or if we needed to keep pressing in, I sensed Him saying that we had the potential to win it but that we should not take anything for granted.

At that point, the vote was going to happen in three days, so that night I spoke to my team of young adult interns and laid out a plan, "OK team, we are in an Esther hour when this bill needs favor with our King in Heaven. We are committing to a three-day fast to petition the higher court of Heaven to ensure that C-484 passes second reading." My team is so awesome. With a twinkle in their eyes, they stepped up to the plate and took this prayer assignment by the horns!

We fasted for the next three days and, just prior to the vote, spent targeted time in prayer together for it to pass. After the prayer time, we hopped into our mini-van and booked-it down to Parliament to watch the vote as it happened. A wild snowstorm had blown in that day, and the streets were white and packed with snow. The wind kept the snow in a constant swirl around the vehicle. It was an extreme winter day. We contended through—determined to get to the House of Commons to pray onsite as the vote happened. We parked and then braved our way through the snow and up the steps of Parliament, making our way into the Public Gallery. Shortly after we arrived, the voting began.

IT WAS CLEAR THAT THE VOTE WAS GOING TO BE VERY CLOSE.

We watched in suspense as the Members began to cast their votes on behalf of their constituents. The Member who had brought the bill forward stood first to vote in support of it, then the next, and the next, and continued down the line. The odd person would remain sitting, meaning that they intended to rise to vote against it. After the first half of the House of Commons had voted, it was looking good. Then the opposition vote began. The first person remained sitting, thereby also indicating that they intended to rise and vote against it, and then the next, and the next. It soon became very clear that the vote was going to be very close. Our team sat in the Parliament praying our guts out for protection of the unborn to prevail through this bill.

When the final Member finished voting, it was still hard to tell if we had won or lost. We waited in eager anticipation as the votes were tallied and continued to set our hearts toward the highest House of the land in prayer: Heaven. After what seemed like forever, one of the Parliamentary staff rose and said, "Yeas 147, Nays 133." Parliament erupted in applause! We were ecstatic! Through the noise, the speaker of the House stood up and declared, "I declare the motion carried accordingly, the bill stands referred to the Standing Committee on Justice and Human Rights." The bill had passed to committee! Even though it was not yet law, this was still a huge victory and a huge indication that the momentum in Parliament was at our back. Because of all the work we had been doing on the bill, we were invited to a private Parliamentary reception that night to celebrate the victory. Several Members of Parliament attended to celebrate and to congratulate one another for their hard work over the last weeks to see it get to this phase. Several Members also thanked our group, knowing that we had worked very hard at the grassroots level.

> THERE WERE SEVERAL MPS WHO HAD NOT MADE IT FOR THE VOTE BECAUSE OF THE HARSH WINTER STORM. MANY OF THEM LIKELY WOULD HAVE VOTED AGAINST THE BILL…[AND] WE MIGHT HAVE LOST.

During one conversation with a key cabinet minister and a parliamentary secretary, the parliamentary secretary looked at me with a smile and said, "So Faytene, what did you think of that snow?" His grin and the twinkle in his eyes told me he was getting at something. The obvious then occurred to me: *the snow!* I then realized that there were several MPs who had not made it to the House of Commons that night for the vote because of the harsh winter storm. Many of them likely would have voted against the bill. The reality is that we might have lost if they had been there. I looked back at him with a big smile (the cabinet minister standing there was all ears) and said, "Well, we had a group of young people praying and fasting for the past three days, and we believe God answers prayer." The smile on my face went so deep. God wins!

Just a stone's throw from Parliament is the National Art Gallery. In front of it stands a massive black widow spider statue that is about 30 feet tall. When you stand on one side of it, you clearly see Parliament through its legs. It is creepy and, in a sense, personifies the spirit of death and destruction. The morning after the vote, the headlines in the city paper pictured a man clearing snow in front of the Art Gallery. The shot was picture perfect. Using a snow blower, he was blowing snow directly at the large black widow spider's head, and the headline: "Winter Packs Another Whallop!" I'll say! What a sweet victory! The papers were even throwing encouragement our way without knowing it. I immediately thought of Isaiah 1:18: "'Come now, and let us reason together', says the Lord. 'Though your sins are like scarlet, they shall be as white as snow; though they are red like crimson, they shall be as wool.'"

Could it be that the Lord was using the prayers of His Church and the faithfulness of some amazing Parliamentarians to begin loosening the grip of a spirit of death off of our nation?

TRIGGERING ELECTIONS, SHUFFLING THE DECK

Five months later, the power of prayer and fasting to shift things governmentally was illustrated even more vividly during TheCRY 2008. Four to five thousand Canadians had gathered in our nation's capitol for a full day of prayer and fasting. Throughout the day, we cried out in prayer for a move of God in French speaking Canada, for a culture of life to prevail, for a purity reformation to fall on the younger generation, for our leaders to make righteous and just choices for Canada, and much more. In the middle of the day, while standing in front of the Peace Tower with the mass of people behind me, I had the privilege of leading a time of prayer for our government leaders. We faced the Parliament of Canada and prayed that the Lord would bless them with a spirit of wisdom, truth, and justice and a revelation of the Messiah. We prayed for their families and their staff and that everything they put their hand to would be led by the will of God. As we continued, faith and the authority of God in our prayers mounted to the point that I wondered if I might explode—that is literally how intense it was. His authority was so present and so serious that you could feel that whatever we prayed in that moment would surely be established. So I did it. I prayed one of our dreams declaring, "God, will You pour out Your favor on the righteous here in our Parliament, and will You remove favor from those whose hearts will not be bent to Your will. Remove anyone from this place that does not represent Your heart" (paraphrased).

A few weeks later, we opened the national newspaper and saw a political graph that tracked Canadian voting intentions from the end of June to the end of September, 2008. This poll was revealing how Canadians would likely vote if an election was called on any of those given days. From the end of June to the *day* of TheCRY, August 23, the two leading parties were neck and neck in the polls. On the day of TheCRY, without a word of a lie, one of the major parties began to shoot up in the polls, the other began to plummet, and within a week, we were in a national election. The gap between these two parties sustained until the day of the election. There was a massive shuffle of Parliamentarians within a matter of weeks.

This is dangerous stuff. It is true: God has given the pen of history into the hands of a praying Church. Here are a few more amazing stories to relay the power of this stuff called prayer.

REWRITING HISTORY

For years now, a group of seasoned leaders has been walking together under the leadership of an organization called Watchmen for the Nations.[6] Leaders have come together in a spirit of deep humility, unity, and sacrifice to seek God together in regard to how to break open His purposes over the land. In various seasons, I have walked closely with this group and have witnessed, firsthand, the fruit of prayer that legislates in the heavenlies. One of the issues that Holy Spirit has brought up over the years at these gatherings of leaders has been the need for repentance to come from the European settlers toward aboriginal people, the original natives of our land.

Throughout our history, in a variety of forms, there have been horrific abuses perpetuated against the native peoples at the hands of the government of Canada and the Christian community. One of the grave national sins that our government and churches committed against the original people of the land was through a rampage of sexual abuse in government schools that the aboriginals were forced to attend. Leviticus 18:24-26 teaches us clearly that these types of things defile the land and even cause the inhabitants of the land to be spewed out of it.

> *Do not defile yourselves with any of these things; for by all these the nations are defiled, which I am casting out before you. For the land is defiled; therefore I visit the punishment of its iniquity upon it, and the land vomits out its inhabitants. You shall therefore keep My statutes and My judgments, and shall not commit any of these*

abominations, either any of your own nation or any stranger who dwells among you.

This is intense, and this was the judgment that Canada would be under, according to the Word of the Lord, because of this historical atrocity. I believe that being "vomited out of the land" speaks not only of being spewed out of our physical land but our spiritual land and destiny as well. As leaders and intercessors in the nation, we knew that this issue needed to be dealt with if Canada was to come into wholeness.

> AS LEADERS AND INTERCESSORS IN THE NATION, WE KNEW THAT THIS ISSUE NEEDED TO BE DEALT WITH IF CANADA WAS TO COME INTO WHOLENESS.

Like Daniel, who bore the sins of his nation in prayer before the Lord, at many leadership gatherings, national leaders were led by Holy Spirit to intercede, repent, and cry out to God to heal this historical wound. A mass breakthrough came at a national event in 2005 where, through a spontaneous move of the Spirit, the Lord began to open up a journey of healing between the church and the First Peoples of the nation—Métis, Inuit, and First Nations. A year later, Christian leaders from various indigenous groups came together in order to declare a covenant that they would walk together and work for healing and restoration of their people, and they even signed an official covenant together.[7] I had the privilege of not only witnessing this with my eyes but of signing as a witness on the official documents.

In a national prayer setting, these indigenous Christian leaders had: (1) granted forgiveness to the European leaders and (2) granted forgiveness to one another for the various historical atrocities that had defiled the land. It was mind-blowing to watch it unfold. All this went even deeper in March 2008 when the large gathering of young people caught the same burden in prayer at one of our prayer gatherings. Hundreds of young people gathered for TheCRY Edmonton for the purpose of crying out in united and fervent prayer for the nation and for their generation. The hand of the Lord was evident on the event from the start. The Lord seemed to be arranging every little detail.

HUNDREDS OF YOUNG PEOPLE GATHERED FOR THE-CRY EDMONTON FOR THE PURPOSE OF CRYING OUT IN UNITED AND FERVENT PRAYER FOR THE NATION AND FOR THEIR GENERATION.

TheCRY was located on Canada's first licensed aircraft field in the original aircraft hanger. It was also held on the 405th anniversary of when Samuel de Champlain set out on his first missionary journey to Canada. Champlain's heart was to bring the Gospel to the indigenous peoples living in Canada at that time and to establish an outpost that would not only be a settlement for France but would also be a constant presence for the Gospel. He was a Jesus freak and a nation builder. The history books recount that he had an amazing relationship with the First Nations and that they had a deep respect for him. The fact that we were gathering on Canada's first licensed aircraft field on such a significant day gave us great faith that God was about to launch something powerful in the spirit-realm. We knew that this was a divine appointment and that we were on assignment.

"FAYTENE, DID YOU KNOW THAT MY GREAT-GRANDFA-THER WAS BORN ON THIS EXACT PIECE OF LAND?"

We felt very strongly that Carol, a mature Christian leader, needed to be with us for this CRY. Carol is an amazing giant of the faith and a Cree elder from that area. As we approached the day, she shared with me, "Faytene, did you know that my great-grandfather was born on this exact piece of land? This is our traditional territory." I did not know this, but realizing the significance, I freaked out with glee! God sets the boundary lines of peoples, and He had, in His divine design, set the Cree people as the founding settlers of that area of the earth. I knew in my spirit that Carol carried a profound authority in the spirit realm because of this.

I BEGAN TO WEEP IN DEEP INTERCESSION, CRYING OUT TO GOD THAT HE WOULD RELEASE HIS HEALING TO THE FIRST PEOPLES OF OUR LAND.

Naturally, we felt honored to give the opening words of this CRY to Carol. She welcomed all of the young people with a powerful prayer blessing. She exhorted the young people about gathering for such a time as this, saying that the day was ordained by God and that the prayers offered in that aircraft hanger would change the nation profoundly. We reciprocated by giving her a gift—a golden maple leaf from our national Parliamentary buildings. The maple leaf is the national symbol on our flag, and Revelation 22:2 says that, "…The leaves of the tree were for the healing of the nations." For years we have heard this verse declared prophetically over Canada, and I truly believe that there is a destiny on my nation to bring healing to the nations of the earth. However, before we can heal others to the extent that God has intended, we need to be healed ourselves as a nation.

ON JUNE 11, 2008, THE DREAM BECAME A REALITY FOR ALL OF US…YOU COULD FEEL CURSES BEING BROKEN…AND THE POWERS OF DARKNESS LOSING THEIR GRIP.

A large group of young adults joined me to surround Carol as I presented her with the gold-plated maple leaf. Carol took my hand in hers, and we all began to cry out and pray for the First Peoples. The heavens opened over us in prayer, and I began to weep in deep intercession, crying out to God that He would release His healing to the First Peoples of our land so that they could be healed and freed to go into the nations, bringing that healing power. Like the experience at the National House of Prayer in the spring of 2006, this was one of the more intense corporate prayer times that I have ever experienced. As we cried out fervently for the First Peoples to be healed, we felt something shifting in the heavenlies. It was riveting.

A few weeks afterward, the Parliament of Canada announced that the long-awaited apology to the First Peoples for the sexual abuse in the residential schools was soon to be coming from the Prime Minister of Canada. On June 11, 2008, the dream became a reality for all of us when the Prime Minister of Canada welcomed the leaders of various indigenous groups—First Nations, Métis, and Inuit—to sit in the center of the House of Commons while the entire Parliament of Canada issued a formal repentance and apology to them.

It was historic. As our Prime Minister repented on behalf of the nation, we could feel curses being broken off of the nation and the powers of darkness losing their grip. Since that time, many of our First Nations, Métis, and Inuit friends have said that they feel a new joy and freedom in their communities that has never been there before. On that day a cloud of darkness and despair was pushed back over our nation!

Our team had the privilege of being present in Parliament when this took place. As I sat there, drinking in this historical moment, I was amazed at the faithfulness of God and the power of prayer. I was watching something play out in the natural government that the Church in Canada had secured in the spiritual realm in the season prior. I was struck again by the power of our prayers to transform nations and even to usher in healing for historical atrocities.

When I meditate on these things, I cannot help but marvel at what a privilege and responsibility it is to be part of the Body of Christ. Jesus truly has put the keys to our nations in our hands (see Matt. 16:19).

Before I close this chapter, I must share just one more story! I can't resist. If this does not convince you of the power of prayer, I don't know what will.

I WAS WATCHING SOMETHING PLAY OUT IN THE NATURAL GOVERNMENT THAT THE CHURCH IN CANADA HAD SECURED IN THE SPIRITUAL REALM IN THE SEASON PRIOR. I WAS STRUCK AGAIN BY THE POWER OF OUR PRAYERS TO TRANSFORM NATIONS AND EVEN TO USHER IN HEALING FOR HISTORICAL ATROCITIES.

A GIANT HAS FALLEN

As previously mentioned, one of the main issues of moral debate over this past season has been the legal definition of marriage. As mentioned in Chapter 2, prior to moving to my nation's capital, I lived in Vancouver,

British Columbia, just a stone's throw away from the constituency where the Member of Parliament who initiated this legislation came from. As pastors and leaders in that city, we often spoke of our responsibility to the nation because this legislative initiative had come out of our political territory and on our "watch." During that particular season, I was extremely involved with city prayer and served at the local house of prayer.[8] The main intercessory leader in the city had been working quite extensively with a group of us in a "swat team" type of prayer format to pray for the city on a regular basis. She had also been working extensively building relationships with the local senior pastors.

During her times of seeking the Lord regarding a prayer strategy for the city, she felt directed to submit a plan to the leaders that would mobilize four swat teams of intercessors, each visiting three key sites in the city over the same time period. They would be commissioned by the citywide apostolic leadership, and as they went to each location, they would decree Scripture, pray spontaneous prayers, and take communion to honor the blood of Christ. There was a strong sense of agreement that this was indeed a strategy that the Lord was giving, and the citywide leadership backed it wholeheartedly. Interestingly, during this same time frame, the Member of Parliament I just mentioned was aggressively pushing forward his legislation to redefine marriage in Canada.

> THERE WAS A STRONG SENSE OF AGREEMENT THAT THIS WAS INDEED A STRATEGY THAT THE LORD WAS GIVING, AND THE CITYWIDE LEADERSHIP BACKED IT WHOLEHEARTEDLY...WE DID NOT KNOW THAT WE WERE TRIP-WIRING A HISTORIC EVENT.

Our fearless leader began to work more extensively with us, and as a larger team, we spent time fasting and seeking the Lord to prepare our hearts for the prayer assignment. The strategy was solid at every turn. On execution day, the citywide pastors blessed and commissioned us, and then finally we all gathered to receive our orders. We were divided into four teams and given our locations; a large group of intercessors stayed behind at the church to cover us in prayer. Those on the swat teams went to the high places—literally and spiritually—of the city and to some of the main gates of influence to carry out our prayer mission. One team went to the very church that had openly endorsed same sex unions and that was one of the main voices spearheading the movement against traditional marriage. We prayed, worshiped, decreed, repented, and took communion on-site. We had no idea that we were trip-wiring a historic event.

That same afternoon, the Member of Parliament of whom I have been speaking entered a public auction where a $50,000 wedding ring was on display. He told reporters later that, "Something just snapped in this moment of total, utter irrationality." He placed the ring on his finger, and with video surveillance cameras all around recording his every move, pro-ceeded to walk out of the auction, stealing the ring. Almost immediately, it hit national media, and this man, who had been a political ace for almost 25 years, was arrested and removed from political office. Over the next days, televisions across Canada broadcast images of this teary-eyed man admit-ting his guilt and openly blaming his behavior on stress and emotional problems. Whatever the reasoning, everything changed that afternoon. That is wild.

173

...EVERYTHING CHANGED THAT AFTERNOON.

What happened? Only Heaven has the instant replay. Only Heaven knows what was set in motion as these intercessors prayed, re-pented, and cried out to God on behalf of the sins of our city. The fact that both the prayers and this Member's slip-up were happening at the exact same time is too amazing to chalk it up to coincidence. It is clear that something massive was shaken—and fell.

As I think about these things, sometimes I have to shake my head and wonder, *Do we really comprehend the power that God has given into the hands of a praying Church?* I'm not sure that I do, but from the little I have seen and the little that I do comprehend, I can say with total as-surance that when we pray God answers. The fervent effectual prayer of the righteous in Christ indeed does avail much.

I finish this chapter with a prophetic exhortation that both relates to all that we have been speaking of, as well as the times we are landing in globally. "I See Sickles" is from one of the most accurate prophetic voices I know, Stacey Campbell.[9]

I feel the Lord saying that, just as with individuals there are certain demons that only come out by fasting and prayer, in nations, when things get so deep and so wrong, there are certain things that cannot be reversed except by fasting and prayer. And there are times in the history of the Church when mission movements come and the Gospel is preached and a harvest is reaped but there are other times, and this is such a time, when the harvest will not come except by fasting and prayer because of the level of demonic strongholds in nations. And I feel like the Lord wants to highlight this to the next generation, that they don't just hear the call to evangelize nations but they hear the higher call of fasting and praying to bind the strongholds of nations, to loose the heart of the Gospel of God, because there are certain times, even in nations, when things will not come out except by fasting and prayer…I feel by the Spirit that God wants to deposit this because I know that many of you are end-time evangelists, and you know that the Lord has called you to gather, and you know that the Lord has called you to reap, but you must know that in this season, you will not gather to the level that is needed except you hear the message of fasting and prayer. It's like your sickle—I keep seeing sickles—Your sickle will only go, like, six inches in front of you, but if you knight it with fasting and prayer, it will go miles and miles and miles, and cities will be gathered. And so Father, I am asking that by Your Spirit, Lord that by Your Spirit, You would give us ears to hear…it's not about other gatherings. All of us have been to gatherings in nations, over and over again, and big gatherings in nations. But there's a time. It's a different time, and your generation will be at the front end of that different time. You know how the Bible says that the cup of iniquity gets filled? There are cups in nations that are filled with iniquity, and they won't be shifted or emptied except by fasting and prayer….

Endnotes

1. http://www.histori.ca/minutes/minute.do?id=14742

2. An incredible book that explains some of this and intercession in general is Dutch Sheets' book, *Intercessory Prayer.*

3. To find out more about the 24/7 Prayer Siege to end abortion, visit www.bound4life.ca.

4. CBC in Canada is equivalent to CNN in the U.S. or the BBC in Europe.

5. Facebook is an online networking tool that many young adults and youth use. See www.facebook.com.

6. To find out more about Watchmen for the Nations, visit www.watchmen.org.

7. Check out TheCRY online to see pictures: www.thecry.ca.

8. Vancouver House of Prayer has now transitioned into a variety of expressions and no longer functions as a physical house of prayer.

9. Find out more about Stacey Campbell and her husband Wesley's ministry at www.beahero.org.

CHAPTER 10

Faith That Subdues Nations

Who through faith subdued kingdoms, worked righteousness, obtained promises, stopped the mouths of lions, quenched the violence of fire, escaped the edge of the sword, out of weakness were made strong, became valiant in battle, turned to flight the armies of the aliens. Women received their dead raised to life again.... (Hebrews 11:33-35).

I think my favorite quote ever is the following one by Mother Teresa:

We, the unwilling, led by the unknowing, are doing the impossible for the ungrateful. We have done so much, for so long, with so little, we are now qualified to do anything with nothing.

When I read this for the first time, I had a good, deep, inner-laugh. I could totally relate to it: *do anything with nothing*—that is the call, isn't it. No excuses and no holding back. When I look at my life with Jesus over the past 13 years—11 of which have been in full-time ministry—I have to say without a doubt that the most fruitful things I have had the privilege of partnering with the Lord to release into the earth have been the things that I was the least qualified for and the least resourced to do. I heard someone say once that, "God does not call the qualified; He calls the willing." There may be truth to that; just read First Corinthians 1:27.

THE MOST FRUITFUL THINGS...HAVE BEEN THE THINGS THAT I WAS THE LEAST QUALIFIED FOR AND THE LEAST RESOURCED TO DO.

I remember when the Lord put it in my heart to begin researching the righteous foundations and righteous covenants that had been made by generations past in my nation. This was hilarious, really. I knew that He was calling me to do it, but I had almost failed research in college! I had good grades in everything else, but research was the one course I almost failed! I thought, *God, You have got to be kidding. There has to be someone else out there who is more qualified to research this than I am. Surely You don't want a hack job on this kind of research compilation!* The Lord simply spoke deeply to my heart and said,

> Faytene, I have called you to do this. You either obey or disobey. Your response should have nothing to do with your self-perceived ability. As a matter of fact, to say that you cannot do this is *pride* because you are telling Me that it is up to you and your natural ability instead of My ability to pour out My grace upon you for the task.

Daaah! I love the rebuke of the Lord. It is so good. So I purposed in my heart to obey, and I did all I knew to do—I asked God to lead me by His voice.

> "TO SAY THAT YOU CANNOT DO THIS IS *PRIDE* BECAUSE YOU ARE TELLING ME THAT IT IS UP TO YOU AND YOUR NATURAL ABILITY INSTEAD OF MY ABILITY TO POUR OUT MY GRACE UPON YOU FOR THE TASK."

I might not have known how to use micro-fiches and reference books very well, but I knew how to recognize the voice of my Father in Heaven. So it was simple. I would just pray and ask the Lord to tell me where to go, what to look for, and how to find it. Time and time again over those months of research, He was faithful. He would lay it on my heart to go to a certain library, talk to a certain librarian, and ask a certain question. A few hours later I would find myself walking out of the library or the archive center having hit the bullseye on some awesome historical find. It was so fun! It was hard work, but fun. Anyone who tells you that walking with God is boring has not really walked with Him.

> ANYONE WHO TELLS YOU WALKING WITH GOD IS BORING HAS NOT REALLY WALKED WITH HIM.

A couple of months later, I had a file about 2-3 inches thick and was prepared to simply hand the research off to mature national leaders who, I presumed, would know what to do with it. I shared with some of these leaders the amazing finds that I had come across regarding our national history. They were intrigued and encouraged me—but no one took the file off my hands to do something with it! Every once in a while, at a national gathering, I would share a historical event that was significant for whatever we were praying into at the time. God would use the things I had found in really amazing ways. However, for the most part, this file of research about our nation's righteous foundations and covenants was just sitting in my room not really being accessed at all. I had done what the Lord had asked of me, and there was satisfaction in knowing that I was obedient. I figured that the rest was up to Him and my part was over—or so I thought.

After keeping this file for about five months, the Lord began to speak to my heart, "You have submitted this information to the leaders around you. Now it is time to publish it so the wider Body of Christ in Canada can have access to it." What!? Publish? That was nowhere on the map when I started this adventure! I had no idea how to go about doing this, and publishing offered another hurdle: I had no money. So problem number one on this obedience journey was that I had no "smarts" about how to take on a project like this. But God had shown Himself faithful on that front. Now, problem number two was that I had no cash. I guess I was learning that a barrier in my eyes is simply a set-up for a miracle. I can just see my Father in Heaven grinning at that moment. I was sweating, but He knew that He had it under control.

179

A BARRIER IN MY EYES IS SIMPLY A SET-UP FOR A MIRACLE.

I did the research and found that it was going to cost about $1,000 to self-publish. For an urban missionary (at the time), this was not pocket change—I had missionary support income of about $500 per month, and rent was $450 per month. Once again, I was faced with the same challenge: I could either obey God, believing Him for the impossible, or disobey Him and live with the regret of knowing I had missed it. I don't really enjoy regret, so I decided to obey once again. I began to put the research into book form.

> I COULD EITHER OBEY GOD, BELIEVING HIM FOR THE IMPOSSIBLE, OR DISOBEY HIM AND LIVE WITH THE REGRET OF KNOWING I HAD MISSED IT.

A few weeks into writing, I was preaching at a church in Seattle, Washington. It was an awesome church, and I met many amazing people while there. One sweet couple told me that they wanted to keep in touch, so we exchanged information. I thought nothing of it and returned to Canada to keep plugging away at my faith project—the book. Shortly after that, a letter showed up in the mail with a note saying something like (paraphrased):

> Hi Faytene. We just wanted to let you know how much we appreciated your ministry here to us this weekend and that we believe in you. Enclosed is something that the Lord put on our hearts to sow into your life and the ministry God has called you for.

Aawwwe, I thought, *this is so sweet of them.* I was expecting perhaps a check of $50. To my surprise, I unfolded the check and before me was a gift for $1,000. With the exchange rate from U.S. dollars, this was more than what I needed! I was overwhelmed and humbled by God's amazing goodness and this couple's faithfulness to obey the prompting of the Lord. This couple did not know what was waiting on the other side of that prompting of the Lord. I had not made mention of the book project or my need to anyone at the church. This gift was directly from Heaven and was such a comfort to me—I was not loony; God was with me in this. I entered, once again, into the experience of the truth that, when we act in faith to His Word, God is totally faithful.

> I ENTERED, ONCE AGAIN, INTO THE EXPERIENCE OF THE TRUTH THAT, WHEN WE ACT IN FAITH TO HIS WORD, GOD IS TOTALLY FAITHFUL.

Ephesians 3:20 says, "Now to Him who is able to do exceedingly abundantly above all that we ask or think...." Well it is true; God is into blowing our circuits of expectation with His faithfulness when we step out. The stories of all that God has done with this book between that point and now are amazing. Within months of it being published, the Lord provided the funding for me to send it to every single Member of Parliament and Senator in Canada. Within a few weeks after that, not only had I received many personal letters from the Parliamentarians that they were thankful to have received it, but I also received a letter from the Parliamentary Library of Canada telling me that they had accepted it into their stacks. I was ecstatic! Right there in the center of political power was this little girl's book—a testimony of all that this nation was founded on and for, a book that clearly testified to the dream that was in God's heart for Canada. I am still amazed when we meet with Parliamentarians and I see the book sitting on their office shelves.

In the months afterward, I received many more letters, including one from a government leader who told me that he had been contemplating quitting politics. When he read my book, God convicted him that he needed to run again and to keep fighting for strong moral values in Canada. Within a matter of months, I was finding myself on national talk shows, addressing the nation and bringing awareness to our righteous history and foundations. It was wild. Even though we were self-distributing we sold thousands of copies. Within the year, the book was plastered all over the nation with no marketing agent other than Holy Spirit! According to the number that we have sold, had it been distributed on the main stream market, I am told it would be considered a best seller in Canada. I was really overwhelmed by the fruit.

WITHIN A YEAR, THE BOOK WAS PLASTERED ALL OVER THE NATION WITH NO MARKETING AGENT OTHER THAN HOLY SPIRIT.

Two Kinds of Christians

I have found that there are really only two kinds of Christians. There are those who live their lives governed by what they can see, feel, and touch with their natural senses, and there are those who live their lives governed by the Word of God. One of the most obvious clashes of these two credos is found in Luke 4:3-4, where satan tries to tempt Jesus to make a decision based on what He feels in the physical realm: the hunger of His stomach. He tries to lure Jesus into turning a rock into a piece of bread in order to appease His physical reality. Jesus refuses to go with it, however. He refuses to live His life governed by the natural realm and, therefore, responds to satan saying, "Man shall not live by bread alone, but by every word of God." This was precisely how the apostle Paul lived as well.

SEEN (BLEPO): TO SEE WITH THE EYES, TO PERCEIVE BY ONE'S NATURAL SENSE, TO FEEL; IT CAN ALSO SPEAK OF THE PHYSICAL NATURE OF THINGS SUCH AS PLACES, MOUNTAINS, AND BUILDINGS.
TEMPORARY (PROSKAIROS): SOMETHING THAT ENDURES ONLY FOR A WHILE OR IS ONLY AROUND FOR A SEASON OF TIME.

Second Corinthians 4:18 says, "While we do not look at the things which are seen, but at the things which are not seen. For the things which are seen are temporary, but the things which are not seen are eternal." I have always been fascinated by the word study of this text. The Greek word for *seen* in this text is the word *blepo*, which means to see with the eyes, perceive by one's natural senses, to feel; it can also speak of the physical nature of things such as places, mountains, buildings, etc. It deals with the natural, physical realm. The word *temporary* in the Greek is the word *proskairos*, which means something that endures only for a while or is only around for a season of time. Like a paper tablecloth that is used for a certain moment and certain function but is discarded after that occasion is over, something that is *proskairos* will eventually pass away.

THERE IS A WAY TO LIVE THAT IS NOT DICTATED BY THE
EARTHLY, TEMPORAL REALM, WHICH IS DESTINED TO BE
DISCARDED.

In the entire chapter leading up to Second Corinthians 4:18, the apostle Paul is speaking of a lifestyle. He is speaking of a lifestyle that prefers Christ, His life at work in us, and His glory perfected in our afflictions. The apostle Paul is speaking of a lifestyle that is governed by a revelation of eternity. Paul seems to be saying that there is a higher place to fix our sights. There is a way to live that is not dictated by the earthly, temporal realm, which is destined to be discarded like a paper tablecloth. There is a realm that has more substance than anything our natural eyes can see. It is wisdom to live our lives in light of that reality, not the one that is temporal and fading. When I ponder these things, I often think of the faith test that Peter was given when Jesus challenged him to get out of the boat and walk on water by faith.

PETER, WILL YOU TRUST MY WORD MORE THAN GRAVITY?

183

I find so many elements of Peter's story (see Matt. 14:22-33) completely typical of the life of a believer. As believers, we are challenged to live lives of supernatural faith, even when all of our senses are bombarded by a physical realm that screams for our attention. The disciples had been walking with Jesus and knew Him intimately. They had seen Him do so many miracles. They had seen Him heal the sick, cast out demons, speak with wisdom and power (time and time again), and even multiply small portions of food to feed multitudes. They had experienced the supernatural through Jesus, up close and personal.

The context of the story in Matthew 14 is that Jesus had told His disciples to go on ahead of Him so He could have some time alone to pray in light of the announcement of John the Baptist's martyrdom. After spending time with His Heavenly Father in prayer, Jesus set out to join His disciples who had already boarded their boat and were traveling across the water in it. He, the miracle Man Jesus, did what made sense: He used His faith to override natural realities and walked on the water in their direction. He took authority over gravity. It made more sense than swimming.

EVEN THOUGH THEY HAD SEEN JESUS DO MANY MIND-BLOWING MIRACLES, THEY STILL STRUGGLED TO BELIEVE HE WAS WALKING ON WATER.

As soon as the disciples saw Him, they freaked out at the paranormal sight and, therefore, concluded that the figure coming toward them must be a ghost. Even though they had seen Jesus do many mind-blowing miracles, they still struggled to believe He was walking on water. When you think about it, logically, it is crazy that they would doubt Jesus' ability to perform the miraculous. He had proven Himself so many times prior in a variety of ways. Knowing they would recognize His voice, Jesus spoke to them saying, "Be of good cheer! It is I; do not be afraid" (Matt. 14:27b). I am sure they were a bit perplexed in that moment. The image walking on the water looked like Jesus and talked like Jesus, but apparently it was all still blowing their mental circuits. What would they believe: their eyes or His voice saying, "It is I"?

Peter, in a classic "seen realm" vs. "unseen realm" moment, put out a tester and said, "Lord, if it is You, command me to come to You on the water." I am sure Jesus must have been delighted by what was about to take place. Like a father looking at his toddler about to take a few wobbly steps toward him says, "Come to me, baby," I think Jesus was eager to see Peter get out of the boat. In all honesty, I have to wonder if Peter's tester-question was inspired by God Himself who, we know, wants His disciples to enter into the same walk of faith in the earth that Jesus was walking.

Jesus responded to Peter's tester-question and said, "Come." What a moment that must have been in Peter's mind! An opportunity to be the main character in one of the most awesome miracles they had seen yet was right before him; all he had to do was trust Jesus more than gravity. He had to come to that place of faith in his heart that says, "I believe the Word of God has more weight and more substance than anything in the natural realm. Jesus has told me to walk on water; His word is all I need. It is more real than anything else." I believe this is the kind of faith that will shift and subdue nations.

HE HAD TO COME TO THAT PLACE OF FAITH IN HIS HEART THAT SAYS, "I BELIEVE THE WORD OF GOD HAS MORE WEIGHT AND MORE SUBSTANCE THAN ANYTHING IN THE NATURAL REALM."

Peter mustered it up and chose to believe. Because true faith acts, he lifted his leg over the edge of the boat and stepped out on the water and began to walk. And walk on water he did! Peter was the man! Of course he walked on the water, what else would you expect when God has spoken?! Well, the truth is that, more often than not, as believers in Christ, we still live our lives as though the natural realm is stronger than the Word of God. When we hear Jesus speak, it is a test of our faith to get out of the boat and begin to walk on the water. It takes guts. It takes confidence in God. I can't tell you how many times I have heard individuals say phrases like, "Oh, I can't do that; I don't have the money," or, "I don't have the time," or "I have never done anything like that before." We should never assume that, because we have not done something in the past, we can't conquer it in the present. All things are possible to those who believe. But in reality, exercising our faith is a lot easier said than done, isn't it? That is why not everyone walks on water. Did you notice how the rest of the disciples stayed in the boat? Not one of them piped up and said, "Can I come too, Jesus?"

185

WHEN WE HEAR JESUS SPEAK, IT IS A TEST OF OUR FAITH TO GET OUT OF THE BOAT AND BEGIN TO WALK ON WATER.

Even the great apostle Peter, when he began to experience the resistance of the wind and the waves, wavered in his faith. As soon as he wavered in his faith, wondering if Jesus' words really had more authority than natural laws, he began to sink. What a lesson for all of us! The lesson: believe God's word is real and you will live a life unrestrained by natural limitations, but put your faith in what you can see—which is one of the backbones of secular humanistic thought—and you will surely sink.

As Peter wavered in his faith and began to sink, Jesus in His awesome mercy stretched out His hand to catch Peter, clearly explaining the reason He was sinking, "O you of little faith, why did you doubt" (Matt. 14:31). He did not attribute the sinking to gravity, water, or any natural thing. The sinking was simply because of Peter's lack of faith.

PUT YOUR FAITH IN WHAT YOU CAN SEE...AND YOU
WILL SURELY SINK.

I believe, with all my heart, that just like Jesus extended the opportunity to Peter, Jesus continues to extend this opportunity to Christians today. The call is to fix our eyes on the unseen and eternal realm, not on the seen and temporal realm. Not everyone who calls himself or herself a Christian is truly a *believer*. True believers will take up the call and live their lives governed by the words of Jesus above anything else. If we live this way, we will shock the world. If we don't, we will simply look like any other human being, the only difference being that we hang out in a church building on Sunday mornings. What is the difference between believers and those who have not surrendered their lives to God? We live a life of supernatural love, joy, and power, defying natural limitations that should, but can't, hold us back.

NOT EVERYONE WHO CALLS HIMSELF OR HERSELF A
CHRISTIAN IS TRULY A *BELIEVER*.

The first mass gathering—TheCRY 2006—was going to cost us well over $100,000. Did I have it? No, I had $700. Did God have it? Yes. God simply said to us, "If you will get out of your boat of comfort, I will take care of the rest. The miracle will manifest as you step out, just like it manifested for Peter *as he stepped out.*" I have found that this is the way God works. He puts a vision in our hearts, but rarely is it within our means in the natural to accomplish it. We either step out, or we don't. If we do, He shows up. If we don't, we spend the rest of our lives wondering if He might have.

Let me sum it up this way: if we are waiting for a bank account, schedule, whatever to "change" before we obey God, we will be waiting forever. He is waiting for us to step out so He can make the water solid under our feet and re-arrange the world on our behalf. The way I look at all this is: we are either crazy or incredibly intelligent. Since there has never been a time yet when Jesus has allowed us to sink, my conclusion is that we are walking in divine intelligence; and yes, it is incredible.

He is waiting for us to step out so He can make the water solid under our feet...

One of my favorite, repeated dialogues over the past years has been with secular media reporters who attend our mass prayer gatherings, or ask us about the work we are doing on Parliament Hill. Looking at the stage, sound system, jumbo-tron, or group of young people who have traveled from across the nation, they almost always ask, "So, how do you get funding? Who pays for all this?" (Interestingly, unbelieving Christians sometimes ask us the same question.)

I simply look in their eyes, smile, and say, "God pays for it."

Then they say, "No, seriously, who pays for this?"

And I look in their eyes, smile, and say again, "No, seriously, our God provides. He moves on the hearts of people to donate, sometimes surprise checks from 'nowhere' show up in our mailbox; it happens in lots of ways. That is how big He is and how real He is."

We have seen reporters and sound-tech people alike rocked by the testimony of this walk of faith. That is fun and easy witnessing. However, for me this is more than just a cool ministry testimony for a book. In my life, it has been a matter of life and death.

187

We have seen reporters and sound-tech people alike rocked by the testimony of this walk of faith. That is easy witnessing.

FAITH: A MATTER OF LIFE AND DEATH

In 2000, I was diagnosed with a terminal illness called auto-immune hepatitis. It is a disorder where your own immune system, for some reason, begins to think that a particular part of your body is foreign. The immune system becomes activated and tries to kill off that part of your body because it believes it is foreign and bad. It does not stop attacking until it succeeds; normally, that means the person dies. Auto-immune hepatitis means that your own immune system is attacking your own liver. This was my situation.

By the time I found out what was happening, my liver was already in bad shape. The doctor did not know what caused it, and he did not know how to cure it. All they could do was try to manage the symptoms and keep me alive as long as possible. I was 25 years old, with my whole life ahead of me. It was an intense announcement.

ALL THEY COULD DO WAS TRY TO MANAGE THE SYMP-TOMS AND KEEP ME ALIVE AS LONG AS POSSIBLE. …IT WAS AN INTENSE ANNOUNCEMENT.

I believed God, though, and went home to seek Him. As I sought Him, I felt Him say that He was going to use this situation to teach me about healing and that He wanted me to press into Him for the answer. As soon as I began to press into Him for the answer, it became clear: the answer was faith. This sounded too "pat-answerish," and to be honest, I am one of those people who does not really appreciate "pat" or "canned" Christian answers to things. In spite of this, I knew it was that simple. I have come to learn that the most powerful things in life are simple; they just aren't always easy. For example, it is simple to say that if you want to be in good shape then you need to exercise and eat well! It is simple to say, but not too easy for some of us to execute. Faith is the same way. It is simple, but we have to sometimes discipline ourselves to really activate it. Sometimes you have to choose to believe, even when everything around you is screaming at you not to. This is faith; it is confidence in that which is not seen (see Heb. 11:1).

AS SOON AS I BEGAN TO PRESS INTO HIM FOR THE ANSWER, IT BECAME CLEAR: THE ANSWER WAS FAITH. …WHETHER OR NOT YOU COME OUT OF THIS ALIVE DIRECTLY DEPENDS ON WHAT YOU CHOOSE TO PUT YOUR FAITH IN.

The Lord spoke clearly to my heart and said,

Faytene, whether or not you come out of this alive directly depends on what you choose to put your faith in. Will you put your faith in the doctor's analysis, or will you put your faith in My Word, which says that because of Jesus' sacrifice on the Cross you are not only forgiven but also healed? Will you choose to believe My Word has more authority than what you see and even feel in your body right now?

After I got over the initial shock and fear of it all, the obvious began to hit me. I had so many prophetic words over my life that were yet to be fulfilled. It had been prophesied over me that there was a missionary call on my life and that I would go to the nations. One very accurate and seasoned prophet had even prophesied over me, at a prophetic presbytery in my Church, that the Lord was saying to make sure my passport was always current and that the Lord was going to be sending me out to the nations a lot. I knew in my heart that these were not fortune-cookie prophecies; they bore deep witness in my spirit, and I knew they were true.

I got on my face in prayer one night and rose into the faith that God was calling me to. I prayed with tenacity saying, "God, either Your Word is true, or it is not. I cannot go to the nations if I have an immune disease, which stops me from being able to get vaccinations, and I cannot go to the nations if I am dead. So, either Your Word is true, or the doctor's word is true. I believe Your Word is true, so show Yourself strong. You have to heal me. It is not an option. Do it."

> GOD, EITHER YOUR WORD IS TRUE, OR IT IS NOT. I CANNOT GO TO THE NATIONS…IF I AM DEAD…. I BELIEVE YOUR WORD IS TRUE, SO SHOW YOURSELF STRONG.

THE MIRACLE BEGINS TO MANIFEST

Within a couple of weeks of this prayer, I was at a revival meeting where a powerful young Christian evangelist was ministering. He stopped in the middle of ministering to the people and said, "There is someone here who is a missionary and the enemy has loosed an attack on your immune system and you have an immune disease of some sort. It is actually preventing you from going to the mission field, but God wants to heal you tonight. Who are you?"

He read my mail! I got up and went to the front of the church. When I got there he looked at me and said inquisitively, "You're a missionary?"

"Yes, I am," I responded, "and I have just been diagnosed with an auto-immune disorder."

"Alright then, let's pray." He laid his hand on me and the power of God went through my body like lightning. It was raw power. This began a journey of revelation where the Lord showed me how this disease had gained entrance to my life through an alignment I had to the spirit of self-destruction—death—and because of some direct witchcraft that had been done against me when I preached at a coffee shop where a witches' coven was meeting in the front room. I was on a fast learning curve, to put it mildly.

THE POWER OF GOD WENT THROUGH MY BODY LIKE LIGHTNING. IT WAS RAW POWER.

I met with some elders at my church, dealt with everything I needed to deal with in terms of renouncing the spirit of self-destruction and repenting for any way I had aligned myself with it in the past, and then I had them anoint me and lay hands on me for healing (see James 5:14). I knew something was happening and that God was going to give me the breakthrough I was after. A couple of days later, some friends prayed for me at a home group meeting, and the power of God hit me again. It was at that moment that I knew, without a doubt, that the breakthrough had been secured.

The assurance that it was "finished" flooded my heart. I still felt the pain in my body at times, but I knew that I knew that I was healed. I also knew that whether or not it manifested was dependant on whether or not I maintained that posture of faith. Would I continue to fix my eyes on the Jesus who says, "Get out of the boat, Peter; walk on water," or would I fix my eyes on the winds and the waves pelting against my skin? By God's grace, I chose to fix my eyes on Jesus.

THE ASSURANCE THAT IT WAS "FINISHED" FLOODED MY HEART...WHETHER OR NOT IT MANIFESTED WAS DEPENDANT ON WHETHER OR NOT I MAINTAINED THAT POSTURE OF FAITH.

A couple of weeks later, I had an appointment with my doctor and "the nurse" (I call her the nurse of the Grim-reaper's doom) who, based on the most recent chart she had for me, was telling me that it was only a matter of time before I would be dead. The nurse was dripping unbelief. As she expressed her "opinion" to me, I guarded my heart and spirit. After my session with her, they proceeded to do what they normally did during a visit—they consulted with me and took my blood. As I was booking my next appointment, I looked at the secretary and said, "You are about to witness the fastest recovery you have ever seen."

A couple of weeks later, it was confirmed. My doctor called me into his office and with a grin from ear to ear said, "Young lady, I am not sure what happened, but I am glad to say that, after your last blood test, for some unknown reason, your liver function is completely back to normal. It seems the auto-immune hepatitis has decided to leave you alone for some reason." I'll say! That some reason was *God* and faith in Him! It was such a sweet moment and testimony—again—to God's faithfulness against all odds.

AS I WAS BOOKING MY NEXT APPOINTMENT, I LOOKED AT THE SECRETARY AND SAID, "YOU ARE ABOUT TO WITNESS THE FASTEST RECOVERY YOU HAVE EVER SEEN."

"IT SEEMS THE AUTO-IMMUNE HEPATITIS HAS DECIDED TO LEAVE YOU ALONE FOR SOME REASON." ...THAT REASON WAS *GOD*.

After this breakthrough, there were days when the enemy would try to come back with what I call "lying symptoms," and I would feel pain in my liver. I knew instinctively that, if I came into agreement with the possibility or fear that the auto-immune disease was back, I would lose my

191

healing. So I fought with all my might. Guess what? We—me and Jesus—won. I am now a healthy 34-year-old, and I have traveled to various nations numerous times. My God, whose Word says that He heals, is faithful. All I needed to do was discipline my heart, mind, and emotions to trust whole-heartedly, with no exception. His word had more authority than anything else the devil, or life, could throw at me.

IT IS IN THE PERSONAL FAITH BATTLEGROUND THAT CHAMPIONS FOR NATIONS ARE MADE. IF WE CANNOT CONQUER THESE MINI-GIANTS, HOW WILL WE SUBDUE NATIONS BY FAITH LIKE THE HEROES OF HEBREWS 11?

Why do I share all these personal stories in a book where the emphasis is supposed to be about a generation of dread champions rising to shift nations? Simple: because it is in the personal faith battlegrounds that champions for nations are made. If we cannot conquer these mini-giants, how will we subdue nations by faith like the heroes of Hebrews 11? These life tests are the training ground for greater things. No matter what the giant, no matter what the mountain, if we are going to become the generation that truly arises in this hour to shake nations, we must come to the simple, childlike place of faith that will not be moved. God's Word has more authority than anything. Period. No debate. Done. Finito.

IF WE ARE GOING TO BECOME THE GENERATION THAT TRULY ARISES IN THIS HOUR TO SHAKE NATIONS, WE MUST COME TO THE SIMPLE, CHILDLIKE PLACE OF FAITH THAT WILL NOT BE MOVED.

If God tells you to take a team of young people to address the political leaders of your nation about issues of righteousness and justice, then He will back you up as you step out of your boat. If God tells you to research the righteous foundations and covenants of your nation and you got a "D" in research class, know that He will back you up as you step out of your boat. If God tells you to plan an event that will cost thousands of dollars beyond your means, He will back you up as you step out of your boat. If He tells you to do it again, then do it again. He will back you up again and again.

God is really God, for real. His Word does not fail, and if we show up with faith in our hearts, He will back us up. No matter how cliché it sounds, we must always remember that *one plus God* is a powerful majority. I will finish this chapter as I began, with a quote from another famous woman of faith. She, with faith as her backbone, brought the rightful heir, in her nation, back to his throne.

This is the kind of faith that will shift and subdue nations.

Every man gives his life for what he believes and every woman gives her life for what she believes. Sometimes people believe in little or nothing and they give their lives to that little or nothing. One life is all we have; we live it and it's gone, but to live without faith is more terrible than dying, even more terrible than dying young. —Joan of Arc

Pass the life tests.

First the bear, then the lion, then Goliath.

By faith, I can see the giant biting the dust already. Many of his friends already have.

CHAPTER 11

Strategic Key #1 to End Abortion: Honoring Authority

Honor your father and your mother, that your days may be long upon the land which the Lord your God is giving you (Exodus 20:12).

I believe, with all my heart, that the generation God is raising up in this hour truly is a generation that is going to be marked with the spirit of reformation and revolution. We are a generation wired for the extreme. It is all over our music, television shows, hair, and practically everything associated with us. We are an extreme generation. We are a radical breed wired to take risks and push the edge.

> IF WHAT IS COMING...IS A MOVEMENT, A REFORMATION, OR A REVOLUTION THAT HAS THE BANNER JESUS OVER IT, I BELIEVE IT IS GOING TO LOOK, SMELL, AND ACT LIKE JESUS.

I don't know about you, but in the Christian circles I am often in, I have heard many prophetic words about a Jesus Movement—a Jesus Revolution—that God wants to release in the Church again. I believe these words wholeheartedly, and I actually believe it has already begun. However, I want to say that, if what is coming, and is already breaking forth, is *a movement, a reformation, or a revolution that has the banner JESUS over it, I believe it is going to look, smell, and act like Jesus. It will not be a revolution that has the odor of accusation, self-righteousness, unrighteousness, or selfish aggression.*

It will be a revolution of love, humility, purity, true righteousness, and power, and it will reflect all the ways of our Father in Heaven. One of those ways, which is highlighted throughout this chapter, is the principle of honor, specifically honor of authority.

LIFE REVOLUTION: WHAT KIND OF REVOLUTION?

THERE IS A LINK BETWEEN HONOR AND LONG LIFE.

Let's face it, in our day, when you think of the word *revolution,* things like rebellion against authority, violence, riots, and these types of things normally come to mind. I recently did a Google image search on the word *revolution,* and the first several rows of imagery were of angry mobs and fists being raised toward established authority. I bring this up for a very pointed reason. I believe one of the "social goliaths" that the Lord is calling our generation to bring down is abortion.

The Word of God clearly teaches us that there is a link between honor and long life—long life is the opposite of abortion. Conversely, there is a link between dishonor and pre-mature death. I believe that one of the reformation assignments that the Lord has for us as a movement, revolution, or whatever you choose to call it, is to see the end of abortion. Because of this, I have spent a good amount of time seeking the Lord and asking Him what it is going to take. In response to this seeking, the link between honor and life has been repeatedly highlighted to me. One of the most significant encounters I have had with the Lord in this regard happened on New Years Eve 2004.

"ASK ME FOR THE KEYS TO END ABORTION."

"ASK ME. I WANT TO POUR OUT THIS REVELATION, AND I AM LOOKING FOR THOSE WHO WILL ASK ME FOR IT."

I attended a young adults' worship service where a friend of mine was leading a time of worship and prayer to prepare our hearts to enter the New Year. At one point, the Spirit of God came upon her and she began to cry out, "There is a window right now to ask the Lord for something. Cry out to Him! Ask Him for the desires that have been in your heart." I was on my knees in prayer before the Lord at this exact time and sensed the Lord speaking to my heart, "Ask Me for the keys—revelation—to see the end of abortion. Ask Me. I want to pour out this revelation, and I am looking for those who will ask Me for it." I knew from the tone of His voice that we were entering into a season in the Body of Christ at large when He was going to begin releasing keys of revelation regarding this whole issue. He was letting me know that it was "time," and He was inviting me to be part of it. When this happened, I did not know that Lou Engle had already begun raising up an army of young people in the United States to pray for the ending of abortion and that they were praying specifically for Canada around that time.

Lord, why is it that the Church in the '60s and the '70s did not have the authority to stop abortion from coming into North America?

As I already shared, I began to cry out to the Lord asking Him for His heart on this issue and for understanding. Because I am a bit of a strategist, and I do not want to waste my life on fruitless labor, I specifically asked Him:

> Lord, why is it that the Church in the '60s and '70s did not have the authority to stop the spirit of abortion from coming into North America? I know that there were many who rose up fervently to protest this when it was entering the gates of our nations. Some of those who arose to fight against it were even thrown into jail for their efforts to protect the sanctity of life. Why did they have such a hard battle? Why did they not have the authority to keep this thing out?

I was really perplexed and did not understand. I knew that there was no lack of effort or fervency by those in the older generation to keep abortion out of our nations, but we still lost. Why? There was a deep hunger in my heart to understand so that we could learn from it and use this wisdom as leverage in our leg of the battle.

> THERE WAS NO LACK OF EFFORT OR FERVENCY, BUT WE STILL LOST. WHY?

REBELLION OF THE '60S

As I pondered these things in prayer, the Lord began speaking to my heart about the rebellion of the late '60s in North America. 1967 was arguably the flagship year of this rebellion as thousands of young people gathered in San Francisco and other communities across the Western world under the banner of the sexual revolution, "peace" movement, women's movement, and the new age movement. It was a summer that launched movements. Two of the hallmarks of these movements were: (1) rebellion toward traditional Judeo-Christian values and (2) rebellion against authority at large.

> THIS DNA HAS INFECTED WESTERN WORLD CULTURES AND CREATED A BREEDING POOL FOR MUCH SOCIAL UNRIGHTEOUSNESS—INCLUDING ABORTION.

From my studies, and from firsthand reports many in the older generation have given me, my perception is that this rebellion against authority was expressed in many ways and most obviously through the anti-war/free love movements. I am not justifying any of the war or anti-war efforts of the time by my remarks here; I am simply pointing out that there was a clear DNA of rebellion against authority that was interwoven throughout the generation and their movements. I believe this DNA has infected Western world culture and created a breeding pool for much social unrighteousness—including abortion. The Lord spoke to my heart saying,

> Faytene, satan is a legalist. He knows the Bible better than many Christians. The first commandment with a promise is this, "Honor your father and mother, that your days may be long upon the land which the Lord your God is giving you." If the promise of honor is long life in the land that I have given you, then the curse of dishonor is a short life, or abortion.

He went on to explain,

The enemy ushered in abortion rights on the heels of a corporate movement of rebellion. This rebellion against authority was even in some Christians at the time. Because they entered into the sin of dishonor, they lost their authority to fight for life. In other words, it was because of the corporate dishonor of authority that the enemy had a legal right to come in and snuff out millions in your generation. This is why the spirit of abortion was so strong. It got access through rebellion.

He went on to encourage me,

In all that you do, you must do it in a spirit of honor—no matter how full of righteous indignation you are. If you raise up a generation that understands the power of honor and learns to walk in it, then you will be gaining authority to take down the spirit of abortion.

This revelation is so solid and so strong. I believe it is Christian insanity to expect God to bless our efforts—the battle for life—when we do it in a way that is directly opposed to His ways—in the spirit of dishonor. Let me share a personal story to drive home my point.

199

FATHER KNOWS BEST: HIS BLESSINGS, HIS WAY

Like most college or university students, during the summers I worked to make and save money for the next school year. While in my second year of school, I decided to take the ambitious route of starting my own business selling books door to door. One day I was praying about my job and asking the Lord to bless me. This was, however, during the season when I was struggling with breaking free from bulimia and, at this particular time, I was willfully losing the battle. I shared with you about this journey in Chapter 7.

The Lord broke into my prayer and said gently, "Faytene, I would love to pour out this blessing upon you, but I can't bless you when you are in willful disobedience." His voice was gentle, but it was strong, and I knew it was indeed the voice of my Father in Heaven giving me the rebuke I needed at that moment. The rebuke was actually His grace being manifested to me as He knew it would encourage me in the direction of personal holiness.

In spite of this, I hardened my heart, and that entire summer I continued to willfully struggle with the sin. I also struggled in my job. Direct link? Most likely. The Lord spoke clearly to my heart in advance that there was a direct link, and His Word backs up this spiritual law—as I outlined in Chapter 4 when I talked about Deuteronomy 28. He is a God of grace, yes; but that grace is the empowerment by His Spirit to live Holy lives. It is not the grace to keep sinning when He has already paid the price for us to be free.

> THAT GRACE IS THE EMPOWERMENT OF HIS SPIRIT TO LIVE HOLY LIVES. IT IS NOT THE GRACE TO KEEP SINNING WHEN HE HAS ALREADY PAID THE PRICE FOR US TO BE FREE.

In my observation of the Western Church, which I love deeply, I think we too often play with God's grace. The apostle Paul warned the churches over and over not to take the grace of God for granted, but to live a life that reflected Christ in all ways. So then let me ask this question, "What is the Christlike way to respond when we see mass social injustice in our nations? What is the Christlike way to respond when we see a massive 'social weed' in our garden?" I believe the answer is this: we either respond like Jesus, or we respond like satan. Call me simple, but I think it actually is that simple.

ACCUSER OR INTERCESSOR?

> SATAN (SATANAS): THE ACCUSER OR THE ONE WHO CONTENDS.

DO WE RESPOND LIKE THE ACCUSER AND RISE UP IN A HARSH SPIRIT OF CRITICISM AND ACCUSATION? OR ARE WE BROKEN AND RESPOND WITH THE TYPE OF INTERCESSION THAT CAUSES US TO LAY DOWN OUR LIVES?

The word *satan* in the Greek is the word *satanas,* which directly translated means the accuser. This is the nature of the enemy of our souls. His nature is to accuse in a mean-spirited way—to put it mildly. Jesus, however, is the greatest of all intercessors. Romans 8:34 explains, "Who is he who condemns? It is Christ who died, and furthermore is also risen, who is even at the right hand of God, who also makes intercession for us."

So when we see a deep social injustice, like abortion, which has been entrenched into the legislative systems of our nations, how do we respond? Do we act like the accuser or the Intercessor? Do we respond like the accuser and rise up in a harsh spirit of criticism and accusation? Or are we broken and respond with the type of intercession that causes us to lay down our lives to work in love to make wrong things right again. Do we lay hold of God's empowering grace and conduct ourselves in a Christlike manner, even when it tests our self-control to the maximum? These are incredibly hard challenges at times. If you are like me, when you see an injustice or unrighteousness, the temptation is to arise in ways that aren't always completely Christlike.

For example, when we feel we are falsely accused, we want to arise in defense of ourselves and lash back—it is our sinful nature. When we are pushed, our sinful nature wants to push back. When we are hurt, our sinful nature wants to hurt back. Let's face it, our flesh gets out of control at times. What we don't always realize in the heat of the moment, however, is that our sinful responses only add fuel to an already bad fire. We cannot expect a righteous victory when we conduct ourselves in an unrighteous way. Whatever you sow you will reap. It is a biblical law, "Do not be deceived, God is not mocked; for whatever a man sows, that he will also reap" (Gal. 6:7).

DO WE LAY HOLD OF GOD'S EMPOWERING GRACE AND CONDUCT OURSELVES IN A CHRISTLIKE MANNER, EVEN WHEN IT CHALLENGES OUR SELF-CONTROL?

I believe with my entire being that we will not win the battle for *life* in our nations through a spirit of accusation and dishonor of authority. The enemy knows this. This is why he has worked so hard to make sure that we get into the extremely bad habit of accusation and dishonor—even to the point that we seem to think it is our "God-given duty" to harshly criticize and accuse the ones whom God has set in leadership over our nations. (Ouch, did I just say that?) I realize that might have been a punch in the gut to some of you, so let me unpack it a bit more to drive it home deeper. [Kidding.]

HONORING OUR POLITICAL FATHERS AND MOTHERS

A couple of years ago, I was at a national gathering where thousands of Christians had come together to contend in the spirit of prayer, worship, and reconciliation for Canada. There was a God-fearing Member of Parliament who had taken time out of his extremely demanding schedule to be with the larger Body of Christ that day. At one point, the leader of the gathering, Dr. David Demian,[1] sensed the Lord saying that someone needed to blow the shofar, and he felt the leading to ask this particular Parliamentarian if he would be willing to do it.

In a beautiful team spirit, the Member of Parliament came up to the stage and picked up the shofar. With humility the man said, "I will do my best, though I am not very good with this." He stepped out to respond to the request of Dr. Demian, even though he was risking making a fool of himself in front of thousands of Canadians. To get a clear, strong, sound blowing of a shofar can be very difficult, especially if you are not practiced.

IN A BEAUTIFUL TEAM SPIRIT, THE MEMBER OF PARLIA-
MENT CAME UP TO THE STAGE AND PICKED UP THE
SHOFAR.

I was standing near the front of the stage next to a man I recognized but did not know very well. He had also traveled to attend this gathering and his heart was also to see God's destiny for Canada break forth in power. After the Member of Parliament gave his disclaimer about not being very good at blowing the shofar, the man next to me leaned over and said in a very mocking and dishonoring tone, "Spoken just like a true politician." I turned and said, "Do you know this man?" I could tell he didn't, so I continued on [paraphrased],

> I know him. He is a good and a God-fearing man who is fighting for righteousness in Canada; that is why he is here with us today. I believe one of the worst things we can do as Christians is dishonor the very ones God has given us as gifts to lead the nation politically. We have to have the fear of the Lord, my friend. We need to break this spirit of dishonor in our nation. Our role is to bless, not curse.

Peering into this man's eyes, I finished my sentence, smiled at him, and turned back to continue to lock into what was happening on the stage with this Member of Parliament. The man lifted the shofar to his mouth and released one of the most pitiful shofar squeals I have ever heard in my life. In spite of the pathetic blow, in all honestly, my respect for him went through the roof. Many in his position would not have even tried. His humility was amazing. It reminded me of the humility that Moses walked in as he surrendered to the call of God on his life to lead a nation. God can work with that kind of humility and not only lead but even deliver a nation with it.

203

In spite of the pathetic blow...my respect for him went through the roof.

It blows my mind that, at least in my nation (and likely in most Western cultures), we so lack the fear of the Lord in reference to honoring authority. I have noticed that as soon as someone is elected to political office the mouths of the multitudes, who in some cases celebrated and cheered them in their campaigns just months prior, can quickly transform into vulture beaks looking for every opportunity to tear them apart, limb by limb. I find it really strange actually. I find it even stranger when I hear it coming from the mouths of Christians in light of how Scripture instructs in this area. A few examples:

Romans 13:1-2 says,

> *Let every soul be subject to the governing authorities. For there is no authority except from God, and the authorities that exist*

are appointed by God. Therefore whoever resists the authority resists the ordinance of God, and those who resist will bring judgment on themselves.

First Timothy 2:1-3 says,

Therefore I exhort first of all that supplications, prayers, intercessions, and giving of thanks be made for all men, for kings and all who are in authority, that we may lead a quiet and peaceable life in all godliness and reverence. For this is good and acceptable in the sight of God our Savior.

(1) GOD SETS AUTHORITIES INTO PLACE, (2) WE ARE TO HONOR THEM, AND (3) WE ARE TO PRAY FOR AND BLESS THEM.

It is clear that: (1) God sets authorities into place, (2) we are to honor them, and (3) we are to pray for them and bless them. All this leads to a blessing upon us in return. This line of thinking naturally invokes the counter question, "What about bad rulers? What about evil rulers who do evil things? What about Jesus—He challenged the authorities of the day." Jesus did challenge the leaders of His day—the religious and self-righteous ones. He challenged them not only to have an outward religion and air of self-righteousness but an inward devotion to God and a pure heart. The leaders He came down hard on were in the religious community, not the political realm. When brought before the political authorities, He spoke the truth in a spirit of honor. I believe that even in His moments of confrontation of the religious leaders He never transgressed the law of honor and love in His heart. He couldn't; He was perfect. Even though He was angry, He did not sin (see Eph. 4:26). Honor does not mean we agree with everything someone is saying or doing. To honor someone is to respect, treat with dignity, and defer to their ordained sphere of rule as long as they have it over us. I can honor, respect, and even bless someone, including a political leader, even when I disagree with them. To behave in this way is an expression of Christian maturity.

THE LEADERS HE CAME DOWN HARD ON WERE IN THE RELIGIOUS COMMUNITY, NOT THE POLITICAL REALM.

I believe we have a mandate before God to bless our leaders, not revile them. Let me put it another way. If the Church has authority in earth through the work of the Cross (see Matt. 28:18-19), and if life and death are in the power of the tongue (see Prov. 18:21), then if satan can get the Church to speak words of death over our national leaders, he can win. Conversely, as we release a blessing of life, wisdom, truth, and compassion over them, it will begin to manifest because of the authority that we have in Christ.

AS WE RELEASE A BLESSING OF LIFE, WISDOM, TRUTH, AND COMPASSION OVER THEM, IT WILL BEGIN TO MANIFEST BECAUSE OF THE AUTHORITY THAT WE HAVE IN CHRIST.

I will never forget the moment that we did this on the steps of our federal Parliamentary Buildings with thousands of Canadians from all across Canada. It was during TheCRY in 2006. We were convinced in our hearts and through Scripture that breaking the spirit of dishonor over our generation was essential to seeing the spirit of abortion fall in Canada and seeing our nation come into divine inheritance. Because of this conviction we took time during our mass gathering to intentionally bless our leaders at the onset of the day. We all turned and faced our Parliamentary buildings in a decree I will never forget. Thousands of us declared in a spirit of unity:

> We bless you; we bless you; we bless you; we bless you; we bless you; we bless you; we bless you. We bless you with a spirit of wisdom. We bless you with a spirit of truth. We bless you with a spirit of righteousness. We bless you with a revelation of the Messiah. We bless you with the spirit of justice. We bless your health; we bless your families; we bless you!…

After TheCRY 2006 was over, we found out that, on the very same weekend in the same location, another group in a spirit of protest was declaring curses over the government. What an amazing contrast, and what amazing timing. I believe our blessings overrode whatever they released and that we gained major spiritual ground through operating in the opposite spirit.

> THE CORPORATE DECREE OF BLESSING…OVER OUR FEDERAL PARLIAMENTARY BUILDINGS WAS A NATION-SHAKING MOMENT.

That corporate decree of blessing, by thousands of Canadians in unison, over our federal parliamentary buildings was a nation-shaking moment. We caught it on video and posted it on our Website in the months following. I was so blessed when I received e-mails from people who worked on Parliament Hill and had either seen us doing this on the day or had watched the video. One secretary wrote, "You have no idea what that did. All we ever hear is criticism and complaining. It happens every time I pick up the phone and every time I check an e-mail. I have never heard of a group of people (Christian or non) bless us." She went on, "As I watched the footage by video, all I could do was cry. You guys are amazing."

If honor leads to a blessing of life and inheritance, then it is no surprise that our little ragtag group of young adults, under the banner of the MY Canada Association,[2] accomplished in three short years what no other group in the history of our nation has—and we did not even realize at the time that what we were doing was a big deal.

During this time, we received audience with more Members of Parliament than any other organization in the nation—Christian or non. To date, we have had well over 300 sit-down meetings with MPs, Senators, and even the Prime Minister of Canada himself. Along with these accomplishments, we have had opportunity to speak into and influence (on a variety of levels) key legislation that will affect the moral and spiritual climate of our nation.

> THE MY CANADA ASSOCIATION ACCOMPLISHED IN THREE SHORT YEARS WHAT NO OTHER GROUP IN THE HISTORY OF OUR NATION HAS.

The purpose of the many face-to-face meetings that we have had with our MPs has been to honor them (are you surprised?) and to speak to them about the issues we care about, including abortion, immorality, environmental stewardship, poverty, Israel, and other foreign policy. Never in the history of our nation has an organization with such a small budget—basically none—and such a low profile—we are not famous or political kids—received such favor and gained such influence in such a short period of time. It is really wild.

On one of our first trips to Parliament Hill, we received audience with about 50 MPs in four days! A lobbyist who has been working on Parliament Hill for years said to me afterward, "You don't understand. That is not normal. You don't just prance onto Parliament Hill and get audience with that many Parliamentarians unless you are a world leader, the President of the United States, or the nation is in crisis and you have the answer!" I raised my eyebrows and responded, "Well, we might be in the third category."

NEVER IN THE HISTORY OF OUR NATION HAS AN ORGANIZATION WITH SUCH A SMALL BUDGET…AND SUCH A LOW PROFILE…RECEIVED SUCH FAVOR AND GAINED SUCH INFLUENCE IN SUCH A SHORT PERIOD OF TIME.

207

The climate around our group of young people who frequent the Parliamentary buildings is such that heads turn in attention and greeting as we walk down the halls. Many days I pinch myself and think, "How in the world did we get here?" But in all honestly, I think the answer is easy: we did it the way God asked us to. We did it in a spirit of honor, and this is one of the reasons He busted open the doors of His blessing before us. A Jesus revolution is going to have a Jesus nature. As I highlighted earlier, the character of Jesus is intercession and honor of authority—He honored His Father in all things. Our Father in Heaven was very clear—walk in honor of authority and you will have life. Because I believe one of our heavenly assignments is to see the ending of abortion in our generation, I am working with all my heart to make sure I am walking in a way that will allow me to take as much ground as I can on every front. I don't want to lose an ounce through dishonor of authority. That would be silly.

A JESUS REVOLUTION IS GOING TO HAVE A JESUS NA-
TURE.... THE CHARACTER OF JESUS IS INTERCESSION
AND HONOR.

I realize that I have been focusing on honoring our "political" fathers and mothers, but I would like to shift gears now and talk about another angle that I feel is essential if we are going to see the Church of Jesus Christ and our nations come into divine destiny. This is something that we have actually heard a lot of talk about in recent years. It is the angle of the generations walking together in Kingdom mandates and relationship: the younger honoring and esteeming the older and the older passing on a Kingdom legacy to the younger.

Endnotes

1. Visit www.watchmen.org to find out more about Dr. David Demian and the Gatherings in Canada.
2. Find out more about the MY Canada Association at www.4mycanada.ca.

CHAPTER 12

Strategic Key #2 to End Abortion: Walking Intergenerationally

Behold, I will send you Elijah the prophet before the coming of the great and dreadful day of the Lord. And he will turn the hearts of the fathers to the children, and the hearts of the children to their fathers, lest I come and strike the earth with a curse (Malachi 4:5-6).

INTERGENERATIONAL RESTORATION AND OVERCOMING THE MASS GENOCIDE OF ABORTION

In early 2008, a strong prophetic friend of mine, Derek Schneider,[1] had a dream. He shared it with me, and I want to share it with you as well. It is very insightful in light of all that we have been discussing. In describing the dream Derek wrote,

> I saw a very large expanse of desert and dry ground. As far as the eye could see, there were bones sticking up above ground. I saw rib cages and parts of skulls coming up from the ground. It was a horrific sight. As I looked on, I heard the voice of the Lord say, "This is the spirit of death in Canada regarding abortion!" I then looked on and saw a father and son digging up these bones and unearthing them. This is referring to the need for the generations to walk together in order to have the authority to expose and deal with the spirit of death in Canada regarding abortion.

In light of what the Lord had been showing me about honor and life, I resonated so deeply with the revelation contained in Derek's dream. Before I go there, however, I want to take a short but important detour. The pages you are about to read contain the treasures of my heart from the school of hard knocks, as far as this topic goes.

WHY ABORTION?
WHY THIS GENERATION?

I believe one of the reasons that abortion has hit this window of human history so hard is because the enemy intuitively knows that God has ordained the current generation of Christians to usher in a major Kingdom advance in the earth—perhaps one of the greatest advances the world has ever seen. Whether in the time of Moses' birth or the time of Jesus' birth, the enemy's strategy has always been the same. He sensed that a deliverer was coming, and he sensed that he was about to lose some major ground. He sensed this, so he roused up the earthly leaders of that time to issue a decree of death and loose a genocide that wiped out masses in those generations.

In Moses' time, the enemy somehow sensed that a deliverer was about to come upon the scene who would usher God's chosen people out of slavery and into their Promised Land. Because of this, he stirred up Pharaoh to issue the decree that activated genocide in that generation. In a short window of time, because of this decree, masses of Hebrew children were slaughtered.

In Jesus' time, the enemy detected that the moment had come when the Messianic prophecies would be fulfilled and a massive Kingdom advance would take place. Because satan sensed this, he stirred up King Herod with the spirit of fear, jealousy, and murder and used this to trigger another mass genocide of Hebrew children, the natural seed of Abraham. Both times genocides happened because satan himself was threatened by what was about to take place in the earth.

BOTH TIMES GENOCIDES HAPPENED BECAUSE SATAN HIMSELF WAS THREATENED BY WHAT WAS ABOUT TO TAKE PLACE IN THE EARTH.

What I am about to say I shared in Chapter 8, but I will say it again. I believe there is a massive destiny on the current generation alive in the earth today. I believe that we are a deliverer generation destined to usher in the greatest ingathering of souls and release of Kingdom reformation that the earth has ever seen. Many solid prophetic voices have been saying the same thing for years and even decades. Some mature and tested prophetic voices have even gone so far as to say that they believe this is the generation that will usher in the second coming of Jesus. I would not be surprised, especially when I look at how the enemy has worked overtime to prevent so many of us from ever being born and how the signs of the time are lining up with Jesus' prophecies about the end of this age.

Furthermore, it seems as though history is repeating itself. When I look at satan's track record with Moses' and Jesus' generation, and compare it with this one, it is chilling to me. Just as with Jesus and with Moses, whatever it is that the current generation is going to usher in, the enemy is clearly terrified of it. There are few other explanations of his behavior, which has been so bent on our destruction.

I BELIEVE THAT WE ARE A DELIVERER GENERATION DESTINED TO USHER IN THE GREATEST INGATHERING OF SOULS AND RELEASE OF KINGDOM REFORMATION THAT THE EARTH HAS EVER SEEN.

DEATH VS. GENERATION

Never to my knowledge has there ever been a generation that has had to contend with the spirit of death on a variety of fronts like the current generation has had to. Let me ask you this: has there ever been a generation that has struggled to survive not only in the face of abortion but also self-induced starvation (anorexia), self-mutilation (cutting), an overt death culture (Goth), suicide, and extreme addiction (which is also a form of self-destruction)? I could be wrong, but I don't think there has ever been a generation that has had to contend against these forces at this level of bombardment. This is all evidence that something is in the "air." I believe this something is satan himself, the destroyer, who has loosed a mass genocide that is wearing different faces. I also believe abortion is one of the key fuels feeding his empowerment in this way.

THIS IS ALL EVIDENCE THAT SOMETHING
IS IN THE "AIR."

The Word of God says that whatever you sow into, you will reap. If we are sowing the spirit of death into a generation through mass abortion—as of the writing of this book, in my nation, a child is killed through abortion approximately every 3-5 minutes, which is low compared to the U.S., China, Israel, and other nations—then we can expect to reap the spirit of death in other ways as well. I will again bring to our minds Galatians 6:7, which says, "…whatever a man sows, that he will also reap." It is not complicated. It is clear in God's Word. Whatever we feed grows. Whatever we plant will surely grow in our garden. We cannot get away from God's principles; they will chase us down in the end.

I believe that, in the same way, whatever a nation sows it will surely reap. If the enemy can trick us into shedding the blood of our own children, he can easily loose a spirit of death on the generation at large. I get grieved sometimes when I hear voices coming down on the youth of this day as though they should just get over their issues and get their act together. *Never* has a generation in my nation or in the Western world had to deal with what they have had to deal with in such mass, including family breakdown, divorce, abandonment, abuse, and the list goes on. Never has a generation had to face what they have had to face at such a high level. Today's young people deserve more credit than they are often given. I applaud them for how much they have overcome, and I applaud so many of you who are reading this that have "seen" them and given of yourselves to love them to life. The youth and young adults who are here have survived a mass genocide, and many of them are still fighting to survive. I don't think they need voices of pity, however; they need voices of faith. The truth and good news is that where death and destruction have wreaked havoc, there the Lord can come in massive resurrection power that will be a display to both earthly nations and spiritual principalities. I believe God is going to do something so awesome in this emerging generation that the earth will shake because of its enormity.

WHERE DEATH AND DESTRUCTION HAVE WREAKED
HAVOC, THERE THE LORD CAN COME IN MASSIVE
RESURRECTION POWER...

When speaking to youth and young adults today about abortion and the onslaught of death that has come against them in so many forms, I tell them to take it as a compliment. There is a time to look circumstances in the face and say, "Thank you devil for confirming the call of God on my life" and then laugh and keep going. The devil has clearly authenticated the call of God on this generation through his mass effort to take them down. But like in the time of Moses and Jesus, the final chapter is yet to be written. I believe this generation will come forth in resurrection power like none the earth has ever seen. I don't know about you, but I am excited! What the enemy has meant for evil, God is going to turn for good in a big way.

I know it like I know the breath inside of me. I believe we are about to witness one of the greatest moves of restoration that the Western world has seen in a generation—other than perhaps the restoration of the nation of Israel after the Holocaust. I believe this restoration and resurrection movement will have as one of its key components the spirit of reconciliation between the generations.

THEY WILL COME FORTH IN RESURRECTION POWER LIKE
NO GENERATION THE EARTH HAS SEEN TO DATE.

The prophet Malachi declared this,

> Remember the Law of Moses, My servant, which I commanded him in Horeb for all Israel, with the statutes and judgments. Behold, I will send you Elijah the prophet before the coming of the great and dreadful day of the Lord. And he will turn the hearts of the fathers to the children, and the hearts of the children to their fathers, lest I come and strike the earth with a curse (Malachi 4:4-6).

> THERE WILL BE A TURNING OF THE HEARTS OF THE FA-
> THERS TO THE CHILDREN AND THEN THE CHILDREN TO
> THE FATHERS.

This is an end-time prophecy for an end-time generation. There will be a turning of the hearts of the fathers to the children and then children to the fathers. This Scripture clearly shows us that, if this does not happen, the land will be cursed. As I think about this, I have to admit that the order of it—fathers hearts being turned first—is interesting and perhaps even logical. Just ask anyone who had a father who was aloof, abusive, or whose heart was hard toward them. Most in that environment will have a suitcase full of negative baggage that they will need to work through. Thank God for His love and grace that is so amazing, healing, and empowering and can set us free from any negative thing in our past. He is so awesome.

Malachi 4:4 seems to be an exact inversion of the Law of Moses from Exodus 20:12. It is interesting that Malachi 4:4 begins with an exhortation to remember this law. Exodus 20:12 explains that, when there is honor from the children to the fathers and mothers, there will be a blessing of long life in the land the Lord will give them. I believe this is all so essential for us to "catch."

> THE OLDER GENERATION WILL LOOK TO THE INTERESTS
> OF THE NEXT GENERATION WITH INCREASING FOCUS.

God is going to have a Church where the younger generation honors the fathers and mothers in the land—political, natural, spiritual, or other. He is also going to have a generation where the hearts of the older generation are "turned" toward the younger. Speaking of the fathers and mothers, I believe the promise of Malachi 4:4 is that the older generation will look to the interests of the next generation with increasing focus. They will seek to lay down their lives to leave their children and grandchildren a "credit" in every way—morally, environmentally, socially, financially, relationally, etc. Some dictionaries call this an inheritance.

Interestingly enough, it is the cultural mindset that says, "Children are a burden," or "Having children will wreck my life," or "It is not the right time for me to have children," or "I am just not ready," or "I don't have enough money for another child," that has been the backbone mindset of the entire abortion genocide. These statements give words to the inner-reality of those whose hearts have been turned away from the next generation, at least in part. I believe God is about to reform our hearts to the level that a massive company is going to emerge who will believe, and walk in, God's Word that says children are a blessing from the Lord and happy is the man whose quiver is full of them (see Ps. 127:5). Yes! God loves babies; they are not a burden but a blessing! I believe that this company is about to burst onto the scene as a mighty movement of fathers and mothers whose hearts are restored to the image of the Father in Heaven. Some of these with the heart of the Father will be in their 20s, 30s, 40s, 50s, 60s, and older—this will transcend age; it is a way of thinking. It will be a company of those who think: inheritance, legacy, and future generations. Father God's heart burns with love for children, and this company will carry His heart.

THIS COMPANY IS ABOUT TO BURST ONTO THE SCENE AS A MIGHTY MOVEMENT OF FATHERS AND MOTHERS WHOSE HEARTS ARE RESTORED TO THE IMAGE OF THE FATHER IN HEAVEN.

The generation that Malachi is talking about is the one that will not bite the lie of the negative mindsets but will, in a spirit of selfless love, give themselves for the next generation, no matter how inconvenient or expensive. Their hearts will be turned. In response, the hearts of the next generation will also be turned. Why do we have rebellious, angry, hard-hearted young people? Well, other than the fact that we have a basic sin nature—which we may wrestle with until the day we die—it is often because they are hurt, abandoned, and ignored, because they feel like a burden and not a blessing. If people feel this way, we all know, their hearts eventually become hard or angry. Sometimes it is the only thing a person knows to do to numb the pain of rejection. This is what has happened to the hearts of many. It is only a matter of time though—God is already starting to melt the ice. It is only a matter of time until their current reality will be challenged and changed; the tide has already begun to turn.

The older generation is, in sacrificial love, turning their hearts toward the next generation. One of the reasons I can say that statement so confidently, other than the fact that Scripture tells us it will happen, is because I have experienced the *life blessing* of walking intergenerationally with functional spiritual fathers and mothers in a very tangible way.

GENERATIONS WALKING TOGETHER: THE KING DAVID / KING SOLOMON MODEL

Walking with spiritual fathers and mothers has always been a very high priority in my heart. Somehow I intuitively knew that I would not come into the fullness of my destiny without it and that the Church at large would not come into the fullness of her destiny without it. I wholeheartedly believe that, as next generation leaders in the Body of Christ, we need the input of those who have gone before us if we are going to be successful in slaying the giants of our day. Furthermore, I believe God is calling us to slay many giants *together*, walking arm in arm as we battle for our nations.

AS NEXT GENERATION LEADERS IN THE BODY OF CHRIST, WE NEED THE INPUT OF THOSE WHO HAVE GONE BEFORE US IF WE ARE GOING TO BE SUCCESSFUL IN SLAYING THE GIANTS OF OUR DAY.

King David had a Samuel. Even though David's biological father did not see the potential and destiny in him, there was a spiritual father who did and who called it forth. Samuel's action in anointing the shepherd boy as King honored God and gave Israel the greatest warrior leader they ever had, other than the Messiah Himself. The prophet Samuel was a man who heard the voice of the Lord and moved out in obedience to anoint and bless the next generation of leadership, even at the risk of being misunderstood by his peers.

In the same spirit, years later, King David did the most incredible intergenerational father-son baton pass that Israel had ever witnessed by one of their kings. I believe this was meant to be a model for future kings as they transitioned the kingdom to their sons. King David imparted vision into his son Solomon, a vision to build the dwelling place of the Lord that had been the dream of his heart. He also imparted courage to Solomon. In First Chronicles 28:20, David charged Solomon saying,

…Be strong and of good courage, and do it; do not fear nor be dismayed, for the Lord God—my God—will be with you. He will not leave you nor forsake you, until you have finished all the work for the service of the house of the Lord.

That is amazing! I can just imagine King David peering into the eyes of his son saying intently, "Solomon, *my* God is with you. The God who was with me when I defeated the great Philistine, Goliath, the God who was with me when I was in the caves, the God who was with me when I overcame thousands of my enemies, the God who met me in the sanctuary and showed me His glory and His might—this same God is *with you.*" What an amazing moment that would have been for both King David and Solomon. I can just imagine the electricity of emotion going through Solomon's soul! This same God was going to be with him. This is so powerful.

However, it did not stop with that. Not only did King David impart his vision to build a dwelling place for the Lord to Solomon, not only did he impart his heart and courage to his son, but he also stored up the supplies and the resources that Solomon would need in order to get the job done. As I stand in the midst of a culture that is somewhat fixated with storing up wealth for early retirement, as opposed to storing up resource to give as an inheritance to future generations, I find David's behavior so enlightening—so moving.

When I saw this in Scripture, I realized that nowhere in the Bible do we see a strong teaching about retirement—correct me if I am mistaken. What we *do* see is legacy, generations, and inheritance. We see men like King David storing up an inheritance for their sons to build a dwelling place for God in the next generation, and, we see the younger generation talking responsibility to care for their parents in their older years. It is beautiful. The conduct was always about God being honored throughout all generations and an intergenerational walk that made sure it happened. From what I see in Scripture, this expression of intergenerational unity, responsibility, and functioning is the backbone of biblical family culture and the backbone of any strong society. Furthermore, in the King David-King Solomon model of intergenerational walking, we see an incredible picture of what it truly means to "pass the proverbial baton" to the next generation.

217

King David walked with Solomon in a tangible way right up to David's last days as king. When the moment was right, King David presented Solomon to the elders and nation at large as king. What is most amazing about this is that King David did this while he was still alive! Wait a second!? This was incredible! Instead of being threatened by the call on his son's life, he celebrated him and set him up to win. This is because King David was not primarily interested in his own grip on power, but in a house being built for the Lord and in a righteous kingdom that would be sustained far beyond his lifetime. As his son was set into his kingly post, King David rejoiced at what his eyes had seen. King David's heart was wholeheartedly turned toward the Lord, and because of this, his heart was wholeheartedly turned toward the next generation of leadership. This is so overwhelmingly beautiful to me.

In later years, after King Solomon had built the dream that had been in David's heart, he turned and declared in the presence of all Israel, "Blessed be the Lord God of Israel, who spoke with His mouth to my father David, and with His hand has fulfilled it…" (1 Kings 8:15). This is now beauty upon beauty! At the completion of the temple, he did not usurp the moment for personal glory or personal credit. He immediately gave glory to God, who had given him the strength, and he gave honor to his father David, who was the original carrier of the vision and the one who had deposited it in Solomon's heart in a spirit of faith. This is intergenerational honoring at its best.

So this is the summary: King David's heart was turned toward the Lord. As a result, the Lord turned King David's heart toward his son. The outcome: King Solomon's heart was turned back to his father, and the dream of God for a nation and a generation was fulfilled in the temple's completion. God had a place to rest His head and a nation had a place to worship and encounter Him. Father God in Heaven + natural father + natural son = divine alignment. Furthermore, God poured out favor and blessing upon Solomon and his reign to the extent that, to date, this era was the high point of Israel's national splendor.

Never in the history of Israel has there been a temple so glorious, a king so wise and full of favor, and a nation so strong as during the time of King Solomon's reign. This is a powerful demonstration of the fruitfulness of walking in intergenerational love, unity, and honor. The relationship between King

David and King Solomon was a demonstration of the divine relay race at its greatest and a tangible demonstration of Malachi 4:4.

This is all so, so, so powerful. I believe that, in this hour of human history, the prophecy of Malachi 4:4 is beginning to be released into the earth in increasing measure. God will have a people who demonstrate this intergenerational unity with beauty. The unity will be manifested within the boundaries of the current generation (I will expand on this more in the next section). But I also believe this intergenerational unity is meant to be manifested through honor of those historical fathers and mothers of the faith who ran with their hearts turned toward God and toward the coming generations.

The Power of Historical Covenant

All throughout Scripture, God reveals His nature as an intergenerational God. The Bible constantly refers to Him as the God of Abraham, Isaac, and Jacob. This is intentional. It was a reminder to Israel that He was the God of their fathers, that He had a covenant with their father Abraham, and that He intended to honor it throughout all of Israel's generations. They were to pass the revelation of that covenant on. They were to tell it to their children and thereby exhort the next generation to live lives of faithfulness to God, who had been so faithful to them. It is all over the Word. Here are just a few of many Scriptures that highlight God's intergenerational nature.

Psalm 78:3-5 says:

> ...our fathers have told us. We will not hide them from their children, telling to the generation to come the praises of the Lord, and His strength and His wonderful works that He has done. For He established a testimony in Jacob...

Psalm 71:18 says:

> Now also when I am old and gray headed, O God, do not forsake me, until I declare Your strength to this generation, Your power to everyone who is to come.

And one of my personal favorites, Hebrews 11:39–12:1 speaks of the heroes of the faith and exhorts us to run as they did, declaring,

219

And all these [biblical heroes of the faith outlined in He-brews 11], *having obtained a good testimony through faith, did not receive the promise, God having provided something better for us, that they should not be made perfect apart from us. Therefore we also, since we are surrounded by so great a cloud of witnesses, let us lay aside every weight, and the sin which so easily ensnares us, and let us run with endurance the race that is set before us....*

For years now, this has been one of my life Scriptures. There is a gen-eration that has gone before us; they ran their leg of the race well and with strength; now it is time for us to run ours. This Scripture even says that they are imperfect without us! That is mind-blowing to meditate on. These ones—Abraham, Isaac, Jacob, Joseph, and others—are the great heroes of the Bible, and it says they need *us* to see their promise fulfilled! Yes, that is what it says.

PERFECT (TELEIOVW): TO COMPLETE, TO FINISH, TO BRING SOMETHING TO AN END, TO ACCOMPLISH, OR TO CARRY THROUGH.

The word *perfect* in Hebrews 11:40 is the Greek word *teleiovw*, which means to complete, to finish, or bring something to an end, to accomplish, or to carry through. These heroes of the faith had a dream, a mission, a mandate. They had a promise in their hearts that they saw by faith. They laid their lives down sacrificially in obedience to God and in pursuit of that promise. They were faithful, but they did not receive the fullness of their re-ward in their lifetime. They did not receive it because God had something better in mind. What was that better thing? That better thing is that we would complete, accomplish, and finish the race for them. In doing so, we would partake in the divine victory together!

Ridiculous Favor

In the fall of 2005, just a couple of weeks prior to taking our second team of young adults to Parliament Hill, a leader friend gave me an incredibly accurate and weighty prophetic word. He said,

> I see the words *ridiculous favor* all over you. Ridiculous favor. God is going to give you ridiculous favor as you take this team of young people to speak to these Members of Parliament and Senators. It is simply ridiculous, get ready. It is going to be stunning.

That prophetic word has proven truer than I ever dreamed possible. As I meditated on this word in the weeks and months after he gave it to me, the Lord deposited an even deeper understanding into my heart. The deposit was:

> I will pour out ridiculous favor upon you as you align yourself with My divine covenant and promise to generations past in this nation. I am looking for a landing pad to pour out the answers to the prayer of generations past, and I am looking for a landing pad to honor My promises to them—promises of a nation that will manifest My dominion.

I was struck to the core. I understood that the burden God was giving me for my nation was not so much about me, it was about Him, and, it was about them—the former generations. The fear of the Lord settled on me as I understood, at a deeper level, the magnitude of the responsibility to run my leg of the race well. Whether or not the investment of their lives bore complete fruit was hanging on my obedience and the obedience of my generation at large. Their reward and their promise were found in us.

Earlier that year, I had released my book *Stand On Guard: A Prophetic Call and Research on the Righteous Foundations of Canada*. As mentioned in Chapter 10, this book was all about what the nation of Canada had been founded on and the call to the current generation to arise and reclaim God's dream for Canada. Through a series of visions, prophetic revelation, and research, I came to find that my nation had been covenanted to God at the foundation. The most notable moment was likely when our political founders chose to name it "The Dominion of Canada" after Psalm 72:8

221

which declares, "He shall have dominion also from sea to sea, and from the River to the ends of the earth." I also learned that many of Canada's founding fathers and mothers were devoted lovers of Jesus Christ. In many cases, they were led by dreams and visions to come to Canada, and they sacrificially laid down their lives to obey the call.

They came to this new frontier with a desire to share the Gospel of Jesus Christ with the First Peoples of the land, to make Canada a model for global evangelism, and to help establish this nation on righteous foundations. The price they paid was intense. They sacrificed their comfort, finances, and time; some sacrificed their reputations, and some lost their lives because of the harsh climate or through brutal martyrdom. I had no idea of this history. These facts were not taught in our schools, and I could not remember even having ever heard a homily or sermon about this part of our nation's history. It was a hidden covenant, a buried inheritance, seemingly dormant in the history books, museums, and graveyards of our land. However, the life of God bound up in these promises was not dead. It was alive.

God began to speak to me about wanting to raise up a generation that would finish the job in Canada. Former generations had been given a promise and a dream. Like in Hebrews 11 and 12, the Lord was saying their promise was intended to be completed by subsequent generations—us. He began to speak to me about how, just like the promise given to Abraham was an inheritance to Isaac and Jacob, and all of Israel, in the same way, there was a covenant at the foundation of my nation that He desired to honor. He was looking for a successor—a landing pad alive in the earth today.

Moreover, just as God led Isaac and Jacob to renew the covenant they had with God through their Father Abraham, in the same way, the Lord was looking for those in my generation that would rise up and renew covenant with Him so that the relay race could continue toward the finish line of history. He was looking for that King Solomon generation in the land that would say:

> God, for the sake of the promise You made to my fathers, for the sake of the promise You made to my mothers, pour out Your favor and establish Your resting place in our day and in our nation. Here is my life, Lord, make it a landing pad to

manifest the fullness of the promise for Canada and Canada's role in the nations of the earth.

I was completely amazed when I discovered that the very region where the first Canadian martyr, Jean de Brebeuf, served was the same region that both Aimee Semple McPherson and John G. Lake were later born in. Aimee Semple McPherson was one of the greatest evangelists of our century. She was a radical pioneer in media and the arts to the point—I have been told—that producers in Hollywood would come to her Sunday services to get creative ideas. Her ministry was full of demonstrations of the power of God and divine healing, and, she established the Foursquare denomination that is still thriving today. If this was not amazing enough, she also built the Angelus Temple—which seated 5,300— during the Great Depression.

John G. Lake had an incredible apostolic ministry in South Africa, where he helped found the Apostolic Faith Mission of South Africa and planted hundreds of churches. Upon his return to North America, he moved to Spokane, Washington, and established healing centers to pray for the sick. His outreach was so powerful that the secular news reported Spokane as being the healthiest city in North America and directly attributed this to Lake's healing ministry.

223

Is it a coincidence that God poured out such an anointing upon two people who came out of a region where a man—Jean de Brebeuf—laid down his life for the sake of the advance of the Gospel in North America? I don't think so. I think this is a demonstration that He is, indeed, a God who keeps His covenant promises from generation to generation. He is a covenant-keeping God, and He is looking to manifest the fullness of His promise to previous generations through subsequent ones.

This rocks our Western individualistic mindset that is so "self" and "now" focused. The truth is that we are not isolated dots on a fragmented timeline of human history. Rather, we are links in a chain. We are not and cannot be separated from the covenant promises He has made to generations past—we either honor them, steward them, and build upon them for future generations, or we are like the wicked servant Jesus spoke of who buried his talent in the ground (see Matt. 25:26) and received a rebuke in eternity for his slothfulness and disregard.

The hearts of these historical fathers and mothers were turned toward us when they, out of a revelation of God's love for the world, laid down their lives as living sacrifices for Him in their time and nations. It is only wise and honorable to turn our hearts back to them, and the promise of God in their hearts, and to cry out like the prophet Habakkuk did in Habakkuk 3:2, "Lord, I have heard of Your fame; I stand in awe of Your deeds, O Lord. Renew them in our day, in our time make them known" (NIV).

The Hebrew word for *known,* at the end of this portion, is the word *yada,* which means to reveal something or to know something by experience. Yes God! This is our cry, "Father, we want to know the promise—not just by faith but by experience. Pour out the fullness of Your promise—make it known."

Whoever you are, I want to encourage you to begin to do some digging into the promises that may be laying in the history books, museums, and graveyards of *your* nation. Start contending for the promises. Our ultimate promise, of course, is found in the inheritance we have been given through Christ. As discussed in the opening chapters of this book, a part of that inheritance is nations. No matter what nation we are from, God wants to restore the revelation of His nature as a generational, covenant-keeping God. He wants to restore our hearts to our historical fathers who, like King David, carried a promise from the heart of God.

As we have laid hold of this revelation for Canada, the doors of ridiculous favor have burst open in a way that has stunned both the secular *and* the Christian community. As I mentioned in the previous chapter, in three short years, we have had more than 300 face-to-face meetings with our Parliamentarians. This is unprecedented. It has been reported to us that we have had more favor and "ear attention" from our Parliamentarians than any other organization—Christian or non-Christian—in the entire nation over the last few years. Fluke? Coincidence? I don't think so. There have been so many times that I, and the young adults I run with, have been on our faces before God praying something like,

> God, You have a dream for this nation. God, You have a destiny for Canada. Pour it out on us, God. Make us the dream-walkers. We align ourselves with the divine inheritance that has been laid up by our founders at the foundation of this nation. We declare

Your word, "You will have dominion from sea to sea and from the River to the ends of the earth." God, we declare Your divine favor, strategy, and grace upon us. Pour out the manifestation of this covenant upon us as we go in Your name.

I believe God has heard these prayers; and as we have aligned ourselves with His heart and destiny for Canada, something has been activated in the spirit that cannot be stopped. It is covenant and, as far as God is concerned, it is unbreakable. He is the God who builds from generation to generation. It is inherent in His nature. He is a Father, and He will turn our hearts toward Him—our ultimate Father— and toward the fathers of our faith. For the remainder of this chapter, however, I would like to bring this discussion even closer to home and talk a bit about what it looks like for the generations alive today to truly walk together.

MANIFESTING INTERGENERATIONAL UNITY TODAY

Along with raising up a generation that will honor the righteous roots of our nations, I believe the Lord also wants to raise up a living expression of intergenerational unity in the earth today. As we come together in functional unity—which begins with our hearts—I truly believe my friend Derek's dream is true: God will pour out the authority to overcome the spirit of abortion in our nations. He will pour out ridiculous favor upon the work of our hands (see Ps. 90:17).

As a young leader I am very aware that I need the wisdom of the fathers and mothers in the faith who have already fought and prevailed against the giants I may face as I seek to serve the Lord wholeheartedly in my leg of the race. I have no desire to learn lessons the hard way or to be a lone ranger. That type of living wastes time and energy and leads to a whole lot of unnecessary heartache, and simply put, it is not the way God has called us to function. We are a Body. One of the manifestations of true Christ-like unity is healthy intergenerational relationships.

Because of this, and the biblical conviction I have that God is a generational God, I have been very intentional about surrounding myself with seasoned fathers and mothers in the faith. The Lord gave me this as a plumb line conviction when we first began to launch out and raise up a tangible movement of reformation in Canada to address the political realm of our nation. I knew that God was calling me to work with my whole heart, to raise up a generation that would rock this nation, and to labor to bring it back to its righteous foundations.

However, I knew that we were not to be a movement of spiritual orphans. Though He was going to begin to raise up young adults and youth in a strong forerunning spirit, He wanted me to surround the movement with true fathers and mothers who could speak wisdom, faith, and life into it at key times. This was not only for our safety, but for the safety of the nation as well. We don't need any more lone rangers causing damage to the Body of Christ with no accountability. If you are a lone ranger, I want to encourage you to find the ones God has called you to be connected to in the Body of Christ. They are out there, I promise you. Just as a kidney cannot function outside of a physical body, in the same way every individual believer's health depends on their connectedness to the whole. It is the way God has made us, and whether we like it or not, we can't get away from it. In my case, the Lord was also saying that these fathers and mothers of the faith would not only speak wisdom at key moments, keep us in check, and encourage us from the sidelines, but that they would also be in the race with us. We would run hand in hand, stewarding our individual mandates in Christ and not burying our talents, but truly walking with our hearts turned toward one another in order to see a nation come to the feet of Jesus.

To be blunt, when the Lord told me to commit to walking this way—intergenerationally—it was flat out terrifying. Like so many, I had been let down in the past and had experienced what felt like broken promises from some leaders who had told me they wanted to walk together and then, for whatever reason, never tangibly followed through—at least not in the way I expected. This inevitably led to hope deferred, confusion, misunderstanding, and a broken heart. All of this naturally resulted in a lack of trust and disillusionment about the whole idea. Looking back, I am convinced this is exactly what the enemy wanted. He wanted me to run the other direction in a spirit of independence and with a bitter-root judgment that would spring up and defile many around me (see Heb. 12:15).

In spite of the pain, when the Lord began speaking to me about intentionally walking with the older generation of leaders again, I knew it was not an option, no matter how scared I was by the thought. He said,

Faytene, everyone has trials they have to face in their Christian walk, but the difference between those who come into destiny and those who do not is how they respond to those trials. You can either get bitter, critical, accusatory, and cynical, or you can humbly forgive and choose to trust again, even when your emotions are screaming at you to run the other direction. If you trust again, I will catapult you into a season of accelerated growth, if you get bitter, you will be stunted in your calling.

At that moment, I saw a vision.

In the vision, I was hanging at the end of a rope outside of a high-rise building's window. The rope was being held by someone's hand (I did not see their face, but I knew it was someone the Lord was calling me to radically trust). Whether or not I fell to the cement ground, several stories beneath, depended on whether or not the other person held onto their end of the rope. My life seemed to depend on their faithfulness, and I had no guarantee that they would be faithful. Scary. The Lord spoke again,

> This is the level of trust I want you to walk in. I want you to wholeheartedly trust, even when there is no guarantee that those I have called you to walk with will handle you well. I want your heart to be turned toward them unconditionally with forgiveness and love.

227

We all have our stories of disappointment to tell. I have learned, however, that the key is not so much in the story itself but in how we respond when we are let down. Are we willing to forgive, dust ourselves off, and trust again? Well, seeing as Jesus said we should forgive 70 times 7, or 490 times, the answer to that question would be a resounding *yes*. For me, it is one down, 489 forgives to go—kidding. The point is that we are called to a lifestyle of forgiveness that has no limit; this is what I believe Jesus was really getting at when He said 70 times 7. The good news is that, even if we are "dropped" and fall to the ground, our God specializes in resurrection—He turns it all for good, and we can trust Him with the truth of that. So either way, we win! It is the economy of God.

As I continued to process this revealing vision with the Lord, He reminded me that He knew what it meant to be abandoned by those He loved. It was what He went through on the Cross. Every one of His disciples, except one, abandoned Him in His hour of greatest anguish; and one other—Judas—even betrayed Him into the hands of His slayers. I began to understand in a deeper way what the apostle Paul meant when He spoke of sharing in the sufferings of Christ (see Phil. 3:10).

This moment was an intimate one with the Lord. It drove me to be thankful that Jesus would allow me to have this depth of fellowship with Him. Needless to say, as He poured this revelation into me, I felt the magnitude and importance of my response to His request that I forgive and trust again. This meant walking intergenerationally as I launched out in the national mandate He was putting in me. I wanted to respond like Jesus, and I wanted to be propelled into accelerated growth, not stunted by bitterness. So with everything in me, I sucked up the courage to move forward instead of getting stuck in the muck of the past.

SCHOOL OF HARD KNOCKS WISDOM

I am happy to say, by the grace of God, that I made it through to the other side and am currently experiencing an oasis of intergenerational support and functional walking with contemporary fathers and mothers of the faith. Some days I feel like the most blessed young leader on the planet, honestly. However, this did not come without a price and a lot of wrestling for wisdom on "how" to do it. Because of this, I want to share a few more pearls of insight with you in the hopes that it may impart something to those of you who perhaps wrestle with how to do this practically. It is one thing to agree with functioning intergenerationally. It is another thing to know how to do it. As I travel in the Body of Christ, preaching and ministering, I can tell that there are so many people out there who are desiring to walk intergenerationally but simply need some input on how to get there. Furthermore, this next section is especially for those of you who, like me, have been previously let down and are skeptical about this topic because of it.

I, of course, bring a "younger generation" perspective here—because that is who I am and what I have walked thus far. What I am about to share is perhaps a little one sided, not because that is my heart, but only because it is my experience. I look forward to being able to write "wisdom from the other side" one day, by God's grace. Finally, I want to say, before we go any further, that the reason I am taking the time to go down this trail is because I believe that, if we are going to take nations effectively and with the least amount of casualties possible, there are certain principles that are wise to activate. Laboring intergenerationally, as Derek's dream so amazingly articulated, is one of them.

As I already alluded to, because of some of what I had been through, almost every shred of idealism about the generations walking together had been knocked out of me. I now knew that what we sometimes trumpet prophetically in the Body of Christ we do not always know how to walk out. I did not want to get crushed again in the gap between hopeful expectations and the reality of human capacity. I have often prayed, "Jesus, I don't mind dying for You. I just don't want to die stupidly." This was one of those times. You might think I am being melodramatic, but the truth is, with a couple things I had come through, it was a miracle I ever stepped foot in a church again after my first round of this. Why am I belaboring my "past pain" a bit? It is intentional. I want you to know that if I can get past the pain, anyone can. So, let's get on with it [smile].

NUTS AND BOLTS

You may have noticed that, when speaking of intergenerational walking, I have used the word *functional* a few times. That's what I was longing for. Not just something that I bore witness to in my spirit prophetically, but something that actually worked like it was supposed to. As I sought the Lord on how to break out of my past, and into my future with wisdom, He gave me a strategy. This is in no way a rigid formula of how every younger leader should walk with every older leader on the planet. I believe what I am about to share with you reflects wisdom from Heaven, but it was also a strategy He gave directly to me in a particular season of my life. Each one of us needs to hear from the Lord regarding the specifics of how He has asked us to conduct ourselves in the details of our callings—being sure to apply the plumb line principles of His Word at all times. Whether we are a small group leader, pastor, or preacher with international influence, the principles of accountability and submission are important at every turn. As a matter of fact, now that I am a few years down the road, I realize that the strategy of accountability He gave me—which you are about to read—is perhaps a good one for leaders of any age.

I believe one of the reasons that the Lord put an urgency in my spirit to get this "intergenerational" walk in place was because He saw what was coming. He knew I would need strong wisdom from the older generation and rear view mirrors in my life and ministry at every turn because of what we were venturing into—the political realm can be nasty and tricky at times. Furthermore, due to the fact that my influence would soon have a much wider reach, the standard of accountability I walked in needed to be more intense. Sometimes we get the idea that, when a leader expands in influence, he somehow doesn't need the same level of input or accountability—I believe it is actually the opposite. The larger the level of influence, the greater the need for each of us to have strong rear view mirrors. We need relationships with those who will speak wisdom into our lives at key times. This is so that we don't hurt others or fall into the prideful attitude of thinking we know it all. We are the Body; we need one another desperately.

The strategy the Lord gave me was clear and had clear components. He told me to surround myself with a core group of older generation leaders who could walk with me, advise me, support me, and counsel me when I needed it. As already mentioned, this was both for my safety and for the safety of the people I would be influencing. He then gave me eight different things I needed to look for in the ones I would ask to walk with me in this way. This is what they were:

1. Because the magnitude of what we were about to take on was national, I needed to surround myself with leaders that were fivefold leaders in the Body of Christ in my nation and at the national level. This meant they were either apostles, prophets, evangelists, pastors, or teachers and were functioning in these roles (see Eph. 5). Thankfully, I already had relationship with many people who fell into this category, so approaching them would be natural, not awkward. Of course, one of these would be my own local pastor, and my local pastor needed to be in agreement with everything I was walking in.

2. They needed to have a genuine relational connection to me. They needed to be the type of people who, when I talked to them, I felt a deep Kingdom connection that can only be put there by the Spirit of God. We knew that God had joined us, and because what God joins is also strengthened

by His grace, the relationship would have a good chance of standing the tests of time. It wasn't a forced relationship but a God appointed one.

3. They needed to be ones who had taken a few major warfare hits themselves (in my nation of Canada), had come through them, and were still going strong with soft hearts and eyes of faith. I felt this was important not only so they could advise me regarding the giants in the land, but also so they would have empathy for me if I were ever in the heat of the battle with those same things. I had a sense that there would be times when I would need coaches who had compassion birthed from the school of hard knocks.

4. They needed to understand my gifting and calling as a young visionary, and they needed to believe in me and what the Lord had called me for.

5. They needed to be from different streams in the Body of Christ. They could not all be from the same tribe of leaders, stream, or denomination where there was the potential of "group think." I wanted leaders who might actually disagree on some points so I would be able to glean wisdom from different angles.

6. They needed to not only have a "heart" for me, but they needed to commit to being hands-on in their advising. I would commit to communicating with them on a regular basis—at least monthly—with a detailed report of all I was doing and what I believed the Lord was calling us to do in the future with the various national initiatives. I would also communicate by phone and e-mail at key times, between the monthly reports, when I had a big decision to make.

7. When they saw something that they felt was, or might be, "off" in my theology, character, or vision, they would tell me. They would not cower back in silence but share openly—in love for the nation, the Body of Christ, and me.

8. When they had a word of encouragement or prophetic insight, they would also share it with me—I am a glutton for the prophetic and, as I expounded on in Chapter 8, I

believe it is one of the key foundational substances for the building of Christ's Church (see Eph. 2:20).

The expression of intergenerational walking needed to have substance, practical function, and accountability. I needed to fulfill my part, and they needed to fulfill theirs. I prayerfully identified the ones—about nine people—that the Lord was highlighting to me and approached them to be a part of my advisory team. I knew—and they confirmed—that, if we followed through in walking this way, there would be safety for me and for the Body of Christ and that, because of their wisdom and strength, I would be blocked from so many things which have taken other young leaders out. I was so excited! I think they were too—this was one of the things they were created for.

Like I said earlier, I now feel like one of the richest young leaders on the planet. Their wisdom and encouragement has been life to me. At times they have slowed me down. Other times they have pushed me forward. At all times it has been beautiful, healthy, pure, and strong—it smells just like Jesus. That is because it is; it is the Body of Christ.

AN AMAZING PEARL OF WISDOM

When establishing the core of older generation leaders with whom I was committed to walking, an incredible piece of advice came from one of my spiritual mothers. As I laid out the eight parameters to them that I believed the Lord was showing me, she responded with this word of wisdom [expounded/paraphrased from memory],

Faytene, we will commit to being "present." We will walk with you in a tangible way, we will pray and consider what you are doing and how you are running before the Lord, and we will respond to you in a prompt amount of time when you are seeking input. However, if we bring something to you in the way of caution on a certain visionary front, and if you take it to the Lord and pray through it and you still feel to go ahead in spite of our caution, then we will support you. As a young visionary, there will be things that God shows you to do, and you need to go for it if you really believe in your heart that this is what He has asked of you. If you miss it, and our caution was valid, then we will

232

pick you up, dust you off, and we will set you back on track with our love and support. We won't rebuke you to death, though we will "process" things so as to glean the highest level of growth and wisdom. We are committed to celebrating the risk-taker in you as long as you are committed to processing, with full integrity before God, all the input we give you—listening to it when it bares witness, but also walking with humility and boldness with whatever you truly believe God is saying. You are a visionary; we know that, and we are not going to try to make you something else.

I honestly could have cried with gratitude when she gave this input. What safe and life-giving words! I have heard it said that a messy house is a house of love. This is not saying that it is godly to be a slob, but that, when children feel at home enough to make mess and are not afraid of being beaten for it, then the priorities of that parent are on track. Well, there was love in this spiritual house, that was for sure, and I was so humbled by it!

My experience in the past made me feel that, if I did not obey everything that the older generation around me said, then somehow I was rebellious, sinful, and dangerous to the Body of Christ. I have learned since that God gives vision to the visionary. If you are a visionary, sometimes the people around you just don't see what you see. They see a forest of trees. You see a path. The clincher is: is your heart rebellious, self-righteous, judgmental, and unaccountable as you forge out to blaze a trail, or are you soft in your heart, even when you are misunderstood, and are you teachable? Are you committed in heart to walking as a functional part of the Body of Christ?

If the answer in your heart is, "yes," no matter what age you are, you are going to kick major devil butt. If we walk this way, I believe we will see something arise in the Body of Christ that will rock the foundation of the powers and principalities that have sought to control our nations. I truly believe that this type of functional walking, this type of intergenerational working together, is one of the strategic keys to seeing life and righteousness prevail.

So let's get down on our knees and dig, shoulder to shoulder, in the trenches of our nations and dislodge the forces that have bound them. The starting point is this: in order to succeed in this "intergenerational" thing, we must be willing to get our hands dirty in it. The older generation needs to be present and accessible. The younger generation needs to have teachable and open hearts. We all need to be willing to extend a hand of authentic fellowship that has legs in reality. In conclusion to this section, I also want to say that I believe functional intergenerational relating is not just about the older generations supporting the younger. I believe it is so important that the younger generation is also present in supporting and serving the older.

Some of the older generation leaders I walk closely with are in their most fruitful and active years of radical pioneering yet. They have soared from glory to glory over the years and are still dreaming big. I am actually huffing to keep up with them at times! I want to be their greatest cheerleader and to help them with whatever strength I have as they rock this nation and many nations of the earth. The bottom line is this: we need to do this Kingdom-thing *together,* and we need to do it in a practical, healthy, and functional way that has integrity. If it truly is together, and it is functional, I am in.

Whoops! There Went the Pendulum!

I am absolutely in love with the Body of Christ and not into "Body-bashing" at all. But let's face it; sometimes we can be quite dysfunctional. There is no point in hiding it. The world knows it. We might as well admit it at the points where it is valid and seek the Lord for wisdom about how to rid ourselves of it. It is not failure to be dysfunctional at points; it is just failure if we are more committed to our dysfunctional behavior than to growing together in God. Just ask anyone who has grown up in a dysfunctional family—and who of us hasn't at some level? Families either persist in their dysfunctionalism, or they get help and move past it. We are learning and growing, and we are on a journey until we achieve the unity of the faith that the apostle Paul spoke of in Ephesians 4:13.

The reason I bring this up is because, as the Holy Spirit has been highlighting the principle of walking intergenerationally in the Body of Christ, I have seen the pendulum swing to a certain extreme that I think might be helpful to address. This dynamic is actually common for any revelation that Holy Spirit is emphasizing to the Body. Sometimes, before we find our "balance" on how to walk in certain revelations, we first take it a bit too far. Inevitably, in time, we correct ourselves and catch our stride; it is a part of the process. One of the dysfunction points I have witnessed on the issue of intergerational walking, even in my own life, is the over-identification with our age demographic. In some cases, I have seen this identification develop to the point of idolatry. Before I am a spiritual daughter or son of any person in the earth, I am a lover of Christ. Before any person in the older generation is a father or mother, they too are a lover of Christ. Christ, not age or role, is the foundation of our identity and unity. We are His and He is ours, and in reality, our spirits are ageless and eternal. As we seek to step into functional roles in the realm of time—where age, race, gender, height, IQ, and more are all real identity factors—we have to make sure we remember that, before anything else, our identity is in Jesus—not in the role we play in the earth or the "earth suit" we wear.

I will use a recent experience to drive home my point here. I was ministering in a church, and at the end of the service, a distraught woman came up to ask for prayer. She was in her mid to late 40s, and her son was just about to graduate high school and leave home. She said, "Please pray for me! I don't know what I am going to do when he leaves. He is my whole life." I am told that psychologists call this the "empty nest" syndrome. As I began to pray for this woman, I felt restrained by Holy Spirit and sensed He was asking me to have a common sense talk with her instead. I encouraged her by saying,

235

> Ma'am, your identity is not in being a mother. You are a child of God. Over the past 18 years of your life, God has given you the privilege of serving Him in the role of motherhood. You have had the honor of mothering an amazing child. It has been an incredible thing that He has entrusted you with, and you have done a phenomenal job at it. God is telling me to tell you that, if you will put your identity in Him, your best years are still ahead of you. You will always be your son's mom, but life has to look different now. Now is the time to get excited, to seek the Lord with all your heart and ask, "God, I have all this time on my hands! How do You want me to pour my life out in service of You in this next season? My life is Yours."

That, in my opinion, is functional. We rejoice in, and should to be thankful for, the roles God gives us the opportunity to play in the earthly realm. However, we need to remember that these roles are for His glory, not our security. Our security must be in Him, not in any function that we perform.

I have noticed that, if we are not secure in our identity in God, when certain revelations are being restored in the Body of Christ, we can take these revelations and process them through a performance-oriented motivation. For example, in the late '80s, when a strong revelation regarding the restoration of the office of the prophet was coming into the Body of Christ at large, I noticed that some who had selfish ambition or insecurity began to have a "need" to be called Prophet so-and-so. I am not saying that everyone that went by that title was doing it because they were insecure. Some of them were truly prophets, and it was totally legit to be called that. However, there were those that seemed to grasp for the title out of a need for recognition.

After that, when the revelation regarding the apostolic ministry in the Body of Christ began to be restored, there were some who had a need, for the same reasons, to be called Apostle so-and-so. Interestingly, they were sometimes the same people. So, were they prophets? Were they apostles? Were they confused? Or did they simply have a "need" inside them to wear the latest and greatest title? We must be so careful. Prophets need to be acknowledged as being prophets so they can function in their full capacity to impart into and equip the Body of Christ. Apostles need to be acknowledged as such so they can function as well. I do believe this is important.

But we do not chase after these titles as though they are the next rung on the Christian corporate ladder. There is no ladder of performance in the Kingdom; there is only promotion through servanthood to God and sacrificially laying down our lives in whatever capacity He calls us to.

In a similar way, when the revelation regarding the restoration of the generations and fathers and mothers walking together began emerging on the scene, I had to weed through some of this. As an emerging younger generation leader, I found that there were certain ones, who are amazing individuals, who wanted to, all of a sudden, "father" or "mother" me. Though I was humbled and thankful, I could feel in my spirit that something was "off"—especially because prior to fathering and mothering becoming buzz words in the Body of Christ, these people seemed to have little or no interest in me at all.

Along with this, I felt patronized at times. Instead of being built up and edified through interaction with them, I felt belittled, patted on the head, and sucked dry through the atmosphere of unbelief that related to me on the basis of my "package"—a young woman. The Word says that man looks upon the outside, but God looks upon the heart. I could often sense that I was being looked at and related to based on my age instead of the Kingdom seed I was carrying on the inside. That is OK—having my flesh poked was good for me.

These situations were a test of how "dead" my old nature was, and I actually rejoice in these types of experiences now. This is not because they are fun, but because they really are tests that, if we walk through with love and humility, will inevitably lead to promotion. I love the threshing of God because it makes me more like Him. These types of experiences also taught me to stretch myself to relate to others as I wanted them to relate to me. These tough times reminded me not to look at those around me through the lens of human packaging, or even my past experiences with them, but to say, "God, give me Your eyes. I want to see what You see in those You have placed around me. Reveal the gift of God inside them to me so I can encourage it, bless it, and make room for it."

I finish this chapter with a famous quote by one of the greatest revivalists and reformers the evangelical world has ever known, William Booth of the Salvation Army.

While women weep, as they do now, I'll fight; while children go hungry, as they do now, I'll fight; while men go to prison, in and out, in and out, as they do now, I'll fight; while there is a drunkard left, while there is a poor lost girl upon the streets, while there remains one dark soul without the light of God, I'll fight, I'll fight to the very end!

I will fight. I will carry the tears of my God and the tears of my spiritual mother. They have been sown on good soil.

Endnote

1. Derek Schneider is a member of the Canadian Prophetic Council and gives leadership to a thriving young adult ministry called Embassy. Find out more at www .embassyonline.ca.

CHAPTER 13

Here Come the Mighty Ones

For at that time they came to David day by day to help him, until it was a great army, like the army of God (1 Chronicles 12:22).

God is Father. I have found that, just like a father in the natural, He uses different approaches to get things across to different children. This is simply because we are all so unique by His design, and He speaks to us in light of the way that He has made us. For some kids, you have to scream to get their attention. For others, all you have to do is look at them and raise your eyebrow. I'm not totally sure why, but one of the ways that God has gotten my attention in the last several years has been by highlighting numbers that directly connect to the Scriptures He wants to speak to me out of. It does not happen every day, but when it does happen, I know it is significant. He wants me to seek Him out to discover what He is saying. Since Proverbs 25:2 says, "It is the glory of God to conceal a matter; to search out a matter is the glory of kings," whenever this happens, I get excited. If I will seek the Lord in these times, I know He will share an amazing treasure of His heart with me.

1222

A few years back, this Father-daughter hide-and-seek game ramped up when it seemed that almost everywhere I looked I saw the number 1222. I would look at the clock, and it would be 12:22 P.M. I would look at it later, and it would be 12:22 A.M. I would look up a phone number and the last four digits would be 1222, or I would see a sign with an address and there would be 1222. It was everywhere I looked during that season! Deep in my gut, I knew God was trying to speak something important because He would not let up! As I prayed and sought Him, I knew the number had to do with a Scripture, so the idea occurred to me to look up all the Scriptures, from Genesis to Revelation, that had 1222 as part of their reference. I trusted that the Lord would speak to me through His Word as I searched for understanding.

When I reached the Book of Chronicles and read First Chronicles 12:22, I knew that I had hit the Scripture He was trying to draw my attention to. My spirit exploded as I read the words of this Scripture. It has now become one of my favorite texts in the Bible. Before I unpack it, however, I want to dive into the context so we can get a fuller understanding of its significance.

This section of First Chronicles recounts an amazing time in Israel's history. King Saul had just died, and the kingdom was about to transition to the new king, David.

First Chronicles 10:13–11:1 describes it saying,

> *So Saul died for his unfaithfulness which he had committed against the Lord, because he did not keep the word of the Lord, and also because he consulted a medium for guidance. But he did not inquire of the Lord; therefore He killed him, and turned the kingdom over to David the son of Jesse. Then all Israel came together to David at Hebron, saying, "Indeed we are your bone and your flesh."*

Even though Saul's death was the clear event that marked the kingdom shift, prior to Saul's death, mighty men had already begun to gather to David. There must have been a sense in many of their hearts that the season had changed—otherwise, why would they move? They were smart warriors with keen sense. Like one can feel the air changing right before a heavy rain, though they could not see it with their eyes, they could feel the national atmosphere shifting. They knew it was time to position themselves for a new national era. So they began to "move" with their intuition, and this meant that they gathered to David.

THERE MUST HAVE BEEN A SENSE IN MANY OF THEIR HEARTS THAT THE SEASON HAD CHANGED.

These warriors came from the tribe of Gad, the tribes of Benjamin, Judah, Manasseh, and so on. Scripture describes some of them as brave warriors who were, "…ready for battle, and able to handle the shield and spear" (1 Chron. 12:8 NIV). They were mighty men of war who were able to use a bow, a sword, and sling stones with either hand. "Their faces were the faces of lions and they were as swift as gazelles…."

Even more impressive than that, many of them were leaders who had single-handedly defeated hundreds of opponents in certain battles. Verse 14 says in reference to some of them that, "…the least was a match for a hundred, and the greatest for a thousand." That is pretty phenomenal! I want to be on their team! First Chronicles 12:22 then declares of this powerful group, "…they came to David day by day to help him, until it was a great army, like the army of God." Did you catch that!? Like the army of God! I have searched throughout the Bible and, other than in Joel 2, I do not see any other group of people directly referred to as being like the army of God! These guys were something special. I believe they were something the earth had never seen before.

"…THE LEAST WAS A MATCH FOR A HUNDRED, AND THE GREATEST A MATCH FOR A THOUSAND." …"THEY CAME TO DAVID DAY BY DAY TO HELP HIM, UNTIL IT WAS A GREAT ARMY, LIKE THE ARMY OF GOD."

As I have said in previous chapters, I believe that what God is releasing upon this emerging generation is something the earth has never seen before. Through this Scripture (1222), the Lord began speaking a flood of encouragement to my spirit saying,

I am rousing the mighty men and mighty women once again in this hour of history. I am going to call the skilled, the fervent, the wholehearted, and the mighty to fight like few generations have for My purposes to be established. They will take their gifts, their strengths, and their talents and, instead of building their own kingdoms or corporations, they will [like the mighty men in First Chronicles] give themselves completely to advance My will in the earth. Though the earth may not know their names, Heaven will record them.

I believe we are in a time like in First Chronicles 10:12. A shift is taking place. I believe that we are in a season when the Body of Christ is being challenged by the Spirit of God to shift away from a personal-agenda, personal-gratification-driven Christianity back to a mindset of radical Kingdom advancement—advancement of justice, compassion, righteousness, liberty for the oppressed, and all that the Kingdom is about. One of the main marks of this shift will be that a remnant will emerge who will not live their lives governed by comfort, religious routine, or personal glory but will, sometimes at great personal cost, misunderstanding, or discomfort, align themselves with God's purposes for their nation.

> IT WAS ONLY A MATTER OF TIME UNTIL EVERYTHING WOULD RADICALLY SHIFT IN THE NATURAL TOO.

I don't know for sure, but perhaps there were some amazing men of war who were alive during the time spoken of in First Chronicles 12 who sensed something was shifting but, instead of adjusting, chose to stay stuck where they were. Perhaps they had a good position in Saul's army, a good salary, and a good pension. Perhaps they were so committed to their routine, and so busy with it, that their ears were deafened to what the Spirit of God was trying to show them and how He was trying to lead them.

The mandate to rule Israel had lifted off of Saul. The shift had already happened in Heaven's court (see 1 Chron. 10). It was only a matter of time until everything would radically shift in the natural too. Certain elements would be the same. They would still fight with their swords. They were still standing for Israel. They were still men of war, but things were different now in the nation. It was essential that they realign. I find it amazing that one of the groups of mighty men that rallied to David were those from the tribe of Issachar who "…understood the times and knew what Israel should do…" (1 Chron. 12:32 NIV). If these men of "discernment" were rallying, surely something authentic was up. In the same way, I believe something authentic is up in our day. I believe that God is going to raise up a new breed who will discern the shifts in our day and, like the mighty men who showed up at David's camp, will move with it. For me, this has been called, *lay down everything and fight for your nation.*

> I BELIEVE THAT GOD IS GOING TO RAISE UP A NEW BREED WHO WILL DISCERN THE SHIFTS IN OUR DAY AND, LIKE THE MIGHTY MEN WHO SHOWED UP AT DAVID'S CAMP, WILL MOVE WITH IT.

In 1997, I walked away from a summer job that had netted $70,000 (Canadian currency) in four months. By God's grace, I was on track to net six figures by the age of 22. If this had continued, by now (34 years of age), I would likely be a millionaire, or at least on that financial track. Even though I was experiencing financial success, my spirit heard the sound of footsteps on another path. It was a sound of change. It was a sound that, when I heard it, caused me to intuitively know who the rightful leader of my nation was and that a shift was on the horizon. That shift was just on the other side of a battle that was beckoning for a few good men and women. It was a sound that challenged me to change my plans, to rally to a cave, and to fight for the rightful Heir of my nation. I didn't just go there to roast marshmallows over a cave campfire—I was expecting victory!

243

> IT WAS A SOUND THAT BECKONED ME TO CHANGE MY PLANS, TO RALLY TO A CAVE, AND TO FIGHT FOR THE RIGHTFUL HEIR OF MY NATION.

It seemed like just me and King Jesus hung out in that particular cave for a couple of years. We came out for the odd battle and had the odd visitor or band of holy zealots to fight on this frontier, but nobody seemed to stay too long. I suppose they did not feel called to sleeping on hard cave dirt, even though Jesus Himself did not have a place to lay His head in His earthly ministry. I find His servant humility so amazing and so beautiful. I am not preaching that poverty equals righteousness. I just think it is crazy to place our comfort above the will of God. The Lord spoke to my heart years ago, "Faytene, your provision is absolutely guaranteed as long as you daily obey Me." God has proven faithful—so faithful. God is faithful, and you really cannot out-give Him.

> I AM NOT PREACHING THAT POVERTY EQUALS RIGHT-EOUSNESS. I JUST THINK IT IS CRAZY TO PLACE OUR COMFORT ABOVE THE WILL OF GOD.

When I first came into this season, however, there were deep times of loneliness in the battle. I would often cry out to God, "Lord, where is everyone? The battlefield is intense. We need reinforcements." At times it felt as if there were many who would cheer by the sidelines, but few who were willing to jump onto the battle zone. Those who were willing did not seem to be able to find the cave. The Lord was encouraging me, though, through First Chronicles 12:22 to keep my eyes on the horizon. I was going to begin to see many other mighty men and women who were hearing the same sound, who would find this and other Kingdom caves, and who would be willing to stand no matter what the cost—for King and for country.

These were the type of people who were coming: they could have been successful corporate lawyers for personal purposes, but instead they would apply their skills and talents to administrate His justice in the earth for the broken and oppressed. They could have been successful corporate giants building their own mega-empires, but instead they surrendered their strengths to the Lord and would use their talents to build His fame and economy. They could have been divas and rock stars whose main pursuit was maintaining gossip magazine headlines; instead they would take their talent and use it to magnify God in a way that would humble powers and principalities at the sound of their voices. Riches, renown, and success would follow them, but it would not be their master. They would live under the Matthew 6:33 anthem, "...seek first His Kingdom and His righteousness, and all these things will be given to you as well." They would be the mighty men and women of our generation.

> THEY WOULD LIVE UNDER THE MATTHEW 6:33 ANTHEM, "...SEEK FIRST HIS KINGDOM AND HIS

RIGHTEOUSNESS, AND ALL THESE THINGS WILL BE GIVEN TO YOU AS WELL."

Finally, they would not be lone rangers. They would band together and, shoulder-to-shoulder, turn nations back to God. The most amazing confirmation of this came years later when one of our team members received her ministry call to join ranks with us through this exact same word even though she had never heard me speak about it.

SARAH'S STORY

After TheCRY in 2006, our leadership team knew that the next strategic step was to own physical land in our nation's capital. Up until that point, I had been based out of Vancouver on the west coast of Canada. There was a clear shift for us as a national movement after TheCRY in 2006, so we moved the ministry and my home to our nation's capitol to drive a stake in the ground through owning land. I believed in my heart, and my advisors agreed, that something would be secured in the spirit realm as we did this. Not only that, but practically it made a lot of sense.

Prior to this, even though my physical home was in Vancouver, I pretty much lived in airports as I traveled the nation calling my generation and the Church at large to take a stand in this hour. Even though I had a heart to run with a strong team, the truth was that, practically, it was very hard for people to keep up with the travel itinerary. Perhaps this was why they could not find the cave, it was too mobile.

During my transition to Ottawa, the Lord began to put on my heart to make room for those He would send to be part of what we were doing on Parliament Hill. Once I had purchased land and laid the ministry roots in the capitol, it would be so much easier to establish a place where young people could come and plant themselves as well. He was setting the stage. He also began to give me faith that He was going to handpick a team and call them by name. They would help carry and build the movement. Along with this, the Lord would give me the grace to pour into them and raise them up as leaders in the nation.

One of the team members the Lord brought to me in this season was a wonderful, talented young woman named Sarah.

I WAS BLOWN AWAY…WHEN…SHE SHARED A POWERFUL REVELATION THE LORD HAD GIVEN HER OUT OF THIS EXACT TEXT!

When Sarah applied to be a part of our three-month ministry internship, I had an immediate witness in my spirit that she was one of the ones God had handpicked for the team in that season. I prayed over her application, and after I spoke with her on the phone and felt a strong confirmation that her involvement was indeed ordained by the Father in Heaven, I accepted her. I was blown away a couple of weeks later when she opened up and shared a powerful revelation the Lord had given her out of this exact text from First Chronicles! It was the pivotal revelation that motivated her to overcome inhibitions and apply.

"DO YOU KNOW WHO THESE PEOPLE ARE, SARAH? …THESE ARE THE MEN WHO CHANGED THEIR NATION."

The year prior, Sarah determined to read the Bible from front to back. She read faithfully every day, and the Lord would speak to her as she poured over the words and stories in Genesis, Exodus, Leviticus, Numbers, and so on. When she came to First Chronicles, where it speaks of David's great kingdom advance, and specifically the section where it lists the names of the mighty men, she started to get a little bored. In her boredom, she began to skim over the names to get back to the action of the story. The Lord spoke to her with a gentle but firm tone of rebuke, "What are you doing Sarah?" She replied, "Lord, reading all these names is boring. Can't I just skim over them?"

He answered, "Do you know who these people are, Sarah?" She was still with alertness and conviction and continued to listen to her heavenly Father. He continued, "Sarah, these are the men who changed their nation. Everyone wants to be a David, but where are the mighty ones who will be willing to fight for their nation even if they are not the main 'name' in the story?"

It then occurred to her that in the Bible there are really only two types of people whose names are mentioned. There are the names of those who were incredibly wicked and the names of those who gave their whole being to see God's will established. The only list that is missing is the group of people who sat back with indifference and did nothing. The Lord challenged her, "Sarah, will you give your life for My Kingdom, even if no one knows who you are and no one knows the significance of your name? Will your name even be in the book, or will it be counted with the masses who were indifferent and never made the book?" Needless to say, it was only a matter of weeks after this when Sarah's application arrived in our office.

"SARAH, WILL YOU GIVE YOUR LIFE FOR MY KINGDOM, EVEN IF NO ONE KNOWS WHO YOU ARE AND NO ONE KNOWS THE SIGNIFICANCE OF YOUR NAME? WILL YOUR NAME EVEN BE IN THE BOOK, OR WILL IT BE COUNTED WITH THE MASSES WHO WERE INDIFFERENT AND NEVER MADE THE BOOK?"

She is amazing, and she is a picture of what God is about to do in many in the rising generation. She is bright, talented, self-taught, motivated, and pretty (I am sure she will blush when she reads this). When she made her decision to come and work as an intern, for free, for a grassroots ministry seeking to impact government, she was totally misunderstood by some of her dearest friends. They thought she was nuts.

I want to say this: everyone is nuts for something. Some people are nuts for their self-comfort and personal glory. Others are nuts for God. If you are going be nuts for something, it might as well be something that will echo in eternity and leave your world better than you found it. The wise will live so that, at the end of it all, they will have the satisfaction of knowing they gave their lives for something bigger than themselves. Sarah was misunderstood—but she knew it was God. She had heard a sound. I was so thankful when I saw her silhouette rising on the horizon as she walked toward the cave of national reformation.

THE WISE WILL LIVE SO THAT, AT THE END OF IT ALL, THEY WILL HAVE THE SATISFACTION OF KNOWING THEY

GAVE THEIR LIVES FOR SOMETHING BIGGER THAN
THEMSELVES.

God is raising up a generation who doesn't care who gets the credit as
long as they get the job done. Actually, their main desire is for *God* to get the
credit. Some prophets have called ours the "nameless" and "faceless" generation. Others have called these ones the dread champions[1] of God. Whatever you call them, I believe they will be—and are already—the modern-day
band of mighty men and women who change the face of the earth forever.

THEY WILL NOT JOSTLE
THEY WILL NOT BREAK RANK
THEY ARE LED BY THE VOICE OF THE LORD

For years now, I have been gripped by Joel 2 for many reasons. One
of the reasons is because of the prophetic picture of the army of God described in its opening verses. This army is awesome, invincible, strong, and
effective in their mandate. Joel 2:2 says, "…A people come, great and strong,
the like of whom has never been; nor will there ever be any such after them,
even for many successive generations." I realize that the army Joel is seeing
is an end-time army of judgment, perhaps even a heavenly one, but I have
always felt that there was something in these Scriptures that was for my
generation. I am not saying that we will administer devastation in the earth,
though I do believe that He has called us to execute havoc against the kingdom of darkness—as discussed in the opening chapters of this book. I believe many of the characteristics that the Joel 2 army demonstrates—unity,
focus, being led by God's voice—are ones that He has called us to demonstrate as well. Not only will we demonstrate it, it will be in our DNA.

I BELIEVE MANY OF THE CHARACTERISTICS THAT THE
JOEL 2 ARMY DEMONSTRATES—UNITY, FOCUS, BEING
LED BY GOD'S VOICE—ARE ONES THAT HE HAS
CALLED US TO DEMONSTRATE AS WELL.

Two of the verses in this chapter that have always connected deeply
with me are Joel 2:7-8:

*They run like mighty men, they climb the wall like men of war;
every one marches in formation, and they do not break ranks.
They do not push one another; every one marches in his own
column…*

I love this! They run mightily. They are strong, forceful, and clearly moving at a fast pace. They are the anti-apathetic. They move with intense motion, but a motion that is self-controlled and focused. They are not jostling one another for position, prestige, or personal glory. They are a team. Moreover, they are God's team.

BREAK (ABAT): TO TAKE SOMETHING, TO BORROW
SOMETHING
RANKS (ORACH): A WAY (AS IN A WAY OF LIVING) A
PATH OR A ROAD.

The words *break* and *ranks* in the Hebrew are the Hebrew words *abat* and *orach*, which mean to take something, to borrow something—and, a way (as in a way of living), a path, or a road. I find this quite profound. The mighty ones of this army do not try to take or even borrow someone else's path. This army is authentic. Instead of competing with others, trying to get ahead of ones they should be working alongside, or trying to become the latest, greatest someone or something, they know who they are in God, and they are at rest in it. They know their strengths. They know their lane. They know their calling and run in it wholeheartedly.

A wise spiritual mother of mine, Stacey Campbell, says this, "You have to know who you are, and you have to know who you aren't. Many in the Body of Christ know who they are, but they don't know who they aren't, so they are running all over doing this and that, but never really focusing into what they have actually been called to do." That is wisdom from a mama.

INSTEAD OF COMPETING WITH OTHERS, TRYING TO GET
AHEAD OF ONES THEY SHOULD BE WORKING ALONG-
SIDE, OR TRYING TO BECOME THE LATEST, GREATEST

SOMEONE OR SOMETHING, THEY KNOW WHO THEY ARE IN GOD, AND THEY ARE AT REST IN IT.

I believe the army of mighty men and women God is raising up to bring nations to His feet will indeed know who they are and know who they aren't. First, they won't buy the lies of our Western world culture that tell them they have to be a certain way and do certain things to be accepted and successful. These ones will already know that they are accepted perfectly by God and that there is nothing they could do to earn His affection. He loves them perfectly and has made them as they are, and they know it. They are secure in who they are so they won't swallow the lies, they won't be seduced into the performance mindset, and they won't be tricked by their flesh into climbing the corporate ladders of our world—whether inside or outside of the Church walls.

If they are successful in worldly terms, it is not because they are chasing or idolizing that success, but because the call of God has led them there. They see earthly success simply as a gift and as a tool to advance the Kingdom of God. Like Daniel in the midst of Babylon, they are consecrated and pure in motive. Their one desire is to be faithful to their God, whether in the dungeons of society or in the highest echelons. They know who they are so they aren't seduced by temptations that appeal to insecurities in others.

THEY WON'T BUY THE LIES OF OUR WESTERN WORLD CULTURE THAT TELL THEM THEY HAVE TO BE A CERTAIN WAY AND DO CERTAIN THINGS TO BE ACCEPTED AND SUCCESSFUL.

Not only will they overcome the lies of a secular culture that tries so hard to define them, but they will also know who they are in the Kingdom. They will know their gifting, their mandate, their path, and they will stick to it, running side by side with others who are doing the same. They do not covet the gifting, calling, or season of anyone else in the Body of Christ, but with maturity, they rejoice in the successes of others and mourn with their losses. They understand the power of unity. They transcend age, gender, and ethnicity and see one another by the spirit. They understand that alone they are a voice but together they are a force. They watch each other's backs.

When one falls, the others pick him or her up. They understand the cost and what it means to pay it.

Sacrifice does not need to be explained to them. They have eyes of fire because they see the end from the beginning. *They never stop.* They are mature sons and daughters of God who know their lanes and keep in them. As they run side by side, they will form the dream teams of God. They are God's mighty ones—the dread champions of the Lord. They are commanded by one thing alone: the voice of God.

Joel 2:11 says of them, "The Lord gives voice before His army, for His camp is very great; for strong is the One who executes His word...." This is so key. I believe that we are living in an hour of human history when we cannot afford to be driven by good ideas and personal agendas. Our strategies and initiatives must be led by the voice of God and nothing else. This is our inheritance as mature, mighty men and women of God. The apostle Paul makes this clear in Romans 8:12-14:

> *Therefore, brethren, we are debtors—not to the flesh, to live according to the flesh. For if you live according to the flesh you will die; but if by the Spirit you put to death the deeds of the body, you will live. For as many as are led by the Spirit of God, these are sons of God.*

There is a way that God has called us to live where we no longer are ruled by the lusts and temptations of our flesh. One of the most powerful lusts of the flesh is selfish ambition that drives its own agenda and seeks to build its own kingdom. This was the hook for lucifer's fall—the lust for power and personal glory. The generation of mighty ones whom God is calling forth in this hour will be made up of those who will be moved by nothing but His voice—as revealed in His Word and by the Spirit of God that testifies in their inner spirits. Good ideas won't move them. Strong salaries won't move them. Fear of others won't move them. They are ruled by God; like the good sheep that Jesus spoke of in John 10, they will not follow the voice of another.

I get so excited about running with a generation like this, and actually I am so thankful to be able to say that they are not only on the horizon, but many are already functioning in their lane. Every day in our ministry and in the various cities I travel and preach in, I see them. Their hearts are pure, their eyes are full of fire, their motive is the glory of God, and their commitment is unswerving. They have caught something and are running with the ball.

A book like this does not need much explanation for them—it simply puts words to what they already intuitively burn for. This is the generation that will bring the Lamb the full reward of His sufferings and not care if their name is ever mentioned in the process. This is the generation that all of creation is longing for; even as I am typing, I can feel the groaning in my own spirit for them to come forth in fullness.

On that vein, I end this chapter with a prayer. If your desire is to see this mature generation come forth as well, please join with me:

> Father, I thank You for this hour of human history. I thank You that You have allowed us to be alive in this hour and to witness all that You are doing and about to do. God, we pray that You will bring forth in even greater measure the mighty men and women of God in this hour. We pray You raise up these ones who will live for You, who will know who You have called them to be and what You have called them to do, and we pray that they will go for it wholeheartedly. Holy Spirit, we ask that You will work in the Church to raise up an army of those who will not jostle one another, who will not play into the competition games and the lies of the culture, but who will run together as a united army for Your purposes. Father, we pray that You will raise up an army like Joel saw. Send Your voice before us; help us to never shrink back. Do what only You can do. Raise up a generation that will give You all the glory that You are due. For Your name's sake and for Your glory, we pray this in Jesus' name. Amen.

Ahhh! I can't wait to meet more of them. Come forth dread champions of God!

Endnote

1. To read a powerful insight by James Goll about the "dread champions" see the Appendix.

CHAPTER 14

You Are a Nation-Changer
—Don't Ever Stop

Before I venture into our final pages together with this conclusion, I want to say what a joy it has been to spend this 90,000-some words with you. I honestly count it an honor that you would invest your time in perusing these pages, and my prayer is that God has spoken to you and deposited something of His heart and ways as you have read stories and pondered the principles that we have been talking about. These pages carry many of the treasures of my heart right now, and I believe in faith that they have been invested in a way that will multiply into yours. God is jealous for the nations of the earth, and my prayer is that we together will make His dreams come true.

With this in mind, I want to share with you one last story from these past years of running for Jesus in Canada. This experience deeply impacted me and often spurs me on to continue to apply the godly principles I have talked about in this book—and to look for more.

YOU ARE A NATION-CHANGER

It happened in the fall of 2006, when we were taking our fourth team of young adults onto Parliament Hill to honor our Members of Parliament and be a voice for traditional Christian values. As I mentioned previously, prior to God's stirring coming upon me to begin to impact government for His glory, I was not politically oriented at all. I did not know the who's who of the current political world very well, and I surely did not know the who's who of former political generations. Because of this, when we met with this particular Senator, I had no idea what we were getting into.

Prior to meeting with any Parliamentarian, we would brief our team as much as possible by going to the Website or Parliamentary profile of the person and trying to discern from it what kind of values they held and what their points of interest were. We would use this information to pray for them in targeted ways, but also to help us discern what topics might be fruitful to bring up in the meetings. In reality, however, the Websites and online profiles often left out key information. This was definitely the case with this Senator.

> NEEDLESS TO SAY, WE WERE A LITTLE STUNNED BY THE REVELATION OF WHO WE WERE ABOUT TO MEET.

When we arrived for the meeting, the Senator's assistant met us with great enthusiasm and took extra time to let us know exactly "who" we were about to speak with. Many of us on this particular team were young women, and because of this, I am certain the assistant thought we would be extremely excited to find out that the Senator was one of the major figureheads of the women's movement, and the socially liberal movement in general, of the late '60s in Canada.

He told us how she had been one of the most powerful Members of Parliament of the Trudeau era. Trudeau was the Minister of Justice, and then the Prime Minister, during the era when sodomy was legalized, abortion was legalized, gambling was brought in, human rights were exalted over the will of God, and no-fault divorce was legislated. This man's era almost single-handedly dismantled the traditional Christian moral fiber of our nation. The current generation was now wading in the ocean of social ruins that came from this dismantling. Now we found out that this Senator had been front and center during much of this, and gauging from her assistant's introduction, she was very proud of it. Needless to say, we were a little stunned by the revelation of who we were about to meet.

As mentioned earlier, one of our plumb line principles as a movement has always been honor of authority. As I listened to her assistant, I thought to myself, *How in the world are we going to honor this lady and not sound like we are saying, "Greetings Senator. We are here to undo everything you gave your life to accomplish."*

This meeting was going to be interesting, to say the least. In my heart, I began to call out to God for wisdom and for His anointing to fall on us in power. Within a few minutes, the Senator came into the room, and we all rose to greet her. She sat at the head of the long redwood caucus table and asked us who we were and what we were doing at Parliament.

> ALL I CAN REMEMBER IS THE PRESENCE OF GOD COM-ING INTO THE ROOM AND THAT I WAS SURPRISED AT HOW MUCH SHE SEEMED TO "TAKE" TO OUR GROUP.

I opened by introducing the team, saying why we were on Parliament Hill that week, and saying that we were honoring her as a Senator—the position, not her accomplishments directly. In all honestly, I do not remember everything that came out of my mouth, all I can remember is the presence of God coming into the room and that I was surprised at how much she seemed to "take" to our group of socially conservative young people. As we always do, I then opened the floor and asked the young people to share their hearts about why they had paid their own way to come to Parliament that week and what issues they were passionate about. Unknown to me, Holy Spirit began speaking very strongly at this point to a young woman on our team who had traveled from the other side of the nation.

The young woman was clean cut, well-mannered, involved in her church, and the daughter of church elders. I never would have guessed that she had ever had a rebellious season in her life. It turned out that she had had a moral slip-up the year prior, had been involved with a guy, became pregnant, and had an abortion. When she received the news of her pregnancy, all the typical things went through her mind: she wasn't ready, what would her parents think, she had her whole life ahead of her, it was only tissue, etc.

As she was sitting around the caucus table that day, Holy Spirit spoke to her, "I want you to share your story with this Senator in this meeting."

She had never shared her story publicly before. Though she had shared it with a close friend for support, she had not even shared it with her parents. Sharing it in front of the team, this Senator, and me was going to take a lot of courage. I am so proud of her because she found it. She said [paraphrased from my memory],

> Senator, I have something very personal to share with you. Not very long ago, I got involved with a guy, got pregnant, and had

255

an abortion. It was the worst decision I have ever made. It was painful, not just physically but emotionally. I was an emotional wreck for weeks afterward. Senator, no one told me what I would go through. No one told me about the pain, the regret, the nightmares. I wasn't feeling any of this stuff because someone was putting a guilt trip on me. I had not even shared it with anyone. Senator, what about my right to know, before I had the abortion, the negative impact it would have on me? If this is all about women's rights, what about my right to know these things beforehand?

This brave young woman had found out, after having the abortion, that there is a high probability of a direct link between breast cancer, cervical cancer, and abortion—and that 8 out of 10 women who have abortions struggle with depression for the rest of their lives (some even commit suicide)—and that 98 percent of women who have had abortions would *not* recommend it to a friend—and that many women who have aborted their pregnancies have related medical complications in later ones.[1]

She did not know any of these important facts prior to having her abortion, or at least she did not understand it fully. If she had made a "choice," it had not been an informed one—this is what she was expressing. I can't tell you how many times I have heard this story in a variety of ways from various young women, and even men, who grieve the loss of their aborted child.

THE AIR WAS THICK WITH SOBRIETY AND CONVICTION.

After the young woman courageously shared her story, you could have heard a feather fall! The air was thick with sobriety and conviction. Her question to the Senator was like having a Holocaust survivor, or a war survivor, share their story and then turn and say, "Why didn't you do something to stop it?" At this point, I felt the Holy Spirit nudging me. I spoke up,

Senator, you are a champion for women's rights. You always have been. If anyone could successfully bring forth legislation that would protect young women, it would be you. Would you be willing to bring forward a law that would make it mandatory that young women accurately understand the potential risks of having an abortion before they have one?

Because there are currently no laws regarding abortion in Canada, there is no strong watch on doctors' behavior in this regard. We knew that this type of law could potentially save thousands of children's lives. The Senator did not answer at that moment, but we could all feel the weight of conviction in the room.

> SOMEHOW, BY THE ANOINTING OF HOLY SPIRIT, WE HAD MADE IT THROUGH THE MEETING IN A SPIRIT OF HONOR BUT ALSO IN A SPIRIT OF TRUTH THAT BROUGHT A REALLY POWERFUL MESSAGE.

We finished the meeting, gave her a gift that we had brought for her, and began to thank her for her time. Somehow, by the anointing of Holy Spirit, we had made it through the meeting in a spirit of honor but also in a spirit of truth that brought a really powerful message. She reciprocated and thanked us for coming to meet with her. As she arose from her seat, she looked at this brave young woman and said, "Young lady, can I speak with you in private please?"

257

As the leader of the team, I was a bit concerned. I thought, "She is going to destroy her." It was clear they were ideological enemies. I had no idea what this Senator would say to her in private and began praying for protection over her heart. She went into the hallway with the Senator and this political matriarch said something to her that has echoed in my spirit ever since. I believe that what I am about to share with you was not only a message for her, but also for our entire generation and the Christian community at large. She looked directly into her eyes and said,

> Thank you for sharing your story. Now I want to share something with you. I am a nation-changer. I know what it takes to change a nation. I know what it takes to change how people think in a nation. I know what it takes to change the laws in a nation. I have changed this nation. Young lady, *you are a nation-changer.* Don't ever stop sharing your story. Keep going. *Don't ever stop.*

Church of Jesus Christ—*you are a nation-changer; don't ever stop.*

Reforming, shaping, making disciples of nations is not as hard as we may think. If there is anything I have learned from the last few years of reformation work in my nation of Canada, it is this: if we show up, God will back us up. Let me reiterate the fruit. Since the Church has begun to arise in prayer and in prayerful action, we have seen our nation shift from one that had a Prime Minister in 2001 who did not even allow prayer on Parliament Hill at the 911 Memorial to one that now has a Prime Minister who, at the end of every major national address, finishes with the decree, "God bless Canada."

We have a nation that has an estimated 40 percent of the Members of Parliament—across party lines—professing to be born-again Christians; this is perhaps the highest percentage that our nation has ever known! We have a government that has raised the age of sexual consent, brought stricter regulations on crime, overtly blessed the nation of Israel, broken historical curses off of our nation through repentance to the First Peoples of the land, and brought forth the first winnable legislation in decades that will bring protection to unborn babies if passed. We have not seen advances on every front yet, but it is clear that the tide has turned and that the wind is at our back.

258

In a very short window of time, we have seen massive progress. I actually believe we are in the midst of the greatest moral turnaround that Canada, and perhaps the Western world, has ever seen. Why? I believe it is because God, in His sovereignty, has stirred His Church to begin to rise up and show up in the moral battlefields of our nation, and by His grace, we are responding to the call. Whether we call it discipling nations or something else, the truth is that we are starting to rise up and to do just that.

What is the dream that God has put inside of you? Rise up into it. Begin to give it flesh. It is time to invade our worlds with the love and truth of our King—no holding back. The political realm is the target the Lord has given me and our team in this season, but there are many targets. Reach inside and find the one that God has given you. Is it the arts, media, science, education, medicine, law, sports, family? Whatever it is, let's rise up into our respective "lanes" and run as though we only have one life to live—because we do. Discipling our nation, culture, or sphere is not as hard as we may think. We only need to be led by the voice of God, walk in the ways of God, and rise up in bold faith and courage that will not give up. We are not as insignificant as we might think, or feel, at times. Furthermore, we cannot get away from our destiny. The very power of God that raised Jesus from the dead, and the very essence that created the earth at the foundation, lives inside of us. He is the ultimate nation-shaker. He is the ultimate dread champion, and He lives in us. It is time to let Him fill us and send us with faith that shifts nations.

As I look at the emerging generation around me, I am more than encouraged. We are starting to catch something real, solid, fresh, and powerful. We are being marked with the revelation that He has called us to shape our world. Our world will not shape us. Furthermore, we are getting past the rhetoric, debate, and emotionalism of it all and actually beginning to do it. We are captured. We have crossed over a line, and we cannot, will not, go back.

It is my earnest prayer that the pages of this book have truly *marked* you. I pray that you have not only been inspired, but also spurred, equipped, and challenged to arise and begin to write the story for your nation. We can't hold back; let's arise in bold faith and bring our nations to His feet. Time is ticking, and right now, someone is contending for your nation.

Champion, get in the ring.

You are a nation-changer. Don't ever stop.

Endnote

1. All these facts can be verified through studies conducted by the Elliot Institute and other research groups.

259

James Goll's Word Regarding "The Dread Champions"

April 2003

As with many believers, the Lord chooses to speak to us in a variety of ways. Often He speaks to me through dreams and visions. Many times, as I quiet my soul before the Lord, He speaks with His internal audible voice in my heart. Yet, other times, He comes more dramatically with His external audible voice and demonstrations of His presence and power.

When I received the following word that I have titled "The Dread Champions," I had awakened out of a vivid dream where He spoke to me that the "enemies of my soul would become like grass hoppers in my own sight." After awakening from this dream and meditating upon it, my mind was flooded with what I call "divine thought." I penned the following as fast as I could.

A Prophetic Word—The Dread Champions

Giants of faith are appearing in the Land! An apostolic, prophetic, and priestly company of men and women, old and young, with no limitations to ethnic background, cultural persuasions, and religious affiliations are arising at this time. These abandoned believing believers who have broken out of the boxes of self-imposed limitations have begun to think "God-sized thoughts."

They will arise with the roar of the Lion of Judah in their camp as the fear of the Almighty falls in that hour. This is the hour when the DREAD CHAMPIONS—true brothers and sisters of Jesus—are released to tread upon the dreary spirits of fear, fainting, and failure. This is an hour when God's enemies shall be made footstools for His feet!

It will not be an hour of boasting of nationalistic pride, but rather an hour when the peoples of the nations and nations of peoples will come to a crossroads to determine if they live or die, rise or fall. This will be determined by the parable of weakness versus strength.

Those peoples and those nations who shall bend the knee of humility to the one true God shall be given strength to conquer. Those peoples and nations that place their trust in the strength of their own arms shall be temporarily humbled.

Yes, blessed are the people whose God is their Lord. They shall not give lip service only to the Master, but rather desperate heart surrender to the King of armies. The Lord Himself will defend His anointed with heavenly reinforcements in that day. Yes, these are the days when the DREAD CHAMPIONS—the Days of Giants of Faith and Humility—shall walk the earth again.

SCRIPTURAL REFERENCES TO THE DREAD OF THE LORD

Exodus 15:16-17:

Fear and dread will fall on them; by the greatness of Your arm they will be as still as a stone, till Your people pass over, O Lord, till the people pass over whom You have purchased.

You will bring them in and plant them in the mountain of Your inheritance, in the place, O Lord, which You have made for Your own dwelling.

Psalm 14:5:

There they are in great dread, for God is with the righteous generation (NASB).

Isaiah 8:13:

It is the Lord of hosts whom you should regard as holy, and He shall be your fear, and He shall be your dread (NASB).

Gaining Understanding—Exercising Faith

The Lord is equipping His people with wisdom understanding for the days in which we live. These sons of Issachar shall also walk in faith, being victorious in the midst of perilous days as authentic, apostolic believers. Remember, we are overcomers through Christ Jesus our Lord.

The Lord is preparing for Himself a people who will know the fear, wonder, and the awesome dread of the Lord. Yet, in part, the shadow of His presence upon the world will be cast from these same people, having been overwhelmed with the beauty, royalty, and authority of His majesty. These humble yet fierce warriors of the Lord will know their God and do mighty exploits in His name as the Days of Acceleration come upon us. The dread of the Lord will fall upon saint and sinner alike in that hour.

It is my conviction that we are crossing another historical threshold in this hour. One in which new names will be written in the Hebrews chapter 11 Hall of Faith. These are the days for the Champions of Faith and Humility to arise afresh.

James W. Goll
www.jimgoll.com
www.prayerstorm.com

About the Author

Faytene Kryskow is a passionate follower of Christ who has been in full-time ministry since 1997. She has pioneered several ministries, published two books, recorded three worship CDs, and produced other resources. In her native Canada, she is the director of TheCRY and the MY Canada Association. She travels extensively preaching, appears on television, and regularly addresses Christian and government leaders.

From serving in the social gutters and inner-city streets to the back woods of West Africa, God transplanted author Faytene Kryskow smack in the epicenter of Canada's political affairs—prophesying to leaders and influencing policy, causing waves of moral reform nationwide.